Labour
in
Asia-Pacific

Labour Relations in the Asia-Pacific Countries

Editor: Roger Blanpain
Guest editor: Luis Aparicio-Valdez

Contributors
Y. Asao
J. Bernedo Alvarado
E. Córdova
A. J. Geare
T. Hanami
R. Lansbury
H.-S. Lee
W.-D. Lee
E. Morgado Valenzuela
B. Parasuraman
J. Rhee
A. G. Ruiz Moreno
D. Taras
M. Thompson
A. Vásquez Párraga
Y. Zhu

2004
Kluwer Law International
The Hague / London / New York

A C.I.P. Catalogue record for this book is available from the Library of Congress.

ISBN 90-411-2239-7

Published by
Kluwer Law International,
P.O. Box 85889, 2508 CN The Hague, The Netherlands
sales@kluwerlaw.com
http://www.kluwerlaw.com

Sold and distributed in North, Central and South America by
Aspen Publishers, Inc.
7201 McKinney Circle, Frederick, MD 21704, USA

Sold and distributed in all other countries
by Turpin Distribution Services Limited
Blackhorse Road, Letchworth, Herts.,
SG6 1HN, United Kingdom

Printed on acid-free paper

All Rights Reserved
© 2004 Kluwer Law International

No part of this work may be reproduced, stored in a retrieval system, or transmitted in any form or by any means, electronic, mechanical, photocopying, microfilming, recording, or otherwise, without written permission from the Publisher, with the exception of any material supplied specifically for the purpose of being entered and executed on a computer system, for exclusive use by the purchaser of the work.

Printed and bound in Great Britain by Antony Rowe Limited

Table of Contents

Editorial   vii

List of Contributors   xxvii

1. Employment Law in the Context of the Changing Pattern of Employment Relations in Australia   1
Russell Lansbury

2. Canadian Industrial Relations   15
Mark Thompson and Daphne Taras

3. Chile: Labour Relations at the Beginning of the Twenty-first Century   27
Emilio Morgado Valenzuela

4. Labour Law and Industrial Relations in China   37
Ying Zhu

5. The Labour Situation in Japan (2001)   65
Yutaka Asao

6. 2001 Annual Review for Japan   71
Tadashi Hanami

7. Industrial Relations in Korea: Recent Changes and New Challenges   83
Won-Duck Lee

8. PDR Systems Theory Perspective on Employment Relations in a Globalizing Asia: A Korean Case   89
Hyo-Soo Lee and Jaehooni Rhee

9. Social Security in México: An Overview   107
Angel G. Ruiz Moreno

10. Employment and Work Culture in Mexico under the Shadow of NAFTA, 1994–2002   109
Arturo Vásquez Párraga

11. Labour in New Zealand   123
Alan J. Geare

12. 2002: The Peruvian Labour Field   131
Jorge Bernedo Alvarado

13. The Labour Relations System of the United States 147
    Efrén Córdova

14. Industrial Relations in ASEAN: A Comparative Analysis 153
    Balakrishnan Parasuraman

Editorial

It is no exaggeration to say that the Asia-Pacific Economic Cooperation (APEC) forum is the commercial integration treaty with the greatest historical significance and the brightest prospects. Not only is it an integration process of great scope and importance, comparable to Europe's eastward march in the wake of Marco Polo's journey to Cathay. The importance of this agreement lies in its attending circumstances of accelerated re-shaping of national economies the world over in the context of national affirmation and subregional integration processes and overarching continental and inter-continental agreements. Rather than an economic, social and commercial process brought about by the natural growth of the economies; APEC it is a strategic realignment made necessary by the pressing need to respond to the challenges of increasingly intense competition between countries and, even more so, between the major multinational corporations.

For economies with a relatively small presence in world trade, the process of continental and inter-continental integration represents a challenge. They must create opportunities for insertion while at the same time promoting their own development, and they must do so by offering in turn their own markets, whose smaller economies of scale expose them to the risk of being confined to productive activities of lower value added, involving less creativity and less stimulation for human and social development.

The historical experience of a number of countries – especially that of the first- and second-generation Asian tigers, but also of some Latin American nations – has shown that this challenge can be met. Indeed, integration without subordination can be achieved by encouraging growth and equity through social, technological and cultural interchange in the broadest sense of the term as much as through trade.

APEC was established in 1989 in Australia and at that country's initiative, as a forum for consultation and economic cooperation, to disseminate knowledge of opportunities and make cooperation activities more effective by acting as coordination centre. Clearly, it was also a response to the specific needs resulting from the growing interdependence among nations.

APEC has played an important role in the promotion of trade and investment in the region. Indeed, the markets of its member nations have grown considerably over the last 10 years, as have employment opportunities.

The founding states of APEC were Australia, the Sultanate of Brunei, Canada, South Korea, the Philippines, Indonesia, Japan, Malaysia, New Zealand, Singapore, Thailand and the United States. In 1991 these nations were joined by China, Hong Kong and Taiwan, thus making all first-generation Asian tigers members of APEC as well as incorporating the reformed and highly dynamic economy of China, which by then had become the world's most impressive case

EDITORIAL

of sustained growth in the late twentieth century. Mexico and Papua New Guinea joined in 1993.

From that time on, APEC's activities have expanded considerably. From acting as a mere clearinghouse for communicating and coordinating initiatives, it has become institutionalized and established agreements more and more reflecting APEC's own initiative and direction.

Thus, the Human Resources Development Working Group was set up in 1990, one of its objectives being to promote general well-being through development and economic growth. At present, the Group's activities are centred on professional capacity building, education, employment and social protection.

Chile joined APEC in 1994, followed in 1999 by Peru, Russia and Vietnam. The register of new members has been closed for the time being, but those already in account for 56 per cent of the world economy at the turn of the century and 40 per cent of world trade, as well as 50 per cent of the world's population and territory.

Nevertheless, a more detailed look at these impressive figures will reveal considerable diversity in terms of social and economic parameters – quite aside from other areas – which should be taken into account in a discussion such as this. This simplified presentation will therefore focus – with an acceptable degree of error – on blocs of countries based on predominantly geographic criteria.

- America: This bloc comprises the United States, Canada and Mexico in the northern part and Chile and Peru in the southern part of the continent. It is the bloc with the greatest economic weight, representing 40 per cent of APEC, due to the obvious preponderance of the United States, which alone contributes 28 per cent of world production and 86 per cent of the bloc's production.
- Major Eastern countries: This bloc includes Japan, China and Russia, which need no further introduction. They represent one third of APEC's economy, with Japan contributing almost 80 per cent of the bloc's total.
- The first-generation tigers: South Korea, Taiwan, Hong Kong and Singapore, known as 'the Four Asian Tigers'. In spite of the obvious differences among them, their economies shared early take-off and rapid expansion second to Japan's alone.
- Southeast Asia (ASEAN): The example of impressive growth of the four Tigers in Southeast Asia was followed by another group of countries in the same region which complete the core of this bloc. Although they had already shown considerable growth potential, only in the eighties the new Tigers – Indonesia, Malaysia, Singapore, Thailand and, somewhat further afield, the Philippines – achieved accelerated trade expansion, driven in part by trade with the original Tigers.
- Countries of Oceania: Australia, New Zealand and Papua-New Guinea are the countries of Oceania which are APEC members. They are also members of the British Commonwealth.

These diverse groups will be mayor players in the trade integration arena during the first half of this century, possibly with their eyes on the European bloc and no doubt working to incorporate the other American and Asian countries in a movement towards world integration, which is seen as the major goal of the twenty-first century – or so it is foreseen as an optimistic scenario. The opposite scenario – worldwide confrontation – must be controlled and left behind if a world order based on peace is to be achieved.

Returning, however, to our problematic present, we should recall that the process of world integration, which ECLAC calls open regionalism, affects us with its social implications, especially from the standpoint of labour standards, the social variable par excellence.

Unsurprisingly, in APEC we find the same economic diversity in the areas of production and labour force, employment and income. Allowing for the variations due to the age structure and labour force participation, the respective size of each member country's economically active population (EAP) is closely correlated to the size of the population. Thus, the most populous APEC member countries also have the largest EAPs, with China as the clear leader with an EAP of 750 million, more than all other APEC member nations put together, followed by the United States and Indonesia with 139 and 99 million respectively.

The group of countries featuring sizeable – 10 or more million – EAPs is the most numerous, including Russia, Japan, Indonesia, Thailand, the Philippines, Mexico and Vietnam. Next come South Korea, Canada, Australia, Peru, Malaysia and Taiwan, followed by the countries with the smallest populations: Chile, Hong Kong, Singapore, New Zealand, Papua-New Guinea and the Sultanate of Brunei.

Income disparities among the APEC countries are smaller than those among the nations of the world in general, with the difference in per capita production between the poorest and the richest – expressed in comparable dollars according to the United Nations system – not exceeding 1 to 20 for APEC as against 1 to 80 for the world as a whole. The United States and Canada rank at the top, followed by the first- and second-generation Tigers. As to China, while it is not included in this comparison given that its per capita income and occupational earnings data are distorted by its national accounting and resource allocation systems, it is nonetheless the nation with the highest future prospects, and whose growth over the last two decades is, in the opinion of many, one of the most powerful drivers of APEC's very existence.

With regard to labour relations, this study will show that points of convergence as well as of divergence exist within APEC. There is a general feeling that labour relations are being driven by a worldwide understanding of the needs of productivity and competitiveness towards scenarios of increasing cooperation within enterprises as well as at the national level. Nearly all nations can point to experiences of social dialogue. Likewise, it is encouraging to note that such ideas as collaboration to raise productivity, the association of goals to benefits, horizontal human relations and social responsibility are becoming the common language – albeit still short of definitive consolidation – of labour relations within APEC and in the world at large.

On the other hand, it would be overoptimistic to hold that this trend towards homogeneity also exists in the sphere of social security, especially in the area of pension plans, where an arduous process of transformation and debate is still under way. There, realities vary from state-funded integral protection, pay as you go, and individual capitalization and mixed systems, to situations in which the very concept of social security is yet to become a part of fundamental public policy.

Last but not least, the fact should be clearly understood that APEC's future commercial integration – according to the Bogor Goals, all restrictions to trade and investment must have been removed by 2010 for industrialized economies and 2020 for the non-industrialized economies – will necessarily proceed from top down in terms of economic size. Any agreements reached by the larger economies will have an immediate impact on the 'second tier economies' – the tigers, Oceania, Mexico, China and Russia, and later, although with diminishing delay, on the small economies given their lower degree of integration.

For these smaller economies, again, the challenge of the future lies precisely in the ability to integrate advantageously by reducing the risks and absorbing the benefits of integration. To successfully meet that challenge, they must solve the following dilemma: while it may be too soon for integration for a country that starts out at a disadvantage, it will certainly be too late if it holds back.

The present study was conceived as a Special Report on Labour Relations in the Member Countries of APEC for knowledge dissemination purposes and to help in the search for opportunities and avenues of growth for our region. It was prepared on the occasion of ANALISIS LABORAL's 25th anniversary, with contributions from several of the region's top professors and experts, to whom we express our deepest gratitude.

As we reaffirm our resolute support for integration and progress, we thank the authors for their efforts and express our hope that they not be in vain. This Bulletin reproduces the main reports.

Roger Blanpain and Luis Aparicio-Valdez

ANNEXES

    I.   Population and Labour Force Indicators of APEC Member Countries
   II. Economic Indicators of APEC Member Countries
  III. Chart: APEC Member Economies
  IV. What is APEC and what can it do for business?
   V. APEC Structure

Annex I. Population and Labour Force Indicators of APEC Member Countries

Country	Population Millions 2001[a]	Population Avg annual % growth 1990–2001[a]	Population Density people per km² 2001[a]	LEB Years 2000[a]	EAP Millions 1999[b]	Labour force Millions 1999[b]	Labour force Average annual growth rate 1999–2010[c]	Female % of labor force 1999[b]
Australia	19.4	1.2	3	79	13	10	0.8	43.5
Brunei	0.3	2.7	65.5	76	NA	NA	NA	NA
Canada	31.0	1.0	3	79	21	16	0.6	45.6
Chile	15.4	1.5	21	76	10	6	1.9	33.2
China	1,271.9	1.0	136	70	844	751	0.8	45.2
Hong Kong, China	6.9	1.7	NA	80	5	4	0.9	37.0
Indonesia	213.6	1.6	118	66	133	99	2.0	40.6
Japan	127.1	0.3	349	81	87	68	-0.3	41.3
Korea, Rep.	47.6	1.0	483	73	33	24	1.1	41.2
Malaysia	23.8	2.4	72	73	14	9	2.8	37.7
México	99.4	1.6	52	73	60	39	2.2	32.9
New Zealand	3.8	1.0	14	78	2	2	0.7	44.8
Papua-New Guinea	5.3	2.5	12	59	3	2	2.1	42.1
Peru	26.1	1.7	20	69	15	9	2.7	31.0
Philippines	77.0	2.1	258	69	46	31	2.5	37.7
Russian Federation	144.8	-0.2	9	65	101	78	-0.1	49.0
Singapore	4.1	2.7	6,726	78	2	2	1.3	39.1
Taiwan	22.4	0.7	677	76	NA	NA	NA	NA
Thailand	61.2	0.9	120	69	42	36	1.0	46.3
United States	284.0	1.2	31	77	179	143	0.9	45.8
Vietnam	79.5	1.7	244	69	48	40	1.7	49.0

LEB – life expectancy at birth; EAP – economically active population; NA – not available.

Sources:
[a] World Development Report 2003, Table 1, The World Bank.
[b] World Development Indicators 2001, Table 2.2, The World Bank.
[c] World Development Indicators 2001, Table 2.2, The World Bank. 10-year estimate.

Annex II. Economic Indicators of APEC Member Countries

Country	GDP Millions of Dollars 2001[a]	GDP Avg. Annual % growth 1990–2001[a]	GDP annual % growth Forecast 2003[b]	GNI Per capita Dollars 2001[c]	External debt Present value % of GNI 2000[d]	Trade balance Millions of Dollars 2001[e]	FDI Millions of Dollars 2000[d]
Australia	368,571	4.0	4.0	19,770	NA	−500	11,527
Brunei	NA	NA	NA	NA	NA	NA	NA
Canada	677,178	3.0	3.6	21,340	NA	33,990	62,758
Chile	63,545	6.4	6.0	4,350	51	481	3,675
China	1,159,017	10.0	7.4	890	13	22,588	38,399
Hong Kong, China	162,642	3.0	3.6	25,920	NA	−11,576	NA
Indonesia	145,306	3.8	4.0	680	96	25,546	−4,550
Japan	4,245,191	1.3	0.8	35,990	NA	54,591	8,227
Korea, Rep.	422,167	5.7	5.5	9,400	28	9,537	9,283
Malaysia	87,540	6.5	5.5	3,640	52	14,137	1,660
México	617,817	3.1	4.9	5,540	28	−17,620	13,286
New Zealand	48,277	2.9	3.0	12,380	NA	419	3,209
Papua-New Guinea	2,959	3.6	NA	580	66	733	130
Peru	54,047	4.3	5.0	2,000	55	−1,516	680
Philippines	71,438	3.3	4.2	1,050	64	2,216	2,029
Russian Federation	309,951	−3.7	NA	1,750	60	49,710	2,714
Singapore	92,252	7.8	5.1	24,740	NA	5,770	6,390
Taiwan	NA	NA	4.8	NA	NA	NA	NA
Thailand	114,760	3.8	3.5	1,970	64	4,033	3,366
United States	10,171,400	3.5	3.4	34,870	NA	−449,600	287,680
Vietnam	32,903	7.6	7.0	410	36	−900	1,298

GDP – Gross domestic product; GNI – gross national income; FDI – foreign direct investment; NA – not available.

Sources:
[a] World Development Report 2003, Table 3, The World Bank.
[b] World Economic Outlook, April 2002, Table 1.2, International Monetary Fund.
[c] World Development Report 2003, Table 1, The World Bank.
[d] World Development Report 2003, Table 4, The World Bank.
[e] Elaboration by Arturo Z. Vasquez on the basis of World Development Report 2003, Table 4, The World Bank. Negative numbers indicate Trade Deficit.

Annex III Chart: APEC Member Economies

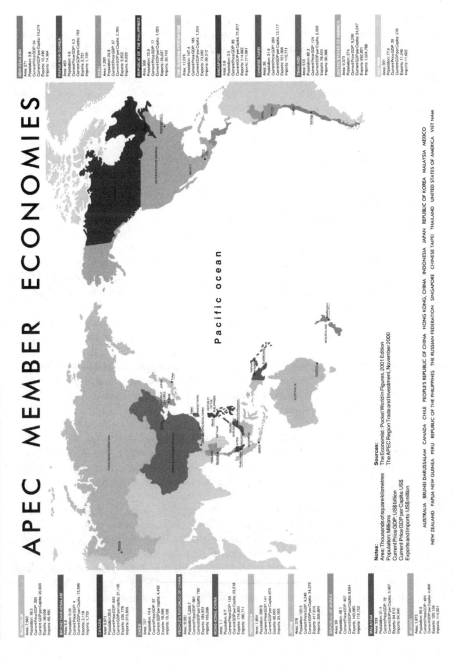

Source: http://www.apecsec.org.sg/

Annex IV. What is APEC and What can it do for Business?[1]

I. WHAT IS APEC?

APEC stands for the Asia-Pacific Economic Cooperation Forum. Today, APEC has 21 members, including all the major economies of the region and the most dynamic, fastest growing economies in the world. APEC members have a combined Gross Domestic Product of over $16 trillion and carry out 42 per cent of world trade. Over the past decade, APEC has become the primary vehicle in the region to promote open trade and economic cooperation. APEC's role has grown in recent years in both depth and scope and now encompasses trade liberalization, business facilitation, economic and technical cooperation, youth and women.

A. APEC's background

APEC was established in 1989 in Canberra, Australia with 12 members. Its origins lay in the desire of the founding members to promote economic growth, foster and strengthen trade, and improve living standards in the Asia-Pacific region. APEC started with a modest program of sectoral and trade negotiations. From the beginning, APEC has seen itself not as a grouping of countries, but of economies, the term emphasizing that the organization discusses economics, not politics. It was also established as a loose consultative forum, with no organization structure or a large bureaucracy supporting it. Indeed, even today, the APEC Secretariat, which is located in Singapore, includes only 23 diplomats seconded from APEC member economies in addition to 20 locally hired staff.

It was in 1993 that an annual meeting of APEC Leaders became a regular feature of APEC. Only one year after this first meeting, which was held in the United States, APEC Leaders took another historic step at their meeting in Bogor, Indonesia. At this meeting, the Leaders declared a bold goal of creating the world's largest area of free trade and investment by 2020. Within APEC, this challenge became known as the 'Bogor Goals'. Under the plan, developed economies would achieve free trade by the year 2010 and developing economies would follow in 2020.

> [APEC's 21 members today are: Australia; Brunei Darussalam; Canada; Chile; the People's Republic of China; Hong Kong, China; Indonesia; Japan; South Korea; Malaysia; Mexico; New Zealand; Papua-New Guinea; Peru; the Philippines; Russia; Singapore; Chinese Taipei; Thailand; the United States; and Vietnam.]

At their meeting in Japan in 1995, the Leaders approved what became known as the Osaka Action Agenda. Under this approach, APEC established three central pillars to its cooperative work: trade and investment liberalization, trade facilitation, and economic and technical cooperation. A more detailed discussion of these three pillars appears below. Building on both Bogor and Osaka, the next year, the Leaders endorsed a 'Manila Action Plan'. In effect, this Action Plan put the flesh on the bare bones of both Bogor and Osaka. It outlined the trade and investment liberalization and facilitation measures needed to reach the Bogor Goals. It also established a system of collective and individual action plans which detail the paths by which economies will reach the Bogor Goals.

---

1. *Source*: http://www.apecsec.org.sg/

Before describing any further what APEC is, it would be useful to make clear what it is not. APEC is not:
- a formal trade agreement like the North American Free Trade Association (NAFTA);
- a European-style 'common market';
- a rules-based organization like the World Trade Organization (WTO);
- a policy think tank group like the Organization for Economic Cooperation and Development (OECD).

B. APEC's first pillar: Trade and investment liberalization

The first pillar is critical for APEC's ability to achieve its Bogor Goal of free trade in the APEC region by the year 2020. It works on the basis of unilateral liberalization, which means that each APEC member voluntarily agrees to liberalize in a particular area of trade and investment. APEC has developed a basic tool for achieving this pillar: individual action plans (IAP). All APEC economies are required to prepare and regularly update these IAPs.

Each IAP includes details on the 15 sectors specified by the Osaka Action Agenda. They include the following areas:
- tariffs
- non-tariff measures
- services
- investment
- standards and conformance
- customs procedures
- intellectual property rights
- competition policy
- government procurement
- rules of origin
- dispute mediation
- the mobility of business people
- implementation of outcomes of the Uruguay Round of trade talks
- information gathering and analysis.

In addition to each IAP describing what APEC members are doing in these areas, there are working-level groups within APEC which work towards making further progress in each of the 15 areas. APEC has made these IAPs more accessible to business by simplifying formats and creating electronic IAPs. These e-IAPs became fully operational in November 2000. In addition to the IAPs, APEC members work together collectively in these same areas through the use of Collective Action Plans (CAPs).

C. APEC's second pillar: Trade facilitation

Basically, trade facilitation is aimed at making doing business in the region easier and less costly. Although work in this area continues on a broad front, APEC has already made substantial progress in many areas including standards, customs, electronic commerce, business travel, telecommunications, energy, fisheries, and government procurement. Some examples will be discussed separately, to better highlight how business can best take advantage of the progress in these areas.

D. APEC's third pillar: Economic and technical cooperation

Within APEC, economic and technical cooperation is described in shorthand by the term, 'Ecotech'. It should first be stressed that Ecotech does not mean development assistance to developing APEC economies. Instead, they are the activities and programs of APEC aimed at achieving its overall goals of attaining sustainable growth, broadening the benefits of that growth to improve the economic and social well-being of all our people and deepen the spirit of community in APEC.

At their meeting in Manila in 1996, APEC Leaders identified six priority areas for APEC's work in Ecotech:
- developing human capital;
- fostering safe and efficient capital markets;
- strengthening economic infrastructure;
- harnessing technologies for the future;
- promoting environmentally sustainable growth;
- encouraging the growth of small and medium enterprises.

Currently, APEC has 250 ongoing Ecotech activities.

II. HOW APEC WORKS

The APEC Forum is not a rules-based organization with trade dispute enforcement powers like the WTO. APEC, instead, works on the basis of consultation and consensus-building. New policies agreed within APEC meetings are voluntary and much of APEC's progress comes through members setting examples for each other and through peer pressure. A key element of the process is open sharing of information between members and the public, an element underlined by the central use of the IAP available to anyone logging on to the APEC website. In Shanghai, the APEC Leaders also launched a 'pathfinder' initiative. The details of this initiative are being worked out this year but the idea is that groups of APEC members will make projects in specific areas where possible, regardless of whether all APEC members are ready.

The apex of each year for APEC is the meeting of Economic Leaders. Since the Chair of APEC rotates each year, there is a different host for each of these Leaders meetings. For example, last year President Bush, President Putin, President Fox, and the other APEC Leaders traveled to Shanghai, where President Jiang Zemin hosted them. This year, Mexico chairs APEC and President Fox will host the APEC Economic Leaders in Los Cabos, Baja California del Sur, Mexico on October 26 and 27. In subsequent years, Thailand (2003), Chile (2004), and the Republic of Korea (2005) will chair APEC.

However, throughout an 'APEC' year, there are many meetings held at different levels aimed at preparing issues for decision by the Leaders, as well as at carrying out directions issued by Leaders in previous years. (The schedule for these meetings can be found on the APEC website under the 'APEC Calendar' at http://www.apecsec.org.sg/whatsnew/calend/calendar.html.) The meetings of APEC Ministers make up the highest level of these meetings. There are regular, although not always annual, meetings of APEC Ministers of education, energy, environment and sustainable development, finance, human resources development, science and technology, small and medium enterprises, telecommunications, trade, and transportation.

Below the level of the Ministers, APEC Senior Officials meet three or four times throughout the year. As with the meetings of the Ministers, these 'SOM' meetings both prepare for the Leaders' Meeting later in the year and respond to directions set by

EDITORIAL

Leaders in earlier meetings. Below SOM are three overarching committees and 23 working level groups that work both in the sectors detailed in the IAP (see Section I.B) and in other areas, including:
- energy
- fisheries
- human resources development
- industrial science and technology
- marine resources conservation
- telecommunications
- trade promotion
- transportation
- tourism
- agricultural technical cooperation
- small and medium enterprises.

There is a Program Director at the APEC Secretariat who supports the working level activities being carried on in APEC in each of these areas as well as those mentioned elsewhere. You can identify each Program Director and contact them by logging on to http://www.apecsec.org.sg and going to the 'APEC Secretariat' page and then to 'Incumbent PSMs and Duties'. In addition, information on the working level groups themselves appears under the WebPages 'Activities by Groups'.

A. The APEC Secretariat

The APEC Secretariat is based in Singapore. The Secretariat is staffed by 23 diplomats seconded from APEC member economies and by 20 local staff. An Executive Director, who is always an Ambassador seconded from that year's APEC host, heads the Secretariat. Since Mexico is this year's host of APEC, the current Executive Director, Ambassador Alejandro de la Peña, is a Mexican. The Deputy Executive Director is always from next year's APEC host and he or she becomes the Executive Director the following year when the new APEC host takes over. The current Deputy Director, Thailand's Ambassador Piamsak Milintachinda, will serve as the Secretariat's Executive Director for Thailand's year as host of APEC in 2003. The other 21 seconded diplomats are currently from 18 of the APEC members and are from Foreign Affairs and Trade Ministries.

The Secretariat works under the direction of the APEC Senior Officials and is the core support mechanism for the APEC process. It provides advisory, operational and logistical/technical services to member economies and APEC forums. It also provides advice on the design of APEC projects, manages project funding, and evaluates the projects after they are completed. It addition to maintaining the website, it produces a range of publications and liaises with the media. Finally, it provides APEC's institutional memory through its Library, Archives and databases.

III. THE CRITICAL ROLE OF BUSINESS IN APEC

A. The APEC Business Advisory Council

There are few international or regional organizations of officials in which the business sector plays such a central role. The members of the APEC Forum have long realized that

Editorial

business is a key constituency for its work and that business must be actively involved for APEC to be successful. During APEC's early years, APEC officials regularly consulted prominent business representatives in the Asia-Pacific region. In 1995, Leaders decided to formalize this relationship and established the APEC Business Advisory Council (ABAC). ABAC's members are chosen directly by the APEC Leaders. Each APEC Leader chooses up to three members. Most APEC economies reserve one of their ABAC positions for a representative from a small- or medium-sized enterprise (SMEs), thanks to the key role that these SMEs play in all APEC economies.

ABAC meets several times during the year and compiles an annual report containing recommendations on ways to improve the business and investment climate in the APEC region. ABAC presents this report personally to the APEC Leaders at the leaders meeting each year. As an example, at the Shanghai Leaders Meeting, ABAC members presented their report in a face-to-face meeting with Premier Jiang Zemin, President George W. Bush, President Vladimir Putin, Prime Minister Junichiro Koizumi Mori, Mexican President Vicente Fox and the other APEC Leaders. There was also a lively question-and-answer session during this meeting.

ABAC's 2001 Report to APEC Economic Leaders was broad-ranging but full of detailed recommendations aimed at addressing problems in a number of different areas.

The ABAC report contains four main themes:

- APEC economies must *accelerate progress towards trade and investment liberalization* as stated in the Bogor Goals. We encourage Leaders to instill the necessary sense of urgency and commitment to fully liberalize trade and investment in accordance with the Bogor Goals and we respectfully urge Leaders to instruct Ministers and Officials to achieve these.
- ABAC strongly advocates that APEC demonstrate its support for the launch of a new WTO round at the WTO Ministerial Conference in Doha in November.
- ABAC alerts Leaders to the impending threat of financial contagion. APEC should counter the current economic uncertainty with decisive measures to stimulate economic growth, and accelerate financial reforms. Economies need to ensure that international and regional financial architecture mechanisms are in place to deal with contagion. These should include key indicators recommended by the IMF aimed at providing early warning signals, and improved policy coordination.
- A balanced approach to globalization that combines market opening, capacity-building and full participation is essential because these three elements reinforce one another. Should any of these three be neglected, the globalization process would lose balance and the goal of common development could not be realized. Therefore, all three elements should develop hand-in-hand as an integral part of the APEC process.

Some of the specific recommendations include:

- Accelerate banking and capital market reforms to international financial standards, improve corporate governance, and further liberalize investment and trade in financial services.
- Intensify capacity-building to promote financial system reforms to deepen markets through the development of domestic bond markets and credible credit-rating agencies, strengthen risk management hedging mechanisms, and when viable, wider use of second board markets.
- Strengthen international and regional financial architecture by participating in:
    - Financial soundness indicators programs to improve surveillance measures.
    - Efforts to mitigate the adverse impacts of short-term capital flows, activities of highly leveraged institutions and moral hazard.

- Encourage regional private–public partnerships in trade facilitation and capacity building as shown by the Shanghai Model Port Project.
- Encourage Leaders to take the opportunity of the Shanghai meeting to renounce the use of food embargoes and to urge their officials to adopt the other action items proposed by ABAC to assist in the implementation of the APEC Food System.
- Align standards and conformance through mutual recognition agreements and the adoption of international standards.
- Strengthen the accessibility and comprehensiveness of the IAPs to make them an essential means of measuring APEC's progress and tools business can use to make strategic decisions.
- Address impediments to trade with emphasis on strengthening the enforcement of intellectual property rights (IPR) and removing barriers to foreign direct investment (FDI).
- Adopt policies that enable the widespread use of e-learning as a tool to develop skills and reduce the digital divide.
- Leading by example, governments should put more information and services online, improving efficiency and access, and encouraging private sector investment in information and communication technology (ICT).
- Facilitate one-window access to SME programs and services through the development of an APEC SME Portal, to provide information on financing, technology and new market opportunities.
- Adopt policies that are 'small business-friendly', with the assistance of a proposed Scorecard for Entrepreneurial Environment.

As a regional economic organization, APEC plays an important role in the economic globalization process. In the past decade, member economies have made remarkable achievements in their pursuit of open and free trade and investment. This year, however, the Asia-Pacific region faces a number of new and serious challenges.

- The terrorist attacks in the United States in September 2001 caused APEC, for the first time, to confront a political issue. The APEC Leaders in Shanghai issued a statement on counter terrorism, detailing a number of steps that must be addressed to respond vigorously to the threat.
- The pronounced slowdown of the global economy in 2001 even before the events of September 11 led to further financial instability and fears of contagion. Market confidence was seriously weakened, slowing progress in globalization. Economies of the region reliant on external demand are lost momentum with their economic recoveries. Financial systems were seen as increasingly vulnerable to a new round of crisis.
- The final launch of a new round of WTO talks, assisted in part by work done in APEC has helped break a logjam in global trade talks. Now progress will be possible in a range of important trade areas. Although APEC as an institution will not be involved directly in those talks, APEC will closely monitor the process and do its best to help it along.
- The deadline for realizing the commitments under the Bogor Declaration by 2010/2020 is quickly approaching. APEC's credibility is at stake unless it can demonstrate political will and decisively translate commitments into concrete actions to achieve the Bogor Goals of trade and investment liberalization and facilitation (TILF).
- Economic globalization is being accompanied by a public debate on its benefits and costs. The time has come for APEC to step forward and contribute to ways of maximizing the benefits for common development and easing the costs of economic globalization, and thus lead the public debate in a constructive manner.
- Website: http://abaconline.org

Editorial

(You can read the ABAC report in its entirety at http://www.apecsec.org.sg/abac/reports/ABAC_Report_2001.pdf.) Past recommendations from ABAC have been adopted as APEC goals. Electronic IAP, the APEC Food System, an E-Commerce Readiness Assessment and many other APEC initiatives owe their genesis to ABAC recommendations.

C. The CEO Summit

As an added opportunity for top business leaders to participate in the APEC Leaders' meeting, a CEO Summit is organized each year. At this year's CEO Summit in Shanghai, Presidents George W. Bush, Vladimir Putin, Vicente Fox, Premier Jiang Zemin, Prime Ministers Mahathir Mohamad, Helen Clark, Junichiro Koizumi, Chief Executive Tung Chee Hua, and WTO Director General-Designate Supachai Panitchpakdi spoke, along with other leading political, academic and business representatives, to a gathering of over 1,000 top business executives. The top business executives included Microsoft's Bill Gates, Hewlett Packard's Carly Fiorino, FedEx's Fred Smith, Toshiba's Taizo Nishimuro, General Motors' John Smith, and AOL Time Warner's Gerald Levin.

D. Business Advising APEC at the working level

Below the level of the APEC Leaders and ABAC, business is active at many levels in APEC and in many of the APEC Ministerial and working-level groups. At the level of the Ministers, the APEC Finance Ministers established the APEC Financiers Group, which consists of representatives of financial institutions from each APEC economy, in 1995. In 2000, the APEC Energy Ministers held a full-day public and private sector dialogue and a separate dialogue with the Energy Business Network, a grouping of energy-related private sector companies. The APEC SME Ministers hold joint meetings with the SME Business Forum and also have met as well with the Women Leaders' Network and an E-Commerce Workshop.

At the working level of APEC, there are many different ways in which business advises APEC officials. For example, business representatives have participated in meetings of the Intellectual Property Rights Experts Group since 1996 and the Fisheries Task Force of the Pacific Economic Cooperation Council (PECC) has worked with the Fisheries Working Group since 1991. Other working level APEC groups hold annual dialogues with the private sector: the Infrastructure Workshop, the Sub-Committee on Customs Procedures, and the Trade Promotion Working Group. As noted earlier, other APEC working groups have established a private sector arm such as the Energy Business Network of the Energy Working Group. Many other groups have *ad hoc* contacts with business and others, such as the Informal Experts Group on the Mobility of Business People and others include business representatives as members of their delegations. These include the Industrial Science and Technology Working Group, the Marine Resources Conservation Group, and the Telecommunications Working Group.

IV. WHAT APEC DOES FOR BUSINESS

The direct and extensive involvement of business in the deliberations of the APEC Forum is critical for APEC's work and for staying on track to achieve the Bogor goals of trade liberalization in the Asia-Pacific region by the year 2020. Business provides APEC officials with a cutting-edge view of entrepreneurial developments and high-technology and helps point APEC the right way in removing impediments to doing business in the region. The business sector has been instrumental in detailing how APEC economies can best make themselves ready for the new economy and e-commerce. With the head-spinning changes taking place not only in technology but the structure of commerce itself, APEC officials would be hopelessly behind the curve keeping up with the changes without the direct ties with those in the business sector at the forefront of these revolutionary changes.

It is often hard to point out a 'top ten' of APEC achievements that benefit the private sector. APEC works in so many different areas that it would be impossible to rank order such a diversity of initiatives. The best approach would be to highlight a few examples from a number of the areas that benefit businesses most directly. The next section, 'Recent APEC Success Stories', attempts to do just that.

V. RECENT APEC SUCCESS STORIES

A. Standards and conformance

- APEC members have committed to align domestic standards with relevant international standards in four priority sectors by 2005 (electrical and electronic appliances, food labelling, rubber gloves and condoms, and machinery). Member economies have also agreed to align all electrical safety and electromagnetic compatibility standards by 2008.
- APEC is eliminating the need for separate testing for compliance with product standards in each importing economy through the adoption of *Mutual Recognition Arrangements (MRAs) on Conformance Testing*. Manufacturers will be able to test importing country standards in approved facilities in their home economy. Key sectors include:
  - *Telecommunications equipment*: The Telecommunications MRA covers trade worth an estimated US$ 50 billion per year. It is estimated that the MRA will save 5 per cent of the cost of new product placement, cut 6 months off the placement of new products in markets and reduce marketing costs for new products by up to 30 per cent.
  - *Food and food products*: The APEC Food MRA is designed to facilitate trade by minimizing food inspection controls at the point of entry into import economies on the basis of assurances provided through pre-export conformity assessment using official and officially recognized inspection and certification systems. It is an umbrella arrangement under which the implementing elements of sectoral arrangements relating to specific foods or food product sectors are to be included.
  - *Electrical and electronic equipment*: The Electrical MRA will be the first truly multilateral arrangement of its type. Unlike the Food and TEL MRAs, it does not require the approval of testing facilities and recognition of test results to be based on a bilateral agreement within a multilateral framework. Rather the Electrical MRA contains parts that are implemented multilaterally.
- APEC has developed guidelines and arrangements for the *exchange of information* in the following sectors:
  - *Food*: The Food Recall Guidelines will help developing members establish their own food recall systems and ensure a consistent approach among all members. As an adjunct to the Guidelines, APEC has endorsed an Arrangement for the Exchange of Information on Food Recalls. The guidelines and arrangement contribute to facilitating trade in food and food products within the APEC region while minimizing the risks to health and safety of consumers.

- *Toys*: The Arrangement for the Exchange of Information on Toy Safety provides a mechanism for the exchange of information on technical regulations dealing with the risks to health and safety of children that may arise from hazards associated with toys.

B. Business travel

- APEC has made business travel much easier within the APEC region. Expanded granting of multiple entry visas and a greater number of visa waiver arrangements have greatly simplified business travel. Instant access to visa requirements within APEC has also been provided through the APEC Business Travel Handbook website (http://www.apecsec.org.sg/travbook/ contents.html).
- The APEC Business Travel Card scheme ensures ongoing visa-free travel and expedited airport processing for holders. After China and Chinese Taipei joined the scheme last year, 12 economies now participate in the APEC Business Travel Card scheme and more are expected to join in the future. The APEC Business Advisory Council is a strong proponent of the Travel Card.

C. Customs

- Economies are implementing both the *WTO Customs Valuation Code* to ensure regional consistency in valuing traded goods, and the World Customs Organization's Guidelines on Express Consignment Clearance. An extensive cooperation program is under way to help all members reach these targets.
- The APEC Blueprint for Customs Modernization maps out APEC's strategic direction in the area of customs and enables business to visualize the future changes and the positive impacts they will have.

D. E-Commerce and 'paperless trading'

- The *APEC Blueprint for Action on E-Commerce* responds to the Internet revolution by committing APEC members to a goal of paperless trading. The computerization of customs and other trade-related procedures through the adoption of the UN/EDIFACT standard is a key step towards paperless trading. The Blueprint also guides governments on the development of legal, technical, operating and trading environments for e-commerce. The *E-Com Legal Guide* (http://www.bakerinfo.com/apec) provides businesses with Internet access to members' current laws on electronic transactions and regulatory barriers affecting e-commerce. The *E-Commerce Readiness Assessment* (http://www.apecsec.org.sg/download/abac/e_commerce_read_guide.exe), developed with extensive private sector input, advises officials how best to make their economies ready to adopt the new economy.

E. Telecommunications

- The *APEC telecommunications interconnection framework* simplifies the negotiation of telecommunications contracts with detailed, non-prescriptive conditions for inclusion in contracts between telecommunications carriers negotiating the connection of services.

F. Energy

- The *Manual of Best Practice Principles for Independent Power Producers* (http://www.apecsec.org.sg/download/pubs/ippmanual.exe) promotes a more certain investment environment for energy suppliers by advocating transparency and consistency in institutional and regulatory structures; tender/bid processes and evaluation criteria; power purchase arrangements and associated tariff structures; and financing.

G. Transportation

- The *Road Transport Harmonization Project* is a multi-phased effort to reduce barriers to trade in the automotive sector by promoting standards harmonization taking into account traffic safety and environmental protection needs. APEC has endorsed a *Model MRA on Automotive Products* to promote bilateral and multilateral arrangements between APEC members on the mutual acceptances of standards.

H. Intellectual property

- APEC's *Guidelines for Simplification and Standardization of Administrative Procedures for Intellectual Property Protection* will lessen the burden on business of complicated procedures when applying to obtain intellectual property rights in different economies. The Guidelines are a step towards standardized APEC trademark applications and, eventually, to 'paperless filing'. The APEC IPR Information Mall and the Intellectual Property Contact List websites provide business with easy access to information on intellectual property protection regimes, including IPR enforcement systems, and contact details for relevant government officials, business people and academics.
- APEC has pursued a cooperation program to assist members in implementing the WTO TRIPS Agreement. Activities undertaken include a symposium to support TRIPS implementation and surveys on the current status of implementation of the Agreement.

I. Trade promotion

- One of APEC's tools in stimulating trade has been the holding of *APEC Trade Fairs*. The APEC Trade Fairs make it easier for member economies to showcase products, services and technologies of APEC member economies, promote trade and investment, and foster closer business and economic relationships among business communities in the region. The APEC Working Group on Trade Promotion has been holding these APEC Trade Fairs once every two years. The last one, the 4th APEC International Trade Fair, was held in Indonesia in October 2000. The date and venue for the 5th APEC International Trade Fair in 2002 is still pending.

EDITORIAL

- The same Trade Promotion Working Group also runs *APECNet*, which allows businesses to search for business opportunities (including business matching services) in member economies, by posting inquiries and accessing member economies homepages.

J. Enhancing access to market information

- The *APEC Tariff Database* (http://www.apectariff.org) includes tariff rates from 17 economies at either the 9- or 6-digit level of the HS Code on all products on which they levy tariffs. The database is not only useful for APEC members but for all importers and exporters worldwide.
- The APEC Directory of Professional Services (http://www.dfat.gov.au/apec/prof_services/index.html) will facilitate trade in services by increasing transparency, making relevant information more accessible and contributing to any future development of common professional standards in the APEC region.
- The Compilation of Information on Food Labeling Laws, Regulations and Standards in the APEC Region benefits food exporters by providing easy access to such information at minimum cost while ensuring the health and safety of consumers.
- The APEC *Manual on Air-Shipped Live and Fresh Seafood* (available for purchase from the APEC Secretariat website) provides customs, health and technical guidelines on preparing and packaging goods for air shipment in APEC markets. With the demand for these products growing worldwide, the contribution that this makes to facilitating trade for fish harvesters, importers, wholesalers and retailers in APEC economies, particularly recent entrants (most of whom are small enterprises) is significant. The current value for trade in live fish alone is estimated at over US$1.2 billion.
- The *APEC Investment Guidebook* (http://www.apecsec.org.sg/download/pubs/invstguide4.exe) provides information on foreign investment regimes in APEC economies, including regulatory frameworks, investment protection and promotion and incentives.
- The APEC Investment Mart and the Cyber Mart provide potential investors with detailed information on investment policies and environments of APEC economies.
- The APEC Government Procurement Homepage (http://www.apecsec.org.sg/govt-proc/gphome.html) details members' policies and procedures for bidding on public procurement contracts and, where available, links to domestic sites listing actual bidding opportunities. Government markets typically represent 10–15 per cent of GDP.
- *APECNet* (http://www.apecnet.org.sg) allows businesses to post or identify business opportunities over the Internet. This provides business with a convenient and cost-effective platform to facilitate business exchange. On average, the site records a monthly hit rate of 45,000 with 8,000 monthly requests for information about member economies.
- The APEC *Ports Database* (*http://www.apecport.org*) provides business with readily accessible, user-friendly information on port location, administration, capacity, and relevant shipping agents.

Annex V. APEC Structure

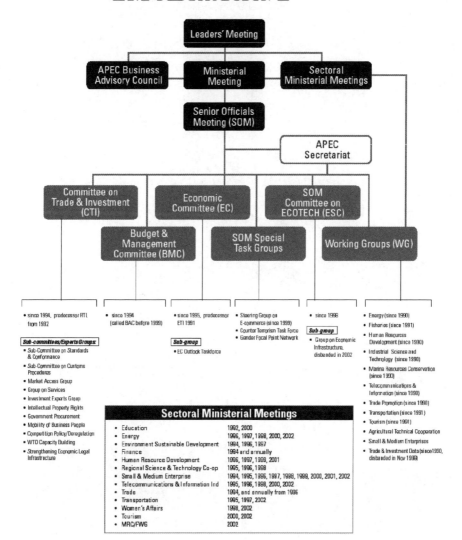

List of Contributors

Luis Aparicio Valdez, Director of Peruvian Journal Análisis Laboral, which recently has celebrated its 25th Anniversary, President of the Instituto Peruano del Trabajo (Peru) and President of the International Industrial Relations Association (2003–2006)
Yutaka Asao, Director of the Research Planning Department of the Japan Institute of Labour
Jorge Bernedo Alvarado, Researcher of Análisis Laboral (Peru)
Roger Blanpain, Professor at the Universities of Leuven (Belgium) and Tilburg (The Netherlands), President of the International Society of Labour Law and Social Security
Efrén Córdova, Professor at the International La Florida University (USA), Former ILO officer
Alan J. Geare, Professor of Management, University of Otago, Dunedin (New Zealand)
Tadashi Hanami, President of the Japan Institute of Labour, Professor at the Sofia University, Ex-president of the International Industrial Relations Association
Russell Lansbury, Professor of Work and Organisational Studies, Faculty of Economics and Business, University of Sydney (Australia)
Hyo-Soo Lee, Professor at Yeungham University (Korea)
Won-Duck Lee, President of the Korea Labour Institute
Emilio Morgado V., Former ILO officer, Professor at Chile University
Balakrishnan Parasuraman, Program of Industrial Relations, Social Science School (UNB), Kota Kinabalu, Sabah East Malaysia
Jaehooni Rhee, Associate Professor at Yeungham University (Korea)
Angel G. Ruiz, M., Academic and national researcher of Mexico
Daphne Taras, Haskayne School of Business, University of Calgary (Canada)
Mark Thompson, Faculty of Commerce and Business Administration, University of British Columbia (Canada)
Arturo Vásquez Párraga, University of Texas-Pan American, Texas (USA), Director of Latin American Companies in the USA project, ex-researcher of Análisis Laboral (1977–1980) (Peru)
Ying Zhu, Senior Lecturer, Department of Management, University of Melbourne (Australia)

1. Employment Law in the Context of the Changing Pattern of Employment Relations in Australia

Russell Lansbury*

Summary The past two decades here witnessed significant changes in the nature and structure of collective bargaining in Australia as the 'social settlement', which characterized employment relations for most of the twentieth century, has been gradually dismantled by successive Australian governments. The long-established system of centralized wage determination has been undermined by growth of enterprise bargaining and the decline of the power and authority of the Australian Industrial Relations Commission. This has been accompanied by a reduction in tariff protection of manufacturing and services with the objective of making Australian industry more internationally competitive. The decline of unionization, resulting from structural change and other factors, has enabled employers to increase their bargaining power and expand the scope of individualized, non-union agreements. The degree of tripartism, which underpinned the social settlement and consensus on industrial relations, has also declined as the Coalition government has reduced its support for tripartite bodies. It seems unlikely that, even with a change of government, there will be a return to a centralized system of industrial relations, although a more coordinated approach to bargaining may be re-established. It is, therefore, an appropriate time to reconsider the kind of industrial framework which is needed for the regulation of work and employment in contemporary Australia. With the decline of collective bargaining and union representation, it is suggested that the Federal government should not only enact positive employee rights into statute law but also legislate minimum terms and conditions for all workers under its jurisdiction. Furthermore, given the decline of union coverage, the introduction of works councils should be considered in order to ensure that employees can participate in workplace governance. Any new institutional arrangements must provide individual workers with a system of industrial justice, while preserving a role for unions in collective bargaining and fostering productive enterprises.

---

*   Professor of Work and Organisational Studies, Faculty of Economics and Business, University of Sydney, Australia.

R. Blanpain (ed.),
Labour Relations in the Asia-Pacific Countries, 1–13.
© 2004 *Kluwer Law International. Printed in Great Britain.*

I. RECENT CHANGES IN THE STRUCTURE OF COLLECTIVE BARGAINING IN AUSTRALIA

The past two decades in Australia have been characterized by significant changes in industrial relations institutions and practices. For much of the past century, Australian industrial relations were considered to be among the most centralized of the industrialized market economies, due to its unique system of conciliation and arbitration. When the Commonwealth of Australia was created in 1901, the Constitution empowered the Federal government to settle interstate disputes by means of conciliation and arbitration while giving it only limited power to directly enact legislation relating to industrial relations and employment matters (McIntyre and Mitchell, 1989). The Commonwealth Court of Conciliation and Arbitration was established in 1904 (later to become the Australian Industrial Relations Commission) with the power to conciliate between employers and unions and, if this was not possible, to unilaterally determine the terms and conditions of employment by 'equitable awards'. Throughout most of the twentieth century, the arbitration tribunals (which operated at both Federal and State levels) provided the main institutional framework for determining employment conditions. Until the late 1980s, Federal and State awards covered around 85 per cent of all wage and salary earners, although these tended to set only minimum rates of pay and conditions and permitted the parties to establish supplementary rates by collective bargaining. Hence, the OECD has referred to the Australian system as one of the 'most highly centralized and highly coordinated of wage determination systems' (OECD, 1994). The Australian system of conciliation and arbitration was, for many years, supported by all the major political parties as providing benefits for both workers and employers. Business accepted the arbitration system in exchange for tariff protection and industrial stability, while unions gained legitimacy and increased membership as part of the established, state-sanctioned industrial relations system. In comparison with some other bargaining systems, the Australian tribunals provided procedures for the orderly settlement of industrial disputes and limited recourse to industrial action. The arbitration system also offered a mechanism whereby broader economic and social concerns (such as equity) could be brought to bear on industrial relations outcomes. Yet critics identified a number of deficiencies in the system, which included: failure of the centralized award system to take into account the particular needs of workplaces and enterprises, frequent appeals to tribunals to settle disputes, which undermined efforts at negotiation and bargaining, fragmentation of bargaining through multi-unionism at the workplace, and failure of the award system to reduce the number of strikes. Another issue which attracted widespread criticism was the existence of separate federal and state industrial relations jurisdictions, although this is a reflection of the particular division of power in Australia between the Federal and State legislatures.

II. FROM CENTRALIZATION TO COORDINATED OR MANAGED DECENTRALIZATION OF BARGAINING

Since the early 1980s, the Australian system of industrial relations has undergone several phases of reform as the long-established system of centralized wage determination has been displaced by a period of *coordinated* or *managed descentralized* (1987–1990), followed by *coordinated flexibility* (1991–1996) and the current phase of *fragmented flexibility* (since 1997).

During the past 15 years, the roles of the Australian Industrial Relations Commission (AIRC) and state-level tribunals have been considerably diminished. Employers generally supported the direction of change but some argued that the reforms, particularly at the federal level, did not go far enough in dismantling the old system. Union leaders opposed reforms which undermined the collective basis of labour–management relations and promoted individualization of the employment relationship. The kinds of flexibility introduced by the most recent reforms, it is argued, leave many workers unprotected and in a weaker bargaining position with employers. Yet, over the past decade, both Labour and Coalition governments have contributed to the dismantling of the institutional structures which underpinned industrial relations in Australia.

Although he AIRC's role was strengthened during the early years of the Hawke Labour government (1983–1986), its powers were eroded under the Keating Labour government (1993–1996), and have been further diminished since the Howard Coalition government was elected in 1996. Critics argue that the AIRC and other traditional industrial relations institutions have become anachronistic and have failed to keep up with changes in the nature of work which require a more deregulated environment. Others, however, regard the diminution of the AIRC's powers as undermining the role of the independent third party between labour and capital, as well as leaving economically weaker members of the labour market less protected. While increased efficiency and productivity may be worthy of national goals, the AIRC is still widely regarded as playing an important role in trying to ensure that equity considerations are taken into account.

From an international perspective, one of the most interesting aspects of Australian industrial relations has been the transition from a centralized system based on compulsory arbitration administered by the Federal and State tribunals to a more decentralized approach of bargaining at the enterprise level. During the initial years of the Hawke Labour government (from 1983–1986), there was a brief return to centralized wage determination as part of the initial Accord (an agreement on wages and other matters) between the Australian Labour Party (ALP) and the Australian Council of Trade Union (ACTU). Indeed, it was argued by the Hawke government during this period that the breakdown of the centralized wage system during the previous Liberal–National Party coalition government (1975–1983) had exacerbated economic problems. The Hawke government wanted to avoid the possibility of a renewed wage/price spiral that had characterized earlier periods of more decentralized bargaining. Furthermore, the government commissioned a review of the industrial relations system, chaired by

Professor Keith Hancock. The Hancock Report (1985) recommended the retention and consolidation of the centralized system, with the continuation of a major role for the AIRC. This was on the grounds that a centralized system facilitated the enforcement of income policies and thereby helped to contain levels of unemployment and inflation.

However, following a balance of payment crisis and other economic problems in the mid-1980s, the Hawke Labour government abandoned its centralized approach and adopted a policy of *managed decentralism*. Full wage indexation was abandoned in 1986 and a two-tier wage system was introduced which not only took account of productivity increases at the industry and enterprise levels, but also maintained a system of national wage adjustments. The AIRC retained an important role whereby the National Wage Cases set the framework for enterprise bargaining between unions and employers. The 1988 National Wage Case Decision by the AIRC, established a 'structural efficiency principle' designed to encourage the parties to reach collective agreements, for example, on the introduction of multi-skilling, broad-based work classifications, and a reduction of demarcation barriers. This period ushered in greater labour market flexibility while retaining the broad institutional framework.

III. FROM COORDINATED DECENTRALIZATION TO COORDINATED FLEXIBILITY

The seeds of coordinated flexibility were sown in early 1990 when the government, employers and unions all submitted arguments to the AIRC in the National Wage Case that 'enterprise bargaining' should become the main process for achieving wage increases. The change of policy by the Labour government and the unions (which had both previously resisted pressure from employers for such reforms) came amid continuing economic uncertainty and a campaign by Opposition parties for enterprise-based bargaining. Although the AIRC initially rejected calls for enterprise bargaining on the grounds that the various parties had different (and contradictory) views on what the new system involved, it endorsed a more decentralized approach in October 1991. The AIRC retained the capacity to scrutinize agreements to ensure that they met 'public interest' criteria. Under pressure from employers, who complained that it was too difficult to achieve enterprise agreements under this system, the government introduced further amendments to the *Industrial Relations Act* which reduced the power of the AIRC to veto agreements and widened opportunities for employers to opt out of the traditional award system. However, the AIRC continued to administer a national 'safety net' of minimum wages and conditions for lowest paid workers by updating awards and conditions and conducting National Wage Case hearings.

After its surprise election victory in March 1993, the Labour government (under the leadership of Paul Keating) introduced further legal reforms to extend enterprise bargaining with the *Industrial Relations Reform Act 1993*. Although parts of the Act were based on International Labor Organization (ILO) conventions and recommendations, which strengthened employment protection and granted a wider range of minimum entitlements, it also included provisions which facilitated employers making agreements with their employees without involving unions. Soon after his government's electoral victory, Prime Minister Keating argued that 'we need to find a way of extending the coverage of agreements to being full substitutes for awards' (Keating, 1993).

Enterprise Flexibility Agreements (EFAs), introduced under the 1993 Reform Act, did not require an eligible union to be involved. Unions opposed EFAs on the grounds that they encouraged employers to avoid unions and facilitated a move towards individual contracts of employment. Such fears were realized in a major dispute during 1995 between a large mining company, Rio Tinto (formerly CRA), and unions at Weipa in the remote north of Australia. This set the pattern for further disputes in the mining and maritime industries during the 1990s, which were designed to break the unions' bargaining strength by persuading workers to accept individual contracts. Hence, the period from 1991 to 1996 was one of transition from the collective to more individualized forms of industrial relations, as some employers sought to take full advantage of the more flexible bargaining arrangements which were permitted under the new legislation and the role of the AIRC was significantly diminished.

IV. FROM COORDINATED TO FRAGMENTED FLEXIBILITY

The most recent phase of industrial relations reform, which has fostered a system of *fragmented flexibility*, began with the election of the Liberal–National Party coalition government led by John Howard in 1996. The Workplace Relations Act 1996 signaled a more radical decentralization of industrial relations to the enterprise level, with broader scope for non-union agreements and further diminution in the role of the AIRC. However, amendments to the legislation by a minority party, the Australian Democrats, which held the balance of power in the Senate, softened some of the provisions which the government sought to introduce. While not going as far as New Zealand's Employment Contracts Act 1991, which dismantled that country's arbitration system, the Howard government nevertheless sought to move the Australian system further away from its traditional collectivist approach, in which there was a strong role for unions and the AIRC, toward a more fragmented and flexible system of individual bargaining between employees and employers. A key element of the Workplace Relations Act 1996, embodied in the new Australian Workplace Agreements (AWAs), sought to enable (and encourage) employers to enter into either a non-union agreement or an individual contract with their employees. While AWAs have so far played only a minor role in regulating wages and conditions, and cover only a few percent of employees, they have been used by employers as a 'threat' against unions in order to gain concessions in enterprise agreements.

Under the Workplace Relations Act 1996, the role of the AIRC underwent further significant change, although it remained a key labour market institution. The AIRC's award determinations were restricted to a list of 'twenty allowable matters', although it could arbitrate on 'exceptional matters'. Yet awards remain an important means by which employment matters are regulated in the Australian labour market. Currently, approximately 25 per cent of all employees have their wages and conditions entirely regulated by awards, while 35 per cent of employees rely on a combination of awards and collective agreements. The remaining 40 per cent of the labour force have their wages and conditions determined mainly by common law contracts, which marks an important shift away from collective forms of agreement making over the past decade or so.

Hence, while there has continued to be a trend toward enterprise bargaining, this has led neither to a total abandonment of awards nor to the elimination of AIRC. Despite their complaints about the system, employers have hesitated to move too far away from the traditional system of awards and collective agreements. Critics have questioned assumptions behind the argument, put forward for enterprise bargaining, that the centralized system lacked sufficient flexibility to achieve economic efficiency. Furthermore, despite constant assertions by its supporters that enterprise bargaining would bring about significant improvements in productivity through greater flexibility and workplace focus, these arguments have not been supported by evidence (Coelli *et al.*, 1994).

V. POLICY IMPLICATIONS OF THE CHANGING PATTERN OF EMPLOYMENT RELATIONS IN AUSTRALIA

A. Winners and losers from recent changes

The most significant change in the structure of collective bargaining in Australia over the past decade has been the movement away from a co-ordinated system, in which the industrial tribunals retained a significant role, towards a fragmented approach dominated by employers. The decline in the role and influence of the AIRC was initiated by the Labour government which sought to decentralize the industrial relations system as part of its program of economic reform. During the early 1990s, the Labour government passed legislation to bypass the AIRC in order to facilitate the introduction of enterprise bargaining. The ACTU supported these reforms, as part of its Accord with the government, in the hope that enterprise bargaining would reinvigorate the union movement at the workplace level. Although the role of the AIRC was weakened, it retained the capacity to scrutinize agreements to ensure they were in 'the public interest'. The Coalition government, however, further reduced the arbitral role of the AIRC to the 'safety net' of 20 allowable matters and opened it up to competition from other regulatory agencies. The overall effect of these changes was to reduce the functions and relevance of the tribunal. Although the ACTU has undertaken a number of reforms to strengthen the organizing skills and capacities of unions, the percentage of the workforce belonging to unions has continued to decline as has the coverage of both awards and collective agreements negotiated by unions.

The Coalition government sought to introduce further legislative changes which would have further reduced the number of allowable award matters over which the AIRC is permitted to arbitrate, but was defeated by a hostile

Senate. The government also proposed changes to the appointment and tenure of members of the AIRC which had the potential to undermine their independence.

The decline in the role and authority of the AIRC has been deleterious for the unions and those members of the workforce whose bargaining power is weak. Unions, in general, have failed to rebuild their membership and bargaining power under a decentralized system in which the AIRC plays a less significant role. While employers have generally welcomed the movement towards a more decentralized system, they do not appear to place as high a priority on the need for industrial relations reform. Some have expressed concern about the reduction in the role and authority of the AIRC, particularly in relation to its reduced capacity to effectively settle industrial disputes.

A report issued by the Business Council of Australia on *Managerial Leadership in the Workplace* (BCA, 2000) noted that Australian enterprises were not grasping new opportunities emerging from globalization, technological change and the knowledge economy, but only 55 per cent of the BCA's members viewed the industrial relations system as a major impediment to improved business performance. While this may reflect sentiment among employers that the decentralization of bargaining has delivered sufficient reforms, it may also demonstrate that other factors are regarded as more important contributors to improving Australia's international competitiveness.

B. The role of government in relation to deficiencies of the prevailing structure of collective bargaining

The Constitution of the Commonwealth of Australia in 1901 assigned limited and specific powers to the federal government in relation to industrial relations. In Section 51, para. 35, it states

> 'The Parliament shall, subject to this Constitution, have power to make laws for the peace, order and good government of the Commonwealth with respect to Conciliation and Arbitration for the prevention and settlement of industrial disputes extending beyond the limits of any one state.'

Hence, the federal government is severely limited in its ability to intervene directly in industrial relations (except in regard to its own employees).

The AIRC acquired considerable influence over industrial relations matters because the Constitution compelled the federal government to delegate its powers of conciliation and arbitration to the tribunal. Although, the Nationalist government led by S.M. Bruce tried unsuccessfully to abolish the Commission in 1929, successive Australian governments have complied with the decisions of the AIRC, even when these were not to their liking. The current Coalition government, however, has raised the possibility of using the Commonwealth's corporation's power in the Constitution to bypass and downgrade the role of the AIRC. So far, the government has been unwilling to do this because it raises a number of possible difficulties and is opposed by the Opposition parties, which hold the balance of power in the Senate. The government has also raised the possibility of the States ceding their industrial relations power to the Commonwealth, but this has been opposed by most of the State governments, including those controlled by the Coalition parties.

While the role of the federal government in resolving perceived deficiencies of the prevailing structure of collective bargaining is limited by the Constitution, it can nevertheless make significant operational changes to the system. Hence, the government's strategy of reducing the arbitral powers of the AIRC has diminished the authority of the tribunal. The government has also created a new regulatory agency, the Office of the Employment Advocate (OEA), to process AWAs, and investigate contraventions of the freedom of association provisions of the Act. The AWAs have provided employers with an instrument which enables them to enter into individual agreements with members of their workforce. So far, AWAs have only been utilized by approximately 4 per cent of employees. However, the effect of the government's action has been to provide the AIRC with a potential, if not actual, competitor as well as facilitating the growth of individual rather than collective employment relations.

If the Labour Party had been returned to government at the federal election in November 2001, it is likely that some of the AIRC's arbitral powers would have been restored and that AWAs would have been brought under its jurisdiction. However, it is unlikely that Labour would have returned to a centralized industrial relations system or even the co-ordinated decentralism of a decade ago. Rather, Labour is more likely to seek some 'middle way' between a collective bargaining system based on trade unions and a stream of individual contracts which are subject to a no disadvantage test administered by the AIRC (rather like the previous EFA). Labour will hesitate to grant monopoly bargaining rights to unions because it will fear alienating business and voters who fear unions gaining too much power. Labour is also likely to strengthen the AIRC's role in adjusting the safety wages and conditions of the lowest paid, should it regain government these would appear to be appropriate measures to take in order to correct deficiencies in the current situation of collective bargaining which have weakened the capacity of trade unions to represent workers, have placed undue restrictions on the arbitral powers of the AIRC and left the weakest members of the workforce with inadequate protection. Given the continuing concerns among many unions about the decline of real wages under the previous Labour government, it is unlikely that a formal Accord-like agreement will be forged between the unions and the Labour Party on wages, prices and other matters.

C. Proposals for changes in the structure of collective bargaining and social partnership

There does not appear to be much interest in developing tripartite approaches to employment relations, such as the social partnership approaches found in some European countries. The Coalition parties are principally concerned with finding means to contain or reduce the unions' influence. The Labour Party tends to favour the establishment of tripartite bodies when in government (such as the Economic Policy Advisory Council, established by the Hawke Labour government) but neither the employers nor the unions have exhibited strong support for these initiatives. It is unlikely that a future Labour government would assign high priority to reviving such arrangements, unless they were strongly supported by the employers and the union movement.

McCallum (2001) has argued that a future Labour government should give priority to reforming labour law using a 'rights-based approach' which would enact positive employee rights and employer obligations into statute law. The Federal parliament should provide a mechanism to require employers to recognize unions and bargain with unions where either 20 of their employees are union members or 40 per cent of the workforce is unionized, whichever is the lesser number. According to McCallum: 'only when enterprises are required to bargain with recognized trade unions will bargaining in good faith laws be truly operative'. Rather that simply relying on collective bargaining, however, McCallum argues that Federal parliament should also legislate minimum terms and conditions of employment for all workers who are covered by Federal labour law. The following issues would be included: hours of work; standards for full-time, part-time and casual employment; major public holidays, annual leave and family leave including enforceable parental, cultural and bereavement leave; minimum period of notice on termination and redundancy payment entitlements. A weakness of the current bargaining system, argues McCallum, is that it has involved employees exchanging their entitlements for cash payments. Such legislation would also clearly spell out the rights of working men and women.

Recently, the ACTU issued a discussion paper which discussed the merits of works councils, similar to those in Europe, which could provide an additional means of influence for workers in decision-making at the enterprise level. While the ACTU Secretary, Greg Combet (2001), argued that works councils could provide an avenue for unions to recruit new members, there was not widespread support for this view within the union movement. Nevertheless, there has been debate among academic industrial lawyers about how legislation could be introduced to provide a 'voice' for non-unionized workers as a means of strengthening 'industrial citizenship' and this proposal could gain momentum under a Labour government.

McCallum (2001) argues that in order for employees to collectively participate in workplace governance, Federal parliament should encourage the establishment of elected works councils in enterprises with 100 or more employees. These bodies could consult with employers on a wide range of issues including the introduction of technological change, rostering arrangements and amenities. The government should establish programs to train employee and employer works council representations to ensure that they understand their rights and responsibilities. Works councils could be voluntary for the first two or three years and encouraged through taxation concessions, but then made compulsory if they prove to be successful.

While any proposals to introduce works councils is likely to be resisted by employers, there has been a steady growth in joint consultative activities and the expanding role of occupational health and safety committees. Management and employee representatives involved at the workplace level, have generally viewed these developments as positive. Any future initiatives in this field, however, are likely to be modest.

Despite the political rhetoric, which tends to highlight differences between the two major parties in regard to industrial relations reform, there has emerged a degree of consensus in favour of incremental rather than radical change in the immediate future. This may be due to uncertainty about the economy and an unwillingness on both sides to create instability. It may also be due, according to Wooden (2000), that the research evidence to date about the effects of industrial relations reform is somewhat inconclusive, and it seems likely that the claims about both the benefits and costs of industrial relations reform have been exaggerated. A similar argument has been put by Justice Giudice (1999), President of the AIRC, that: 'Perhaps surprisingly, on examination of the legislation changes initiated by both sides of politics in the 1990s demonstrates a degree of consistency in the direction of reform which is not evident from the political debate'. While the President notes that there are policy differences between the parties, the political process emphasizes differences rather than areas of common agreement. Giudice raises two issues on which he perceives there is common ground. First, that the AIRC's award making function should be confined mainly to the provision of a safety net, with primary emphasis being given to bargaining by the parties at the enterprise level. Second, that the arbitral role of the Commission should be restricted to instances when enterprise bargaining has not been successful.

Nevertheless, there remain philosophical differences between labour and capital (and those parties which represent them) as to how the industrial relationship is to be regulated and the means by which this is to be achieved. The labour movement will continue to lobby whichever government is in power to extend their rights to recruit members, to bargain on their behalf and to undertake industrial action in support of their claims. The employers will seek restrictions on union activities and promote individual rather than collective forms of employee representation and action. Labour government will tend to favour the industrial relations tribunals having broader powers to negotiate employment issues, compared with Coalition governments.

VI. CONCLUSION

It is timely to consider whether a new social settlement or social partnership between employers, organized labour and the government is possible. Given the importance of labour market issues for both economic and social policies, as well as the need to foster creative human potentialities in the workplace. This must be a worthwhile goal for the new millenium. It is almost a century since an 'historic compromise' was forged between labour and capital in Australia, after the disastrous strikes of the 1890s, with the enactment of the Commonwealth Conciliation and Arbitration Act 1904, which gave birth to the federal tribunal and industrial relations system. It is an appropriate time for reconsidering the kind of institutional framework which is needed for the regulation of work and employment relations in contemporary Australia. Any new institutional arrangements must provide individual workers with a system of industrial justice, while preserving a role for unions in collective bargaining (for those workers who wish to utilize this option) and ensuring employers can develop productive enterprises. The federal government can play an important role in providing mechanisms for dispute settlement and protection of those in a weak bargaining position. There should also be encouragement for the parties to develop innovative approaches to conflict resolution without relying solely on the State. This may involve the development of independent agencies and third parties to assist the coordination of bargaining and dispute settlement. Any new and lasting social settlement will require the contributions of all interested parties to determine how best to achieve both equity and efficiency in the workplace and labour market.

REFERENCES

ACTU (Australian Council of Trade Unions) (2000), *Unions at Work*. ACTU, Melbourne.
ACTU (Australian Council of Trade Unions) (2001), *Our Future at Work*. ACTU, Melbourne.
ACTU/CAI (Australian Council of Trade Unions/Confederation of Australian Industry) (1988), *Joint Statement on Participative Practices*. Australian Government Publishing Service, Canberra.
ALP/ACTU (Australian Labor Party/Australian Council of Trade Unions) (1983), *Statement of Accord between the ALP and ACTU Regarding Economic Policy*. ALP/ACTU, Melbourne.
Australian Productivity Commission (1999), *Microeconomic Reforms and Australian Productivity: Exploring the Links*, APC, Melbourne.
Bamber, G.J. and Lansbury, R.D. (1997), 'Employment relations in the Australian auto industry: A question of survival', in: Kitay, J. and Lansbury, R.D. (eds.), *Changing Employment Relations in Australia*. Oxford University Press, Melbourne, pp. 81–101.
BCA (Business Council of Australia) (1999), *Managerial Leadership in the Workplace*. BCA, Melbourne.
Brett, J. (1997), 'Politics and Business Parted', *The Age Newspaper* 17 July, p. 15.
Calmfors, L. and Driffill, J. (1988), 'Bargaining structure, corporatism and macroeconomic performance', *Economic Policy* Vol. 6, pp. 13–61.
Coelli, M., Fahrer, J. and Lindsay, H. (1994), 'Wage dispersion and labour market institutions: Across country study', *Reserve Bank Discussion Paper*, Sydney.
Combet, G. (2001), 'Employee participation in an Australian Context, in: *Conference on Works Councils in Australia*, Royal Melbourne Institute of Technology, Melbourne.

Committee of Review into Australian Industrial Relations Law and Systems, *Report*, Chaired by K. Hancock (1985), Australian Government Publishing Service, Canberra.

Cooper, R. (2000), 'Organize, organize, organize! ACTU Congress 2000', *Journal of Industrial Relations* Vol. 42, No. 4, pp. 582–594.

Dabscheck, B. (2000), 'The Australian Waterfront Dispute and Theories of the State' *Journal of Industrial Relations* Vol. 42, No. 4, pp. 497–518.

Davis, E.M. and Lansbury, R.D. (1998), 'Employment relations in Australia', in: Bamber, G.J. and Lansbury, R.D. (eds.), *International and Comparative Employment Relations*. Allen & Unwin, Sydney pp. 144–169.

Ellem, B. (2001), 'Trade Unionism in 2000', *Journal of Industrial Relations* Vol. 43, No. 2, pp. 196–218.

Giudice, Justice G. (1999), 'Keynote Address' in: *National Convention of the Industrial Relations Society of Australia* Freemantle, Western Australia, 22 October.

Higgins, H.B. (1915), 'A new province for law and order', *Harvard Law Review* Vol. 29, p. 1.

Howard, W.A. (1977), 'Australian Trade Unions in the Context of Union Theory' *Journal of Industrial Relations* Vol. 19, No. 3, pp. 255–273.

ILO (International Labour Organization) (2000), *Year Book of Labour Statistics*. ILO, Geneva.

Keating, P.J. (1993), Speech to Institute of Directors, Melbourne, 21 April.

Kelly, P. (1992), *The End of Certainty*. Allen & Unwin, Sydney.

Kelly, D. and Underhill, E. (1997), Australian steel: A corporatist transformation?' in: Kitay, J. and Lansbury, R.D. (eds.), *Changing Employment Relations in Australia*. Oxford University Press, Melbourne.

Kitay, J. and Lansbury, R.D. (1997), *Changing Employment Relations in Australia*. Oxford University Press, Melbourne.

Kyloh, R. (ed.) (1998), *Mastering the Challenge of Globalization: Towards a Trade Union Agenda*. ILO, Geneva.

Lansbury, R.D. and Bamber, G.J. (1998), 'The end of institutionalized industrial relations in Australia?', *Perspectives on Work* Vol. 2, No. 1, 26–30.

McCallum, R. (1997), 'Crafting a new collective labour for Australia', *Journal of Industrial Relations* Vol. 39, No. 3, pp. 405–422.

McCallum, R. (2001), 'Legislating Workers' Rights', *Worksite*, Spring, p. 4.

McIntyre, S. and Mitchell, R. (eds.) (1989), *Foundations of Arbitration*. Oxford University Press, Melbourne.

Morehead, A., Steel, M, Alexander, M., Stephen, K. and Duffin, L. (1997), *Changes at Work: the 1995 Australian Workplace Industrial Relations Survey*. Addison Wesley Longman, Melbourne.

OECD (Organization for Economic Cooperation and Development) (1994), *The Jobs Study*. OECD, Paris.

OECD (Organization for Economic Cooperation and Development) (1997), *Economic Outlook*. OECD, Paris.

OECD (Organization for Economic Cooperation and Development) (2000), *Economic Surveys: Australia*. OECD, Paris.
OECD (Organization for Economic Cooperation and Development) (2001), *Review of Labour Market Policies in Australia*. OECD, Paris.
Peetz, D. (1998), *Unions in a Contrary World*. Cambridge University Press, Melbourne.
Poole, M., Lansbury, R.D. and Wailes, N. (2001), 'A Comparative Analysis of Developments in Industrial Democracy' *Industrial Relations* Vol. 40, No. 3, pp. 490–525.
Salmon, I. (1996), 'A business perspective' in: *National Summit on the Future of Work in Australia'* Sydney, May.
Watson, B. (1996), 'Commentary' in: *National Summit on the Future of Work in Australia*, Sydney, May.
Wiseman, J. (1998), *Global Nation? Australia and the Politics of Globalization*. Cambridge University Press, Melbourne.
Wooden, M. (2000), *The Transformation of Australian Industrial Relations*. Federation Press, Sydney.

2. Canadian Industrial Relations

Mark Thompson* and Daphne Taras†

I. INTRODUCTION

Industrial relations in Canada rest on several fundamental characteristics. A large proportion of the labour force is subject to the influence of collective bargaining, directly or indirectly, and legal protection for collective bargaining is strong. Traditions of adversarialism and high levels of strike activity exist in labour–management relations. Industrial relations are highly decentralized. Canada has incorporated employers, unions and public policies that originated in the United States but produced a distinctive industrial relations system.

II. THE HISTORICAL, POLITICAL AND SOCIO-ECONOMIC CONTEXT

Canada's federal system of government is very decentralized in the world, vesting authority for most employment matters with the 10 provinces. Federal authority is limited to regulation of the federal civil service and employment within federal industries such as inter-provincial transport. Less than 10 per cent of Canadian workers fall within this domain.

The history and traditions of French Canada, offer alternative social, economic and legal visions that are quite different from those elsewhere in North America where English is spoken. Canada is regionally fractured into a primarily French speaking province of Quebec and parts of adjacent provinces, and primarily English speaking provinces. A pro-independence party governs the province of Quebec.

Canada has a multi-party system reflecting these interests. For decades, the country was dominated by a rivalry between two parties, the Liberal and Conservatives, with a powerful third party, the New Democratic Party (NDP), able to achieve some of its left of centre agenda when it occasionally held the balance of power. The Liberals dominate federal politics, occasionally forming a minority government or yielding power to the Conservatives, who won large majorities in 1984 and 1988. The Liberals are a pragmatic, reformist party, with

---

*   Faculty of Commerce and Business Administration, University of British Columbia, Canada.
†   Haskayne School of Business, University of Calgary, Canada.

a traditional base of support in Quebec. The Conservatives are a right of center party, normally drawing votes from the Eastern and Western regions. While it had a market orientation, the Conservative government did not embrace the social and economic policies of the Thatcher or Reagan administrations.

The politics of each province are quite unique. None of the federal parties is strong in all the provinces, and purely provincial parties have normally governed in two large provinces, Quebec and British Columbia. While the NDP never gained power in the federal arena, it has won elections in four provinces, and while in power was able to influence the development of labour policy.

Canada enjoys a standard of living equal to the more prosperous nations in Western Europe, but depends heavily on the production and export of raw materials and semi processed products – mineral ores, food grains and forest products. Markets for these commodities are unstable, markets are unstable and primary industries do not generate substantial direct employment. Despite a large manufacturing sector in Ontario and Quebec, manufacturing accounts for about 20 per cent of the gross domestic product. Because Canada lacks a large domestic market, it signed a Free Trade Agreement (FTA) with the United States and the North American Free Trade Agreement with (NAFTA) Mexico and the US, in 1988 and 1994, respectively. The immediate impact of free trade was to accelerate the integration of the manufacturing sector into a larger North American economy. Levels of activity in traditional industries, such as textiles and furniture fell substantially, while other sectors, such as automobiles and chemicals, expanded.

Canada's most pressing economic problems in the 1990s were high government deficits and unemployment, difficulties it shared with most other developed nations. After a period of inflation in the mid-1970s, unemployment, always substantial by international standards, rose sharply and only began to drop off in the mid-1990s, Canadians were less well off financially in 1999/2000 than a decade earlier, with real disposable income decreasing over the previous decade. More Canadians took part time jobs than ever before. Unemployment rates in 2002 hovered at about 8 per cent, lower than the previous decade, but nevertheless were higher than in many developed economies.

III. THE PARTIES IN EMPLOYMENT RELATIONS

A. Unions

The Canadian labour movement has displayed steady, though unspectacular, growth since the 1930s, despite a long-standing tradition of disunity. The number of employees covered by union bargaining arrangements was approximately four million throughout the 1990s, which at the end of the century constituted 32.3 per cent of paid non-agricultural employees. While absolute numbers of employees represented by unions grew by 1.4 million since 1960, the proportionately greater increase in the labour force as a whole has meant that the union density figure has declined moderately since 1984. This membership was divided between two national centres and a large number of unaffiliated unions.

The Canadian density figure reflects growth in female union members and high union density rate in the public sector. The greatest penetration of unionism is in primary industries, construction, transportation, manufacturing, plus the public sector. In the late nineteenth and early twentieth centuries, Canadian unions were established first in construction and transportation mostly on a craft basis. During the 1930s and 1940s, industrial unionism spread to manufacturing and primary industries, without including white-collar workers in the private sector. Since the late 1960s, the major source of growth in the labour movement has been the public sector. First public servants, then health and education workers, joined unions. Professionals, notably teachers and nurses, had long been members of their own associations, and these transformed themselves into unions as their members' interest in collective bargaining grew.

Approximately 275 unions operate in Canada, ranging in size from less than 100 to more than 460,000 members. Two-thirds are affiliated with one of the central confederations discussed below, with the remainder, principally in the public sector, are independent of any national body or are in Quebec. Recent mergers have created 'mega' unions, concentrating union membership in fewer and larger organizations. A variety of union philosophies are represented. Most of the old craft groups still espouse apolitical business unionism. A larger number of unions see themselves fulfilling a broader role and actively support the NDP and various social causes. A few groups, principally in Quebec, are highly politicized and occasionally criticize the prevailing economic system from a socialist perspective. But rhetoric aside, the major function of all unions is collective bargaining.

The role of US-based 'international' unions is a special feature of the Canadian labour movement that has affected its behaviour in many ways. Most of the oldest labour organizations in Canada began as part of American unions – hence the term 'international'. Often these unions are affiliated with the American-based AFL-CIO. The cultural and economic ties between the two countries encouraged the trade union connection, while the greater size and earlier development of US labour bodies attracted Canadian workers to them. For many years, the overwhelming majority of Canadian union members belonged to such international unions, which often exerted close control over their Canadian locals. But the spread of unionism in the public sector during the 1960s and 1970s brought national unions to the fore, as internationals were seldom active among public employees. Beginning in the 1970s, many Canadian unions seceded from internationals, the results of poor service in Canada, protectionism of American unions and Canadian nationalism. As a result of these factors, the proportion of international union membership declined from more than 70 per cent in 1966 to less than 30 per cent in 2000.

The most important central confederation in Canada is the Canadian Labour Congress (CLC), representing almost 69 per cent of all union members belonging to 93 national and international union affiliates. Members of CLC affiliates are in all regions and most industries. It is the principal political spokesperson for Canadian labour, but is weaker than many other national centrals. It has no role in bargaining or any substantial powers over its affiliates. The CLC's political role is further limited by the constitutionally weak position of the federal government, its natural contact point, in many areas the labour movement regards as important, such as labour legislation, regulation of industry or human rights. In national politics, it has supported the NDP. The poor electoral record of the NDP federally (discussed earlier) further weakens its political role. The Confederation of National Trade Unions (CNTU) represents 6.2 per cent of all union members, virtually all in Quebec. It began early in the twentieth century under the sponsorship of Catholic Church as a conservative French-language alternative to the predominantly English language secular unions operating elsewhere in Canada and in Quebec. As the province industrialized during and after the Scond World War, members of the Catholic unions grew impatient with their lack of militancy and unwillingness to confront a conservative provincial government. The Catholic unions abandoned their former conservatism and moved into the vanguard of rapid social change in Quebec in 1960. Since then, ideological competition has prevailed in the Quebec labour movement, and the CNTU has become the most radical and politicized labour body in North America. It has supported Quebec independence and adopted left-wing political positions.

B. Management

Although the majority of unionized firms accept the role of labour grudgingly, open attacks on incumbent unions are rare. In industries with a long history of unionism – for example, manufacturing or transportation – unionism is accepted as a normal part of the business environment. However, non-union firms strive to retain that status, some by matching the wages and working conditions in the unionized sector, others by combinations of paternalism and coercion. A number of firms have union substitution policies, which replicate many of the forms of a unionized work environment with grievance procedures, quality circles or mechanisms for consultation. Unionized firms in Canada normally have a full-time industrial relations staff, though seldom a large one. Major industrial relations decisions, such as decisions to take strikes or the level of wage offers, are highly centralized, that is, taken at the corporate level.

The high degree of foreign ownership in the Canadian economy affects the Canadian economy generally, but seldom industrial relations. About 25 per cent of the assets of all industrial firms are foreign-owned, chiefly by US corporations. Foreign ownership clearly affects a number of strategic managerial decisions, such as product lines or major investments. But the impact of non-Canadians on industrial relations decisions in unionized sectors is almost non-existent. Foreign owners prefer to remain in the mainstream of industrial relations for their industries rather than impose corporate policies.

C. Government

The government in Canada has a dual role in industrial relations – it regulates the actors' conduct and employs about 18 per cent of the labour force, directly and indirectly.

Government regulation of industrial relations is very extensive, although it rests on an assumption of voluntarism. Each province, and the federal government, has at least one act covering labour relations and employment standards in the industries under its jurisdiction. Employment standards legislation generally set minima for such areas as wages, vacations or holidays. In a few areas, such as maternity leave, the law has led most employers. Although the details vary considerably, labour relations legislation combines many features of the US National Labour Relations Act (Wagner Act) and an older Canadian pattern of reliance on conciliation of labour disputes. Each statute establishes and protects the right of most employees to form trade unions, sets out a procedure by which a union may demonstrate majority support from a group of employees in order to obtain the right of exclusive representation for them. The employer is required to bargain with a certified trade union. A quasi-judicial labour relations board administers this process and enforces the statute.

Labour relations legislation imposes few requirements on the substance of a collective agreement, though the exceptions are significant and expanding. For many years, Canadian laws have effectively prohibited strikes during the term of a collective agreement, while also requiring that each agreement contain a grievance procedure and a mechanism for the final resolution of mid-contract disputes. Several statutes required the parties to bargain over technological change and that management grant union security clauses.

Separate legislation exists federally and in all 10 provinces for employees in the public sector. These statutes may apply to government employees and occasionally to quasi-government workers, such as teachers or hospital workers. They are patterned after private sector labour relations acts except for two broad areas. The scope of bargaining is restricted by previous civil service personnel practices and broader public policy considerations. In a majority of provinces, there are restrictions on the right to strike of at least some public employees, such as police and fire fighters. Employee groups without the right to strike have access to a system of compulsory arbitration. While a statute requires arbitration, the parties normally can determine the procedures to be followed and choose the arbitrator.

IV. THE PROCESSES OF INDUSTRIAL RELATIONS

The major formal process of Canadian employment relations is collective bargaining, with union power based on its ability to strike. Joint consultation is sporadic. Other formal systems of worker participation in management are rare, although in an era in which employee involvement systems became popular more collective agreements have developed novel clauses reflecting this thrust. Arbitration of interest disputes is largely confined to the public sector.

A. Collective bargaining

Collective bargaining in Canada is highly decentralized. The most common negotiating unit is a single establishment – single union, followed by multi-establishment-single union. Taken together these categories account for almost 90 per cent of all units and more than 80 per cent of all employees. Company-wide bargaining is common in the federal jurisdiction, where it occurs in railways, airlines and telecommunications, and in provincially regulated industries concentrated in a single province, such as automobile or lumber manufacturing.

Despite the formal structure of negotiations, bargaining often follows regional patterns. National patterns in bargaining are rare. Instead one or two key industries in each region usually influence provincial negotiations. In larger provinces, such as Ontario and Quebec, heavy industry patterns from steel, paper or autos often predominate.

The results of bargaining are detailed, complex collective bargaining agreements. Negotiated provisions typically include: pay, union security, hours of work, vacations and holidays, layoff provisions and miscellaneous fringe benefits. Grievance procedures are legal requirements and invariably conclude with binding arbitration. In addition, there are often supplementary agreements covering work rules for specific situations or work areas. Seniority provisions are prominent features in almost all collective agreements, covering layoffs, promotions or transfers, with varying weight given to length of service or ability.

Given the detail in collective agreements and the parties' preference for litigation, rights arbitrations are frequent and legalistic. In turn, this emphasis on precise written contracts often permeates labour–management relationships.

B. Strike and settlement methods

Another outcome of collective bargaining is labour stoppages, the most controversial single feature of Canadian industrial relations. Historically, strike levels have been cyclical.

There was a wave of unrest early in the twentieth century, another around World War I, a third beginning in the late 1930s and a fourth in the 1970s. The latest wave abated in 1983, and most measures of labour disputes have fallen sharply since then. By international standards, the two salient characteristics of Canadian strikes are their length and the concentration of time lost in a few disputes. Involvement is medium to low (3–10 per cent of union members annually), and the size of strikes is not especially large (350–450 workers per strike, on average). The largest five or six strikes typically account for 35 per cent of all time lost. In recent years, the average duration of strikes has been 12–15 days.

Conciliation or mediation have long been a feature of Canadian collective bargaining. In most jurisdictions participation in some form of mediation is a precondition for a legal strike. Over half of all collective agreements are achieved with some type of third-party intervention.

Outside of the public sector, compulsory arbitration of interest disputes is rare. However, special legislation to end particular disputes is not uncommon in public sector or essential service disputes. Back-to-work laws are extremely unpopular with the labour movement and have contributed to the politicization of labour relations in some areas. In the public sector, interest arbitration is common. Arbitrators are usually chosen on an *ad hoc* basis from among judges or professional arbitrators, who are usually lawyers or academics. The process is legalistic without the use of sophisticated economic data.

C. Issues of current and future importance

The future of collective bargaining is being questioned in most industrialized countries. In large measure, this debate revolves around the ability of labour organizations to retain, or even expand, their traditional bases of strength in heavy industry and blue-collar occupations. Though union density in these industries in Canada has fallen, it remains not declined materially and is twice as high as that of the United States, for instance. However, Canadian unions have had the same difficulty as their counterparts elsewhere in extending their membership base into the more rapidly growing areas of the service sector and technologically advanced industries. Historically, the organized elements of the labour force have led the non-union employers in the expansion of employee rights and improvement in wages and conditions of employment. If collective bargaining becomes confined to declining sectors of the economy, this role also will diminish.

Traditional centers of collective bargaining are also under pressure from foreign competition and deregulation, factors common among developed nations. Canada has long relied heavily on foreign trade, so foreign competition is not new. Tariff barriers eroded slowly in the 1960s and 1970s and more rapidly after the FTA took effect in 1989. Canadian manufacturing sector, aided by a depreciating currency, responded well to these challenges. The decentralized structure of collective bargaining seems to have facilitated adaptation to economic change. Exports rose steadily, while manufacturing employment was stagnant. These developments were sources of stress to industrial relations institutions, but changes were incremental.

The immediate future of collective bargaining will be a function of the actions of government and management in the face of trade union economic and political power. Both federal and provincial governments continue to respect the legitimacy of collective bargaining and an active labour movement. A review of labour relations in federally regulated industries completed in 1995 found strong support for the institution of collective bargaining among the industrial relations parties for instance. Legislation and other public policies reflect that commitment, even when most right-of-center political parties govern. Few major changes in labour legislation occurred in the 1990s.

On balance, however, it appears that the legislative support for collective bargaining will not change markedly across Canada. Given the tilt of the country towards a more right-wing agenda a more likely scenario is further modest reductions in labour's legal position without a wholesale dismantling of the collective bargaining regime.

D. Management and collective bargaining

Canadian employers faced many of the same market forces to reduce costs in the 1980s and 1990s as their private sector counterparts in other developed nations: foreign trade, increased domestic competition in services and deregulation. Public sector employers were required to either limit or reduce wage expenditures. The FTA with the United States and NAFTA added to competitive pressures. Many responses by employers to these changes were traditional. Layoffs dramatically reduced employment in many industries. The use of part-time and casual workers rose substantially. But there was no general movement to escape unionism.

In industries where unionism was well established, a combination of cultural and legal forces caused Canadian employers work within the collective bargaining system to meet competitive pressures. Militant anti-unionism is not a popular public position among Canadian employers, although many managers privately express hostility to labour organizations. At the level of the firm, surveys of industrial relations and human resource managers show little interest in unseating incumbent unions, although resistance to the spread of unionism may have strengthened.

Legal restrictions on employer tactics make de-unionization very difficult, and protections for union organization are effective. Employer success in bargaining has diminished pressures for structural changes. The decentralization of bargaining structures in the private sector, driven by employers, effectively put wages into competition. Negotiated changes in work rules have been frequent, and in the mid-1990s negotiated wage freezes and concession bargaining became more common. With low rates of inflation, it is difficult for unions to bargain for anything other than very modest wage increases.

At the level of the workplace in unionized industries, radical reorganization of work and the implementation of work systems based on high levels of employee commitment have been limited, due to both union resistance and lack of management commitment. Where changes have been introduced, the failure rate is relatively high. However, many employers are seeking to move away from the traditional adversarial system of labour relations, especially in manufacturing. Increased consultation and communication between management and unions is a common development, for instance.

It is unclear how much Canadian employers acceptance of collective bargaining in the face of difficult economic conditions is due to legal protections for unions and collective bargaining or to a philosophical acceptance of the legitimacy of these institutions. If employers are merely obeying the law, then support for collective bargaining obviously is subject to changing political and legal circumstances. If the support for collective bargaining is cultural, then industrial relations institutions will probably survive and evolve gradually.

E. Labour disputes

Historically, the most important issue in Canadian industrial relations has been time lost due to strikes. Governments have attempted to deal with labour unrest in a variety of ways. One model is to encourage consultation. During the 1970s and 1980s, several governments took initiatives directed at establishing labour–management consultation as practised in Western Europe. In cases of large-scale layoffs, joint labour–management committees (in union and non-union workforces) were mandated. Later the Federal government sponsored tripartite sectoral committees to deal with the effects of restructuring. These committees function well, and their number has expanded, slowly, but there still is no evidence that cooperation at this level of the industrial relations-system affects the parties' actions at other levels.

A second model for dealing with labour unrest has been to impose legislative controls on the exercise of union power. Two provinces enacted labour relations amendments along those lines, and others considered the same policies. As in Britain, governments in these jurisdictions are more anxious to legislate against labour than most employers, so the long-run prospects for this model are not good. There simply is little groundswell of support that would seriously threaten the legitimacy of the current collective bargaining regime.

By the turn of the twenty-first century, the incidence of labour disputes had fallen considerably. The decline in labour unrest diverted interest from this issue and labour relations in general. Beginning the mid-1980s unions demonstrated that they could mount large strikes and win concessions on significant issues, almost invariably involving job security. In a time of low inflation and high unemployment, the incentives to strike over other issues fell and the costs confrontation rose.

V. PUBLIC SECTOR EMPLOYMENT RELATIONS

The area of Canadian employment relations most subject to change is the public sector. From the mid-1960s to the 1980s, mature systems of collective bargaining developed in all provinces and the federal government. Beginning with the 1982 recession, governments in several jurisdictions addressed budgetary shortfalls by restricting public sector compensation. In general, governments dealt with their fiscal problems by legislation rather than bargaining. By 1987, legal restraints had been removed. Early in 1991, the federal government led another round of restrictions on public sector bargaining and compensation. By 1995, a majority of all provinces had imposed restrictions on public sector bargaining as part of programs of fiscal restraint.

Public sector unions protested all the restraint programs, but generally in vain. Governments found that restricting public sector wages and bargaining rights were politically popular. Reliance on legislation or other means to impose freezes or reductions have brought into question the commitment of Canadian governments to collective bargaining systems enshrined in many statutes. Under these circumstances, labour's responses to government initiatives are likely to be political. In the 1980s, public sector unions in Quebec, Ontario and British Columbia (the three most populous provinces) organized major demonstrations and work stoppages that brought pressure on governments to moderate their policies. A major national strike by a federal public sector union with a tradition of moderation showed that public sector workers could be mobilized when they faced restrictions they regarded as unfair. In the end, however, government employers prevailed. Led by the federal government, controlled by the Liberal Party since 1993, deficit reduction became a dominant theme in the nation's political orthodoxy. Employment in the federal government fell substantially, and several provincial governments also cut employment as well as compensation. In these conditions, the labour could do little to resist these losses.

VI. POLITICAL ROLE OF THE LABOUR MOVEMENT

Although many Canadian unions and union leaders are active in partisan politics, the labour movement has been unable to define a political role for itself. Officially, the CLC supports the NDP, but this alliance has presented problems. Federally, the NDP has been unsuccessful in raising its share of the popular vote (and legislative seats) beyond about 20 per cent and was left without official party status in the Parliament elected in 1993. The labour movement has been unable to deliver large blocs of votes to the federal NDP, though financial contributions and the diversion of staff to the Party are invaluable. In Quebec the NDP has minimal influence, as most labour leaders support pro-independence parties. Even when the NDP enjoyed greater success, the CLC has been left to deal with governments whose election it had opposed. For example, labour opposed the FTA, a central issue in the 1988 national election. When the pro-free trade Conservatives triumphed, the CLC was in a poor position to secure assistance for workers who lost their jobs as a result of new trade patterns. The tensions created by this situation have hampered consultation on economic policies.

Provincially, the situation is different. The New Democrats have governed in Ontario and three western provinces. Labour's political role is better defined when the NDP is a viable option provincially. However, the labour movement's partisan position provincially risks making labour issues more political and subject to sharp variation after changes of government. Quebec unions have supported independence for the province and have enjoyed great political influence when pro-separatist parties have governed the province.

VII. CONCLUSIONS

The Canadian industrial relations system is caught up in the central concerns of the nation – the division of powers between provinces and the national government, the relative importance of the public and private sectors, relations with the United States and other trading partners and the performance of the national economy. While employment relations will contribute to the resolution of these issues, the future direction of the system is likely to be determined by broader trends in Canadian life. But decisions on economic policy, changes in industrial structure and political shifts will ensure that flux and unrest in the Canadian industrial relations system remain high in the future.

The employment relations system itself displays few of the overt signs of structural changes found in other developed nations. Unlike the United States, unionism and collective bargaining have not been subjected to an attack by management. By contrast with the United Kingdom, it is a rare situation in which any government has undertaken a sustained anti-union campaign. (The most concerted efforts to limit the power of unions through legislation occurred after 1996 in Ontario.) The labour movement has a high degree of legitimacy in Canadian life. It has close ties with the women's movement and consumer groups, for instance. The labour movement is recognized as the spokesperson for workers in economic and social consultations.

Canada's record of slow but steady economic growth, combined with more than a decade of stagnant wages, provide scant support for politicians or employers who wish to blame collective bargaining or unionism for the economy's performance. The collective bargaining system has responded successfully to most of the changes in economic conditions. Yet a decade of high unemployment has reduced the militancy of Canadian workers except when job security is the central issue in dispute. The elimination of trade barriers undermines the bargaining power of Canadian workers in their manufacturing and transportation sectors, two major sources of industrial strength. Continued reductions in government service employment affect another pillar of collective bargaining. The lack of any crisis in the system has stifled debate over the broader questions of worker representation outside of the traditional strongholds of the labour movement. In the absence of a direct challenge to the system, the recent pattern of incremental adaptation will continue.

3 Chile: Labour Relations at the Beginning of the Twenty-first Century

*Emilio Morgado Valenzuela**

I. ECONOMY AND LABOUR MARKET

The macroeconomic index is very positive. Between 1988 and 1998 gross domestic product (GDP) grew at 7.6 per cent annual rate. The following external crisis since then have affected its growth which, nevertheless, is still one of the highest in Latin America.

The annual average rate of inflation between 1990 and 2000 was 10 per cent. In 1989 it was 26 per cent and in 1999, 3.3 per cent. In May 2000, it was slightly higher than 2 per cent.

During the 1990s average unemployment rate fluctuated around 7.3 per cent. Between 1990 and 1998 it came down to 8.1–6.1 per cent. As a result of the adjustment due to the Asian crisis it rose to 10.6 per cent (August 2000). In May 2002 unemployment was 8.4 per cent. At the beginning of the 1980s, open unemployment was 33 per cent.

The real remuneration index for working hour rose 27 per cent in the 1993–2000 period. The highest raises come from skilled labour. The less qualified workers are affected by unemployment rates and high underemployment.

During the 1993–2000 period the minimum wage – in the form of 'monthly minimum income' – rose over the national wage average and was an important factor in the reduction of poverty levels, and at the same time a stimulus for increasing average market wages.

Remunerations in the national finances that were 52 per cent in 1972 and 30.9 per cent in 1988, now represent to 38 per cent.

Real productivity in the 1988–1998 decade (at steady 1986 prices) had a 5.2 per cent annual increase and employment rate had 2.3 per cent annual growth. The growth of real remunerations was 3.4 per cent annual accumulative.

Chile is part of APEC. It is a Mercosur's associated state. It has finished negotiations to establish a treaty of association with the European Community and has signed free trade treaties with Canada and Mexico. It has negotiated a treaty of free trade with the United States of America and also takes part in several commercial, economic and social cooperation agreements.

---

* Former ILD Officer, Professor at Chile University.

R. Blanpain (ed.),
Labour Relations in the Asia-Pacific Countries, 27–36.
© 2004 *Kluwer Law International. Printed in Great Britain.*

II. LABOUR RELATIONS

Taking into account the main distinctive features characterizing collective labour relations in Chile, the following stages can be distinguished in its evolution:

(1) *The beginnings (1885–1890)*: Influence exerted by intellectual's analysis on social situations in Chile. They are substantiated through organizing activities carried off by organizations such as Equality Societies, which encouraged the birth of the first workers' organizations: 'mutual aid societies' (cooperative bodies for members' protection and training).

(2) *The construction (1890–1915)*: Mancommunal reinvidicative workers organizations that resort to strikes as means of action are born. Their activities are repressed with extreme violence. 'Societies for resistance', of anarchic origin and inspiration are born in parallel. At the same time, first labour laws are adopted.

(3) *The expansion (1915–1924)*: It is characterized for union organizations' growth in number and strength in several sectors of economic activity such as mining and seaports. The Chilean Workers Federation (FOCH), replaces their 'mutualist' characteristics for 'mancommunal' reinvidicative ones, competing at the same time with anarchist organizations.

(4) *The backward (1924–1931)*: The political events and its unstable consequences seriously affected the development of union organizations and so did the effects of the world economic crisis and the dictatorial policy established by President Ibañez.

(5) *The reconstructing (1931–1938)*: The political and economic circumstances fastered the rebirth of unionism and enforcement of the 1924 Labour Legislation and 1931 Labour Code made working relations more dynamic.

(6) *The political participation (1938–1945)*: Labour relations coexisted with governments of center left. The exchange that took place was mutually advantageous. Public administration workers' organizations and the recent economic public sector were strengthened. Several reforms to the Labour Code and prevision laws were carried out. Nevertheless, the former did not prevent the existence of conflicts.

(7) *The division and reunification (1945–1955)*: The national and international events, particularly polarizations resulting from the Cold War, brought about the division of Chile's Central of Workers (CTCH). Strikes were repressed with violence after these events, rival unionism tendencies and other social groups agreed to establish a Central Única de Trabajadores (CUT; Single Workers' Central).

(8) *The confrontation (1955–1970)*: It is characterized by strong and growing labour confrontations in private and public sectors. The inflationary process made labour agreements difficult. Agricultural workers were unionized and workers' bargaining power, especially in copper mining sectors, were strengthened. Labour legislation was not effective to attend to new realities.

(9) *The participation and confrontation (1970–1973)*: CUT had an active role in the Popular Unity Government; its most important leaders held ministerial offices. A national agreement CUT/Government was subscribed. Social

areas of economy grew. The country became polarized. Labour conflicts multiplied and in some occasions they answered to non-labour interests not only on the governments' but on the opposition's part as well.

(10) *The repression (1973–1990)*: The great political and economic changes of the military government had a strong impact in labour relations. Union organizations were intervened or broken up and collective bargaining was frozen. The old legislation was partially replaced or not observed. In 1979, that legislation and also social security laws were replaced by other harmonizing with government economic and political policies.

(11) *The new social practices*: Since March 1990, under democracy, open conflicts have yielded way to dialogue and participation. There is a growing presence of labour influence on the changes in economic, technological and production systems, in part derived from the process of globalization.

In general, it can be considered that notwithstanding the advances reached since 1990, to promote a greater presence of collective autonomy, the Chilean labour relations system is still characterized for the pre-eminece of heteronomous establishing of working conditions and employment.

Legislation is still the principal source of rights and obligations, mainly due to the existence of strong legal traditions along with the persisting attitudes of social parties to prefer, as an strategy, that labour relations and their contents be ruled by law and not by themselves. To the former is added the existence of certain inadequacies that prevent or render difficult bargaining at appropriate levels matters to be negotiated and harmonize with existing suitable union organizations, which are not sufficiently protected from management and government interference.

Labour legislation established during the military regime has been subjected to many reforms governed by the following objectives: (a) established equitably and appropriate balance among aims for protection and flexibilization; (b) bring near national laws to international labour laws; (c) harmonize legislation to the new needs linked to increasing production and quality in a growing environment of globalization along with and driven by economic and technological changes – and resulting needs maintain and increase levels of competitiveness.

The first reforms were about termination of labour relations (Law 19.010, November 1990); central unions; whose existence had been forbidden during the military government (Law 19.049, February 1991), union organizations and collective bargaining (Law 19.069, July 1991).

The most recent reforms are contained in the Law 19.759, October 2001. With respect to individual labour relations, the law introduced changes in matters such as: (1) incorporating new standards to dependent workers conditions; (2) improving regulations that forbid and sanction discrimination; (3) Sanctioning transgressions due to alterations of the juridical conditions of employer, worker, independent worker and enterprise; (4) respect to workers' constitutional guaranties as a limit to the exercise of faculties acknowledged to employers by law, especially in matters related to privacy, private life and worker's honour; (5) contractual determination of polifunctionality; (6) Gradual decrease to 45 h of weekly work time; (7) incorporating telework as a labour relation not subjected to working timetable limitation; (8) special regulation of working time and rest time of certain categories of workers; (9) in advance agreement for extra working hours to attend to temporary enterprises' needs; (10) new regulations for Sunday's rest in mining operations and in services that demand continuity due to the nature of their processes or for technical reasons or needs to satisfy or to prevent great damage to public or industrial interests as well as for workers of commercial establishments and services that directly deal with the public according to establishments' modalities; (11) the faculty of the Director of Labour to authorize – subject to previous agreement with workers – exceptional distribution systems of working time and rest; (12) celebrating part-time work contracts and ordinary working day regulations, agreements for extra working time and systems to calculate benefits entitled to part time workers; (13) control for those who act as intermediaries of agricultural enterprises or agroindustrial enterprises derived from agriculture, lumber wood exploitation or similar activities; (14) taking root in the employer costs derived from the fulfillment of legal obligations for housing, feeding and transportation of temporary or seasonal workers; (15) new regulations concerning internal standards that must exist in enterprises of 10 or more employees clearly, stating that all control measures can only be carried out by suitable means that agree with the nature of labour relations and guaranteeing impersonal measures to insure worker's self-respect; (16) employer's obligation to keep in strict confidence all information and private data concerning workers as well accessible information due to labour relations; (17) modifying some of the disciplinary causes for terminating working relations; (18) procedure for contesting causes invoked for terminating labour relations or to declare that the causal invoked is unjust, illegal or irrelevant or that the working relation has terminated without invoking any legal cause. The amount of indemnizations was also increased in those cases and in the special situations when dismissal is declared lacking of any admissible reason. (19) The new standards for indemnization payments and the possibility that employers assign payment for compensation benefits to the direct cost of training given to young workers.

Law 19.759 also incorporated important reforms in legal standards of collective working relations. With regard to union organization, it made flexible and liberalized strictness of a great part of the pre-existent legislation. Thus, for example:

(1) Classical enumeration and legal characteristics of types of unions that can be constituted have no longer exclusive and excluding nature, workers can constitute unions with different characteristics from the ones stipulated by law.
(2) Acknowledge unionization rights to officials in states' enterprises and depending on the Ministry of Defense, with no detriment of especial standards in matters of collective bargaining.
(3) Increases the numbers of persons that can act as Ministers of Faith in union meetings and activities as well as unions' faculties to appoint them.
(4) Gives priority to union representative role in collective bargaining.
(5) Protects with union protection ('fuero'), workers attending constitution of unions in enterprises, in establishment enterprises, inter-enterprise or temporary workers for variable periods of time established by law.

(6) Modifies jurisdictional regulatory standards of union leaders and stipulates matters concerning their faculties, duration and termination.
(7) Submits to union's statutes the determination for affiliation and non-affiliation, members rights and obligations, settling union dues, requirements needed by union leaders in order to be elected; modification of statutes, union mergers, internal disciplinary regime, summoning and settling frequency of ordinary and extraordinary assemblies; updated members' records; institutions for verifying elections and other actions in which collective will is expressed; number of votes each member is entitled to and consideration for non-permanent workers' votes and, annual financial accounts and bookkeeping control mechanisms. The new legislation clearly stipulates that statutes must grant safeguards to allow union members to express their opinions and their right to vote, and also safeguard minorities' rights as well as guarantee members' access to information and union documentation.
(8) Regulates assembly's decision to merge with other union organizations.
(9) Determines number of workers – and percentage in relation to total number of workers in the enterprise – that are necessary to constitute enterprise or enterprise establishment unions. Whatever percentage they represent, 250 or more workers of an enterprise may constitute a union. Twenty-five its the minimum number to constitute a union in an enterprise with more than 50 workers, provided they represent at least 10 per cent of the total employees working there. However, in enterprises with no union organization at least 8 workers are necessary to constitute a union and this number must be increased to 25 in the maximum term of a year. If the enterprise has less than 50 employees, 8 of them can constitute a Union. Unions different than an enterprise or stablishment union need at least 25 worker members to be constituted.
(10) Regulates conditions for electing union delegates in case they are inter-enterprise union members or temporary workers, provided they are more than 8. Delegates enjoy 'fuero' and their number varies according to size of group they represent.
(11) Establishes that number of union directors legal and protected with 'fuero' varies from 1 to 9 according to union's size, regulating at the same time all matters concerning such legal protection of trade union freedom.
(12) Establishes duration of union mandate to no less than 2, and no more than 4 years and allows reelection of directors. At the same times regulates replacement of directors terminating office during mandate. It also regulates especial situations such as matters pertaining seamen's unions.
(13) Demands presentation of candidacies in all elections subsequent to the first directory election. Such presentation will be regulated in union statute. In the absence of statutory standards regarding elected candidates, pertinent legal regulations will be applied.
(14) Stipulates that statute will establish seniority requests for electoral voting and censure for union directory.
(15) Establishes that a federation joins three or more unions and a confederation joins three or more federations or 20 or more unions. At the same time modifies matters concerning faculties of union federations.

(16) Redefines union centrals' objectives, as well as all matters pertaining the discounts of fees. It also stipulates that all union regulations apply to federations, confederations and centrals provided they do not oppose special standards ruling them.
(17) Stipulates that union organizations will not be subjected to administrative suspension or dissolution. At the same time, regulates procedures and effects of dissolution.

Law 19,759 also rules with greater accuracy and force all pertaining to disloyal or anti-union practices, and at the same time establishes new and greater sanctions, for example, in the following reformed standards:
(1) It is established that employers incur in disloyal practices when they refuse to provide – in time and form – union leaders with required information regarding the indispensable antecedents for drafting collective bargaining contracts such as: balances of two previous years, financial information on current months, global costs of labour force, and information on enterprise's future investment policy (except those considered of confidential nature).
(2) Amount of fines is raised and the Labour Office's is authorized to denounce in Court facts it deems anti-union or disloyal practices. Its inform constitute legal presumption of truth. Any interested party will be able to denounce such conduct and take part in the proceedings without lawyers' sponsorship. The law stipulates special procedure to know about denunciations and establishes that judges will rule immediate reinstatement for workers protected by 'fuero'. In the sentence the judge will rule payment of indemnizations determined by law. Respect to workers not protected by 'fuero', the law establishes additional indemnization to the one established for unlawful dismissals.
(3) Orders the Labour Directorate to have records of condemnatory sentences and publish lists of transgressing enterprise and union organizations.

As to collective bargaining, Law 19759 introduced the following main reforms:
(1) Establishes more accurately all matters concerning the beginning and termination of 'fuero' for workers engaged in collective bargaining.
(2) Stipulates that in case of non-ruled collective bargaining only union organizations can intervene representing workers. Non-ruled negotiation is the one that at any time and without any kind of restrictions is initiated with one or more employers – through direct bargaining and not subjected to procedure regulations – to agree on common working conditions and remuneration for a determined time. Non-ruled negotiation does not confer the privilege rights and obligations of regulated negotiation in the Labour Code, it especially does not grant 'fuero', nor rights to strike or lock out.
(3) Establishes that when a non-unionized group of workers joins to bargain in a non-ruled negotiation the following minimum procedure regulations must be observed: (a) the group must be composed of 8 or more workers; (b) workers must be represented by a bargaining commission of no less than 3 nor more than 5 participants, elected by secret vote in an election

conducted before a Labour Inspector; (c) employer must answer to bargaining proposals in 15 days term; (d) approval on employers' proposals at workers' secret voting conducted before a Labour Inspector. If agreement is reached without accordance to these rules, it will have the nature of individual contract and will not have collective agreement effects.

(4) Introduces special standards for non-regulated collective bargaining in which agriculture seasonal workers' unions participate. Its duration will be determined by parties, but will last no less than duration for corresponding season.

(5) Introduces special standards to regulate counselors' participation in cases where the workers' negotiating commission is composed of board members of one or more unions or it is made up by workers belonging to an inter-reenterprise union.

(6) Determines documentation on corresponding project of collective contract to be handed over to workers' bargaining commission.

(7) Establishes rights of inter-enterprise unions to present to employers that hire workers affiliated to unions – a collective bargaining project in representation of its members and workers supporting it provided it represents a minimum of 4 workers in each enterprise. If the employer decides not to bargain, he should make his decision known in a term of time stipulated by law. If he decides to negotiate there must be a joint common commission, made up by an authorized representative for each enterprise. If they are more than 5, they can delegate representation to a bargaining commission of up to 5 members. When stipulations applicable to a particular enterprise are discussed, the negotiating union commission will include in it the corresponding union delegates or, if they do not exist, it will include a delegate elected by workers of the enterprise involved. The law regulates in detail matters concerning presentation and transaction of respective projects of collective contracts.

(8) Perfects standard that obliges non-union workers payment of union dues, if the employers grants them benefits achieved through collective bargaining in which they did not take part, at the same time establishing such obligation to workers leaving unions.

(9) Stipulates 4 years as the maximum duration for collective contracts and arbitral sentences.

(10) Establishes the flexibility for any of the parties to request a Labour Inspector's conciliatory mediation, if they have decided to appeal to mediation or voluntary arbitration.

(11) Modifies regulation for strikes, stipulating that once a strike is declared, only the negotiating commission can convoke new voting to submit matters to mediation or arbitration or to rule on employer's new current or last offer. Decisions must be adopted by absolute majority of workers involved in negotiation. A majority is needed to agree on censure for the negotiating commission. Moreover, along with emphasizing prohibition to replace workers on strike, the present regulation is modified on conditions to be observed in order that said contract is made possible. Among

these modifications, 'replacement bonus' for workers involved in the strike is highlighted.

According to official statistics in 1999/2000, population over 15 year of age was 10,810,560, and labour force was 5,883,400 persons. Unionized workers added to 581,633 which in relation to wage earning population represented a 15 per cent union affiliation rate. Of total number of unionized workers 360,212 were affiliated in 9,469 enterprises unions. At the same time, these comprised the majority of 14,779 existing unions.

According to the same sources, the number of workers protected by 1,375 collective agreements achieved through negotiations having unions as negotiators was three times higher than number of workers involved in 946 agreements achieved through collective bargaining in charge of non-unionized groups of workers. In decreasing order, workers involved in collective bargaining were grouped in the following activities: manufacturing industries; community services, social and personal services; commerce; transport, storage and communications; mining and quarries exploitation; financial establishments, insurance and banks, construction; agriculture, forestry and fishing; electricity, gas and water. A similar concentration is noticed in the number of agreements achieved where changes in location showed differences in the size of negotiating groups. Such is the case, for example, of agriculture, forestry and fishing that rise from penultimate to sixth place and mining and quarries going down from sixth to eighth place.

III. SOCIAL DIALOGUE

Social dialogue dates from the end of the 1930s. It began mainly in the tripartite and bipartite body organizations such as councils of the then Social Security Administrative (public bodies in charge of pension systems); Conciliation and Arbitration Boards (administrative organizations in charge of solving collective working conflicts); Qualifying Employees and Workers Board (in charge of determining juridical workers condition, including the existence of a labour relation); Copper Conciliation Board (in charge of solving collective working conflicts in the Great Cooper Mining enterprises); Minimum Wage Fixing commissions (then in charge of settling minimum wages).

A participant dialogue took place in economic and development institutions, such as the Economic National Council and regional and provincial commission of the Production Promotion Corporation (CORFO).

There were also dialogue and social participation in joint commission of economic or industrial activities sectors in charge of settling 'wage tariffs' and other employment and labour conditions.

Those and other diverse forms of dialogue and social participation were 'frozen' or suppressed during the military government (September 1973–March 1990).

A decided boost has been given to social dialogue during the Democratic Government of Presidents Patricio Aylwin, Eduardo Frei and Ricardo Lagos. The most important actions are:
(a) Workers' Unitarian Central (CUT) and Production and Commerce Confederation (CPC) bipartite declaration (December 1989) where top employers and workers representative organizations stated their will to establish dialogue and agreements this securing that transition to democracy would not have the effects foreseen by some political sectors;
(b) January 1990 agreement framework, in which CUT and CPC established basis and methodology for dialogue;
(c) National tripartite and intersectorial agreement CUT–CPC–Government (April 1990), where parties reached important agreement on mutual acknowledgment of their existence, objectives and relations and principles that would govern them, and at the same time, agreeing on substantive and adjective important aspects on processes for legal reform and incorporation of aims for equity in the growing and development model;
(d) National tripartite and intersectorial agreements (1991, 1992 and 1993);
(e) Sectorial agreements on forestry port traffic and public administration activities, especially those subscribed since 1994, as well as national sectorial agreement on specific matters such as security and occupational health; and
(f) Establishing and functioning of the Productive Development Forum (1994–1998) and Council of Social Dialogue (2000 until now).

The principal parties of dialogue are the most representative enterprise and union organizations. Depending on the level and subject of dialogue, top employers and workers institutions (CPC and CUT) participate in it, as well as representative bodies of management and unions, as is the case of small, medium and micro entrepreneurs and workers organizations such as the National Association of Public Employees.

In addition to 'macrodialogues' above mentioned, there are various formal and informal dialogue modalities enterprise level. It can be maintained, without reservations, that there is a growing level of acceptance and practice of dialogue in Chile. It does not exclude the possibility and practice of conflict, but it constitute an alternate road to it, generally preferred to prevent and solve it, and at the same time to direct social participation in all great national decisions.

IV. SOCIAL COSTS

Without detriment of costs derived from individual and collective contractual clauses, legislation imposes obligations and their enforcement also constitutes labour costs.

Some of them are incidental costs and one is obliged to them only if the conditions established by law are given, as in the case of fines due to infractions to labour regulations or indemnization for unlawful dismissals. On the other hand, others are obligations strictly speaking.

Among them, it is worth mentioning, monthly minimum income payments, profit sharing, wages for extra working hours and social security costs.

By Decree Law 275 (1974) the military government repealed legal standards on workers' minimum wages and employees' vital salary and replaced them with a minimum monthly income, thus remunerations settled according to former, legislation were no longer effective, especially remunerations regarding to automatic adjustment of minimum wages and vital salaries according to consumer prices (IPC). It was also stipulated that the amount of monthly income would become the value applied to all indexation referring to minimum wages and vital salaries, whatever the source of adjustment.

Workers of 21 years of age or younger, subject to training contracts were excluded from monthly minimum income. Between 1981 and 1984 this exception extended to all workers younger than 21 years of age. At present, all workers younger than 21 are excluded and special standards for part time workers and workers in private homes have been established. Since May 2002 IMM is $105,500 and $81,661 for younger than 18 or older than 65 (approximately US$161 and US$125).

Before 1990, periodicity of minimum monthly incomes adjustment were irregular and amounts not always corresponded to raises experienced by IPC.

Since 1990, annual IMM readjusting is previously consulted with representative of employers' and workers' organizations with the purpose of insuring that amounts stipulated by law represent their positions and, if possible, their consensus.

In general, IMMs are established taking into account present productivity and inflationary indicators, including those foreseen during their period of enforcement.

Of course, in determining IMM debate is raised on its effects on employment, productivity, labour costs, competitiveness and inflation, with opposite arguments on negative or positive effects.

Finally, it is possible to say that at present, nothing prevents actors parties from exercising their individual or collective autonomy, to establish one or more minimum monthly incomes higher than the amounts stipulated by law.

4. Labour Law and Industrial Relations in China

*Ying Zhu**

I. INTRODUCTION

China is presently undergoing a tremendous social and economic transformation as it diverges from its 'socialist planning system' towards a market economy with consequent economic reforms and an opening up of the economy to international trade and investment (the 'open door' policy). The commencement of this process can be traced back to December 1978, as a result of the decisions of the Third Plenum of the Central Committee of the Chinese Communist Party (CCP) (Zhu and Campbell, 1996, p. 29). The reform has proceeded in pragmatic steps in subsequent years, but the consistent goal has been a movement away from a command-economy towards the market (Naughton, 1995). Since 1992, this has been couched in terms of the need to establish a 'socialist market economy with Chinese characteristics'[1] (Zhu and Fahey, 1999; Zhu, 2000).

The transformation from the central planning system towards a market-oriented economic system requires an adequate legal framework to ensure that the process is stable and controllable. The process of economic reform does not proceed according to a blueprint, and the decentralisation of economic decision-making needs a legal environment both to legitimize the Party/State leadership and to provide a set of rules for governing market-oriented economic activities. The introduction of a system of labour market regulation is one of the established agendas set under the banner of establishing the 'socialist legal system' (*shehui zhuyi fazhi*).

Under the guidance of these over-arching economic and legal reforms, labour market and employment relations policies have been focused on the reform of wages, employment, welfare and management, and introduction of new systems of labour market regulation and labour law (Child, 1994; Zhu, 1995; Warner, 1996). Labour market reform began with the design of 'breaking the three irons', namely the so-called iron rice-bowl (i.e. life-time employment), iron

---

*   Senior Lecturer, Department of Management, University of Melbourne, Australia.
1.   Zhu and Fahey (1999) claim that the term 'socialist market economy with Chinese characteristics' is a mixed slogan which provides the legitimacy for the Communist Party's political control (maintaining the 'socialist' identity), creates an opportunity to introduce the market mechanism for economic development while at the same time allowing the traditional values such as Confucianism to fill the ideological vacuum and rejecting 'westernisation'.

wages (i.e. fixed wage system based on the 8-grade scale for manual workers) and iron position (i.e. unchangeable official position) (Warner and Zhu, 2000, p. 121). New systems of labour market regulation were required, which would develop a labour contract system, a structural/floating wage-system, an enterprise dismissal system, and a social insurance system (Yuan, 1990; Zhu and Warner, 2000a). In the 1990s, the implementation of the new Labour Law (1994) and the formation of a tripartite system through the so-called 'collective negotiation and collective agreement' (CNCA, a Chinese version of collective bargaining) were seen as the central task for regulating labour markets and reforming employment relations systems.

II. THE DEVELOPMENT OF THE CHINESE LABOUR MARKET SINCE 1978

China has the largest population in the world. In 1999 alone, there were 19.09 million new births in the country. At the end of 1999, the national total population was 1.26 billion. Of these, about 25.4 per cent are aged between 1 and 14, 67.7 per cent between 15 and 64, and 6.9 per cent above 65. The aging population is an obvious problem. Those aged over 65 reached 86.87 million in 1999 (CNSB, 1999). The Chinese labour market is facing severe pressures from such a large population, many of whom are underemployed or unemployed. In the past two decades, in excess of 10 million persons have been newly entering the labour market every year. Of these, less than 8 million per year have been able to secure jobs (LSSM, 2000).

One major outcome of economic reform and the open door policy has been the emergence of a variety of ownership forms, and a diversity of employment opportunities (Naughton, 1995). Since the 1980s, the domination of public sector production, through state-owned enterprises (SOEs) and collective-owned enterprises (COEs), over the national economy has been declining; at the same time in the private sector, domestic private enterprises (DPEs) and foreign-owned enterprises (FOEs), have become increasingly important. For instance, the private sector has contributed more than 50 per cent of GDP since 1995 (Zhu, 2000). In terms of employment creation, the public sector experienced negative growth, in contrast to the positive growth in the private sector.

Under the market-oriented economic reform, competition has become more severe. Many SOEs and COEs have been driven to the edge of bankruptcy, causing widespread redundancies in those sectors. For instance, at the end of 1998, over 17 million workers in SOEs had been laid off (*xiagang*), representing more than one in five urban employees (Benson and Zhu, 1999). Urban unemployment had, by this time, risen to 8 per cent (Wilnelm, 1999, p. 12). Taking into account both urban and rural areas, the unemployment rate has been estimated at between 21 per cent and 23 per cent (Biffl, 1999, p. 5). These figures are substantially higher than the official unemployment rate of around 4 per cent (CNSB, 1999).

Great change has also occurred in the distribution of employment according to industrial sector. In 1978, 70.7 per cent of the employees worked in primary industry, 17.6 per cent in secondary industry and only 11.7 per cent in tertiary industry. This position was substantially transformed over the following 20 years. By 1998, the proportion of employees in primary industry had dropped to 49.8 per cent and that in tertiary industry had increased to 26.7 per cent.

There were also less substantial changes in the gender constitution of the labour market. In 1978, the ratio of urban female staff and workers to total staff and workers was 32.9 per cent. By 1997, the urban female participation rate had increased to about 38.8 per cent of the workforce (CSP, 1999). According to a statistical report of the International Labour Organisation (ILO) in 1998, the total female labour (including the rural workforce) participation rate of China was 56 per cent, which was the highest among 26 countries including Russia and the United States (ILO, 1996).

In the area of compensation, the Chinese wage system was very rigid until the wage reform started in 1985. All the work units – the so-called '*danwei*', including SOEs, COEs and government offices and agents – were governed by a uniform wage system with eight grades for manual workers, fifteen grades for technical workers and twenty-five for cadres (Zhu and Campbell, 1996). After 1985, this uniform system was gradually replaced by a new system of wage fixation. The so-called structural wages (or floating wages) include three basic components: basic wage, skill/position wage, and bonus. Piece-rate pay was also introduced in many work units but mainly for production workers, not for office staff (Zhu and Warner, 2000a). In 1998, the national average annual wage is RMB 6,664 (about US$ 812), which is 9.8 times higher than that of 1978. Over that 20-year period the real wage level has increased 126 per cent after deducting for the influence of inflation.

As far as trade union organization is concerned, there are 16 industrial unions and 30 provincial trade union federations under the leadership of the All-China Federation of Trade Unions (ACFTU) (see Ng and Warner, 1998, p. 44). In October 1998, there were approximately 586,000 grassroots trade unions with 102.12 millions members around the country. About 91.3 per cent of all employees are members of trade unions. The number of trade unions in rural enterprises had increased from 19,000 in 1992 to 76,000 in 1997. The number of trade unions in FOEs rose from 4,274 in 1992 to 53,634 in 1997. There were also 29,132 private enterprises that had established trade unions (*People's Daily*, 15 October 1998). The dual roles of 'protecting the interests of working men and women' and at the same time 'promoting productivity' are the two fundamental aspects of the trade union's function in China as stipulated in the Trade Union Law (1992) and Labour Law (1994) (see Warner, 1996; Ng and Warner, 1998).

III. LEGAL REFORM AND LEGAL CULTURE IN CHINA

The process of economic reform and the establishment of a new legal system in China commenced in the late 1970s after 10 years of the chaotic 'Cultural Revolution' between 1966 and 1976. In 1976, following Mao's death and the Gang of Four's removal from power, the PRC faced tremendous pressure, both politically and economically. The increase in population which had occurred during the Cultural Revolution, combined with a reduction in the production of consumables, resulted in shortages of food and clothing. In urban areas, wages had not risen for more than 10 years (Zhu and Warner, 2000b). A political and ideological struggle continued among the party leadership, between the extreme left wing led by Mao's successor Hua Guo-feng and the reformists led by Deng Xiao-ping.

The eventual outcome of the struggle was that Deng's ideology gained the support of the party and the people. His economic reform initiative, and the 'open door' policy, were formally adopted in December 1978 as the central party policy (Korzec, 1992). However, China had no blueprint for such reforms, and the concern to maintain political stability under the leadership of CCP at the same time as developing a market-oriented economy has been the most important factor for decision-making at the highest level. Hence, a gradualist process of reform has been carried out, described by Deng himself as 'crossing the river by feeling the stones' (Zhu and Warner, 2000a).

A. Legal reform in China

To complement the government efforts at both political stability and economic reform, legal reform was introduced with the purpose of establishing a society governed by the 'rule of law'. The terms 'rule of law' (*fazhi*) or 'governing the country by relying on laws' (*yifa zhiguo*) have been used widely and loosely in the PRC, but certainly in a conceptually different way from how these terms would be understood in the West. The rationale of establishing a socialist legal system was based on the lessons learned during Mao's period of government when political campaign and class struggle determined the life of citizens and legitimized the action taken by the regime without the protection and constraint of law.

After more than two decades of reform, China has made a significant progress towards establishing a new legal framework and an institutionally oriented legal process. For instance, in 1978 China had fewer than 5,000 legally trained personnel and less than a dozen functioning university law departments (Alford, 1990, p. 183). By the early 1990s, it had some 215,000 staff working at over 3,000 courts, including 125,000 judges (Clarke, 1991, p. 21).

The National People's Congress (NPC) led by its Chairman Peng Zhen played an active role in matters of legal reform in the 1980s (Alford, 1990). Commencing with the most skeletal of frameworks, China's legislative drafters have drawn on an array of foreign sources in developing codes and individual laws covering criminal law and procedure, civil law and procedure, domestic and foreign economic activity, marriage and the family, the environment and much more (Alford, 1990). In all, the NPC has passed over 390 pieces of legislation, the State Council has implemented over 800 administrative regulations and the local People's Congresses and governments have introduced more than 8,000 local laws and regulations (*The Independence Daily*, 10–11 March 2001, p. 6).

However, problems still exist in terms of the legal framework, including an effective law enforcement mechanism. These problems raise questions about the purpose of legal reform and the effectiveness of the new legal system given that China has its own historical path, cultural roots and political system which are quite different from the 'West'. Further questions arise about the inter-relationship between legal and non-legal forms of regulation.

The purpose of establishing the 'socialist legal system' for the CCP is aimed to some extent at addressing a more immediate challenge of retaining legitimacy of the Party's leadership in order to maintain such 'political stability' (Lo, 1999). Therefore, the regime has attempted to ensure that the legal system remains subservient to the political needs of the Party by aggressively disseminating its version of socialist legality (Potter, 1994, p. 326). However, in any society, the views of the ruling regime and the general population on the three basic tenets of equality, justice and civil obligations may vary widely. In China, the reality is that the difference between the regime and popular views on these matters are more often in conflict than in unity.

From the point of view of the PRC rulers it seems that law is more about maintaining control over the society (Potter, 1994, p. 358). However, the CCP understands that a sustainable leadership requires support from the masses and that compromise is also sometimes necessary. In this regard, the development of the legal system in China may have a dual-function: control and compromise, and traditional Chinese culture may facilitate these needs (see Lo, 1999, pp. 168–187).

B. Economic development and labour market regulation

Some researchers have tackled the issue of the relationship between economic development strategies/stages and industrial relations/human resource policies and regulations in Southeast Asia and claim that they are closely intertwined and mutually reinforcing (see Kuruvilla, 1995; Sharma, 1986; Verma *et al.*, 1995). The general argument is that the focus of industrial relations policy changes when there is a change in economic development strategies, such as the shift from import-substitution policy to export-orientation policy. This leads in turn to changes in industrial relations/human resource policy over such matters as trade union organization and action, compensation and training. These two aspects, economic development strategies on the one hand, and industrial relations/human resource policies on the other hand, are linked in a variety of ways and form a mutually sustaining system (Kuruvilla, 1995, p. 145).

However, the situation in China is different from other Asian newly industrialising countries (NICs). The major shift in China is from a centrally planned economic system towards a market-oriented economic system. As China moves towards this 'socialist market economy', it needs rules to regulate the social, political and economic environments. Generally speaking, the transformation is in an early stage and there are two issues related to the role of the legal framework during this transition period.

The first is to re-define the relationship between the government and enterprises in the transformation from the central planning system to a market-oriented system. Under the central planning system, the relationship was based on the government's direct control over enterprises and the labour force through the allocation of funds, and the distribution of final products according to government plan. However, under the market-oriented economic system, government control is through indirect means such as tax, interest rates, licenses to import and export, exchange rates and so on. Enterprises increasingly secure autonomy over capital, material supply, labour, production and marketing. In the labour market, a key aspect of the reform policy is the devolution of decision-making power to the level of the enterprise in terms of employment allocation, employment contracts, wages and welfare, and the dismissal of employees (Zhu, 1995). The outcome is, on the one hand, that certain laws aim to make enterprises and their managers accountable for their decisions, but on the other hand, other laws attempt to increase the independence of enterprise managers, thus making it more justifiable to hold them accountable following the market-oriented economic development (Clarke, 1991, p. 36).

The second issue is to develop a rule for enterprises with diversity of ownership to compete in the market. As mentioned earlier, since the 'open door' policy was implemented, many foreign companies have invested in China and they have introduced many new practices in the area of employment relations into China, such as employment contracts, performance-oriented pay systems and so on. By introducing a universal labour market regulation, local enterprises have been able to adopt these new practices and improve their flexibility and competitiveness. At the same time, the law enables the labour administration of the PRC to manage and supervise the labour market consistently among the different types of enterprises.

In fact, labour law and labour market regulation have been important issues throughout the history of the PRC. The CCP historically held itself out to be the vanguard of the proletariat and the leading edge of the working class, and it has remained important for the Party/State leadership to be at the forefront on labour issues (Feinerman, 1996, p. 119). The evidence shows the significance of laws as a political means for controlling the working classes and reflecting party policy and ideology throughout the history in the 1950s, in the 1960s, and even into the 1970s.[2] In the 1975 constitution, which was written at the end of the Cultural Revolution to replace the earlier 1954 constitution, the right to strike was actually included, the first such constitutional right in the history of the PRC. However, it did not last very long. Although the right to strike was reiterated in the 1978 constitution, that constitution was subsequently amended to remove the right to strike in 1982 under Deng Xiao-ping's regime (Zhu, 1995). The change

---

2. For example, in 1950 the CCP introduced the Trade Union Law which established the All China Federation of Trade Unions (ACFTU). Following this a series of laws were put into place in the early to mid-1950s that governed everything from labour insurance (1952) (Wang, 1976) to the establishment of the eight-grade wage scale (1956), and the creation of staff-worker congresses (1957) (Chan, 1992).

was justified on the ground that since the workers were the masters of the people's state, who else would they be acting against except themselves if they were to go out on strike? In the light of this logic, the right to strike was superfluous and unnecessary (Feinerman, 1996, p. 120).

Following the ascendancy of Deng Xiao-ping and the dawning of the 1980s along with the period of 'open door' policy and economic reform, the era of market economic reform has given rise to new labour legislation from temporary regulations in the 1980s to relatively formal laws in the 1990s. The most important initiative among such developments was the establishment of the 1994 Labour Law.

The historical evolution of legal development in China shows that the Party/State always has maintained political and ideological influence over Chinese society. In this respect the situation in China is different from other Asian States. The status of labour law may not be reducible to the link between economic development strategies adopted by industrializing elites and industrial relations/human resource policy (Kuruvilla, 1995). The picture in China is as follows. In the pre-economic reform era, laws and other forms of labour market regulation were established mainly for political purposes and used as a political means for control based on communist ideology. In the economic reform era, the economic agenda became more important, and law and labour market regulations thus took on different functions, including providing a framework for enterprise management and market competition. However, political and ideological influences of the Party/State have remained an important factor in shape of the labour market regulation. As the ideology of the Party/State shifts from a centrally controlled orientation to a more market-based orientation, the establishment of the new labour market regulation is to facilitate such shift.

This process is still in the early stages of its legal development. It is characterized by a mixed system of legal and non-legal regulation, and other 'hidden rules' such as *guanxi* (the necessity of acting through connections) and by corruption. Unlike other East Asian States, China is in a transitional stage with a hybrid economic system, namely the combination of market-orientation and Party/State-intervention. The laws regulating the labour market are accommodating the needs of social, political and economic transitions in quite complex ways reflecting both economic and ideological imperatives.

C. Legal culture in China

It is to be expected that attitudes to law will differ between countries according to cultural difference among other things. The legal culture in China in many respects is quite different from that in the West. Many Chinese people still place law in opposition to themselves, viewing it only as a restriction rather than the means of asserting rights (Liang, 1989, p. 91). In contrast to the ancient Greek concept of the 'rule of law', and its close links between the terms law and rights, justice, and freedom, the ancient Chinese concept of '*fazhi*' (rule of law) only embodied the meanings of the two characters 'punishment and reward' (*xing shang*)

(Liang, 1989, p. 80). The legalization of morality and the moralization of law are the fundamental essence of ancient Chinese law, and law was above all a tool of suppression according to traditional ideas (Liang, 1989, pp. 88–89). The dynasties in ancient China show that there were rulers who had power to set up rules and interpret them. This was the source of what the ancient Chinese political system considered the 'rule of man' (Liang, 1989, p. 89).

Since 1949, especially in the recent years of economic reform, China has gradually established its own system of jurisprudence and numerous modern legal institutions. However, it would be naive to believe that because of this change, the surviving influences of traditional ideas have automatically been eliminated (Liang, 1989, p. 90). In fact, during the post-1949 PRC period, the traditional influence still existed, a good example being the inter-relationship between legal and non-legal forms of regulations. For a relatively long period, say between 1949 and 1979, China failed to differentiate administrative commands from rules of law, to develop a legal profession, and to distinguish legal discourse from moral or political discourse (Lubman, 1991, p. 317). In China, formal legal institutions are neither functionally well-differentiated from other institutions wielding state power, nor permitted to operate with a high degree of regularity. Law and policy remain linked and legality is necessarily weak. In criminal cases the Party/State still dominates the work of the courts, police and procuracy, and the same seems true in civil cases (Lubman, 1991, p. 317).

Even in the post-Mao era when the government has emphasized the importance of developing a 'socialist legal system', legal norms have been relatively weak in China. There may be several reasons for this. First, no evidence exists to suggest that courts have more real power now than they did a decade ago, and court judgements for many institutions remain essentially voluntary. Second, courts remain essentially the creatures of the level of government that appointed their personnel. They cannot be used to overcome the obstacles to reform caused by local protectionism and particularism when they are part of the very structure causing the problem (Clark, 1991).

The problems which China is facing, such as the conflict of its authoritarian political tradition with modern ideas of mass political participation (Alford, 1990, p. 194), may make the social-economic transition more difficult than the initial wishes of the government and people. Difficulties exist in managing legal reform by inducing popular assimilation and acceptance of the views of Party/State, and at the same time, adapting official doctrine to make it fit more closely to popular views and ideals. The latter would entail political sacrifices that the regime does not appear prepared to make at the present moment (Potter, 1994, p. 358).

IV. THE DEVELOPMENT OF CHINESE LABOUR LAW AND INDUSTRIAL RELATIONS SYSTEM

In China, it is possible to distinguish the evolution of reform into five phases: 1978–1984, 1984–1988, 1988–1992, 1992–1995, and 1995–present. In the first phase, many reforms and regulations were introduced as experiments in carefully selected parts of the country, including in the Special Economic Zones (SEZs), before being extended from around 1985 to the national level (White, 1987, p. 375; Ip, 1995, 1999; Zhu and Campbell, 1996, p. 34). A brief period of retreat from further reform occurred from 1988 until 1992, when Deng Xiao-ping made his famous Southern Trip Speech on the goals of a 'socialist market economy' and an acceleration of the process of economic reform (Bell *et al.*, 1993, pp. 3–4; Zhu and Campbell, 1996, p. 34). Since then, the revised Trade Union Law was adopted in 1992 and the new Labour Law was introduced in 1994. Some of the previous temporary regulations were adopted as legal Articles within those new laws.

A. Labour market regulation in the 1980s

Legislative initiatives were consistently used throughout the 1980s in order to consolidate economic reform and cope with changes in the labour market. For instance, when SOEs and COEs were still formally operating under the lifelong employment system (namely the 'iron rice bowl'), FOEs began to utilize contract employment practices in SEZs in Guangdong and Fujian provinces following the introduction of special regulations made by the State Council and by governments of local SEZs in 1980 (see Zhu, 2000 for details). For example, on the 26th July 1980, the State Council promulgated the Decree on the Administration of Employment in Joint Ventures (JVs) with foreign investors. Section 2 of the Decree requires JVs to sign labour contracts with their employees on wages, duration of work, working conditions and welfare, and so on. Under these regulations, management in FOEs enjoyed an autonomy which management in SOEs and COEs did not have in terms of recruiting employees independently (out of the allocation system controlled by the local labour bureau), hiring and firing employees, arranging working hours and shifts, determining pay systems, and promotion. After several years experimenting with such special regulations, the government took the view that it was necessary to set up a consistent national regulatory system to cover all kinds of enterprises.

In 1986, 'Four Temporary Regulations' were introduced (Zhu and Campbell, 1996, p. 34; Zhu and Warner, 2000a, pp. 120–126). The first of these – the Regulation on Labour Contracts – was directed at instituting a system of fixed-term contracts in place of the previous system orientated to permanent status among the SOEs and COEs. It provided a detailed provisions on such matters as duration of labour contracts, job description, job security and working conditions, wages, labour discipline, termination of contracts, and liability for breach of labour contracts.

The second temporary regulation – on the Employment of Staff and Workers – was aimed at reforming the recruitment system from one of administrative allocation and internal recruitment to open job-application and selection through objective standards. It provided enterprise management with the autonomy to recruit, select, and allocate new employees based on the needs of business and the quality of the potential employees.

The third regulation – on Discharging Employees – gave the enterprises the power to dismiss workers. Compared with the pre-reform 'iron rice bowl' system under which the enterprises were basically unable to dismiss any employee, the new regulation empowered the managers to exercise the right of dismissal in the case of employees who were not able to fulfil the requirement of production, or who severely damaged enterprise property, or were involved in criminal activities.

The final regulation concerned the Insurance of Employees Scheme. It was directed to establishing a system of social insurance for unemployment, insurance for injury and illness, and old age pensions for retired people. Generally speaking, it required the enterprises to pay up to 25 per cent equivalent to the employee's salary as social insurance contribution (Hu and Li, 1993; Zhu and Campbell, 1996, pp. 34–35).

B. Labour market regulation in the 1990s

During the immediate post-Tian-an-men Square Incident (June 1989) period, both political and economic reforms stopped and there were no further labour market initiatives until 1992 when Deng Xiao-ping made a tour of southern China and made several speeches about continuing economic reform and establishing the so-called 'socialist market economy'.[3] This further impetus to the process of economic reform resulted in further labour market developments, particularly a speeding up in the process of drafting the new Labour Law, and the encouragement of the tripartite system for regulating industrial relations and settling disputes between management and labour.

With the support of the ILO's Asian Pacific Project on Tripartism (APPOT), the Chinese government began to introduce the tripartite system in 1993 (Zhu and Fahey, 2000). It adopted the ILO's definition of tripartism as 'the interaction between government, employers and workers as equal and independent partners in active participation at efforts to seek solutions to issues of common concern' (Unger and Chan, 1995). Tripartism has since been promoted by both ILO and Chinese government as a strong tool to develop industrial democracy, to improve industrial relations and productivity, to ensure safety and health, and to contribute to stability in working life. Under the financial and professional support of ILO, regional and national workshops were conducted and the Labour Ministry and local Labour Bureaux played a crucial role in the formation of tripartite committees at both national and regional levels (Unger and Chan, 1995). At present, the tripartite committees comprise the government representatives from the labour administration, the workers' representatives from the trade unions, and the employers' representatives

---

3. After Tian-an-men Square Incident, the conservative force control the CCP and media. Deng Xiao-ping remained silence for several years until 1992 when he visited Shenzhen and Zhuhai SEZs and started to fight back for further reform agenda. His speech was published by local newspapers in Guangdong province first and the pressure was built up on the media in Beijing to publish his speech, e.g. *People's Daily*, the mouth-piece of the CCP media.

from enterprise management associations (Zhu, 2000). The major functions of these committees so far have been restricted in practice to the mediation of labour disputes and collective agreements, and providing views on new labour laws.

In addition, the government began to draft the new Labour Law in the 1990s based on the experience of the temporary regulations of the 1980s. In fact, the draft was revised more than 30 times prior to Deng Xiao-ping's 1992 speech on the 'socialist market economy', following which the State Council hastened up the drafting work and submitted the final version to the National Congress on 28th February 1994. The National Congress soon passed the Act on 5th July 1994. The establishment of the new Labour Law can be seen as a response to three factors: the government's concerns about ideological transformation and labour market stability, the needs of different interest groups in China and the pressure of external influences from international organizations (e.g. the ILO as noted above) and multi-national companies (MNCs).

The process of economic reform has meant that there is a strong need for institutionalization and legalization of employment relations within the domestic economy. The economic reform of SOEs provides more autonomy for management at the enterprise level in decision-making of investment, type of production, recruiting employees, wages and other rewards, marketing, and so on, which in turn has required a new legal system to replace the old administrative means of control. For instance, the old employment allocation system through labour administrative control has been gradually replaced by free recruitment by individual work units from the labour market. The old wage system based on the administrative ranking for manual workers and carders (the so-called 'iron wages') has been gradually replaced by structural or floating wages which are more related to the performance of individual work units and their employees (Zhu and Warner, 2000a). At the same time, the diversity of ownership forms has necessitated clear legal guidance for business operation and competition in the market.

Another major factor influencing the development of the Chinese labour market and labour law is economic globalization. In response to globalization the Chinese government has endorsed an 'open door' policy which in some respects may be seen as the core of the great economic reform. It is said that MNCs have created more than 10 millions jobs in the Chinese labour market (Zhu, 1995). Hence, Chinese labour law and regulations are required to facilitate the interests of foreign investors whilst at the same time protecting local employees. Furthermore, with the development of foreign trade, China has been influenced by international pressure from other countries and international organization such as the ILO to promote labour standards and improve labour conditions. By 1999, China had ratified 20 ILO conventions and will ratify more in the near future.

V. KEY FEATURES OF THE 1994 LABOUR LAW

As argued earlier the purpose of establishing the new labour law in China was for accommodating a complex set of needs, including, most importantly, political control, economic reform and the maintenance of social stability. Under the

CHAPTER 4 LABOUR LAW AND INDUSTRIAL RELATIONS IN CHINA

> 1. Principles
> 2. Employment Promotion
> 3. Labour Contracts and Collective Contracts
> 4. Working Hours and Holidays
> 5. Wages
> 6. Labour Safety and Hygiene
> 7. Protection of Women and Young Workers
> 8. Vocational Training
> 9. Social Security and Welfare
> 10. Labour Disputes
> 11. Monitoring and Inspection
> 12. Legal Obligations
> 13. Supplementary

Figure 1: The contents of labour law.
Source: The Labour Law (1994).

process of globalization and developing market competition, companies push hard for workplace flexibility and competitiveness. At the same time, motivating people for high productivity and commitment have become crucial to such a reform agenda. However, as we mentioned before, there was no blue print for China's legal reform. Drawing upon experience from legal systems in other countries with market-based economies thus became an integral part of the legal formation process (especially the experiences accumulated in advanced social democratic countries in West Europe).[4] Combining various international models with existing Chinese concepts a framework was eventually developed, which took its form in the 1994 Labour Law (see Figure 1).

The guiding principles of the 1994 Labour Law (see Appendix) set out the main purpose for regulating labour relations, and establishing and maintaining a labour system compatible with a 'socialist market economy' (Chapter I, Art. 1). These principles sketch the guiding ideology of the socialist market economy and the legitimate rights and interests of labourers (Art. 1); the role of state in promoting employment, training, labour standards and other regulatory functions of labour administration (Arts. 5, 6 and 9); the participation of trade unions and workers congress in safeguarding the rights and interests of labourers; and the independence of trade unions in conducting their activities (Arts. 7 and 8).

Broadly speaking, the law aims to clarify and to codify the relations of the three parties: the State, the employers (in Chinese terms the so-called work unit or employing unit '*danwei*') and the trade unions that have been affected and challenged by the reform. Less broadly, the law clarifies relations between labourers (*laodongzhe*) and the employers – whether the state-, collective-owned or recently established private enterprises including domestic- and foreign-owned firms. At first sight, the rights of workers appear of central focus in the

---

4. The Chinese Labour Ministry sent several delegations to Germany, Sweden and Switzerland, including a visit to the ILO in Geneva in the early 1990s, to study the legal framework and labour market regulations of other countries (Zhu and Fahey, 1999).

new law (see Appendix). However, the devil is in the detail. Many basic rights are not guaranteed in the new formulation and several previously guaranteed provisions of protection were omitted from the new legislation.

The detail and scope of the new law is extensive, so it is impossible to do more than summarize its main points and relate them to current developments while remaining within the constraints of this chapter. It is also necessary to appreciate that in addition to the 1994 Labour Law, there is a large number of special and local rules also covering labour market concerns, including administrative regulations (*xingzheng fagui*) made by the State Council at the national level, local rule and regulations (*difang fagui*) established by the provincial governments and their People's Congresses and their Standing Committees, and rules (*guizhang*) stipulated by the governments at and above the county (*xian*) level. Among these laws and regulations, overlap and inconsistency do exist and the concept of 'policy from above versus counter policy from below' (*shangyou zhengce xiayou duice*) reflects the situation on the ground in terms of the different interests between central government and local governments over matters of different interpretation of particular regulations. However, given that China is a huge country with regional and demographic disparities, such legal outcomes may be inevitable. Certainly, there are cries for ironing out these discrepancies through a consistent process of legal interpretation among the legal professionals, but the difficulties will remain well into the foreseeable future.

The following section briefly illustrates several core provisions of the 1994 Labour Law, including labour contracts; the role of trade unions; remuneration, benefits and working conditions; and labour disputes, mediation and arbitration.

A. Labour contracts

The 1994 Labour Law defines the labour contract as an 'agreement reached between a labourer and an employing unit for the establishment of the labour relationship and the definition of the rights, interests and obligations of each party' (1994: Art. 16). The provisions relating to labour contracts are notable in two respects. First, they take a significant step in the direction of generalization, by extending the concept of labour contracts to *all* employees. Second, they open up the possibility of *different forms* of labour contract. Three main forms of contract are suggested (Labour Law, 1994: Article 20). These are fixed-term contracts (*dingqi hetong*), 'flexible term' or open-ended contracts (*budingqi hetong* or *yongjiu hetong*) – what we call a 'permanent' contract – and 'temporary' contracts (*linshi hetong*), defined in terms of the completion of 'a specific amount of work'.

The Labour Law offers only a limited definition of the content of individual labour contracts. Art. 19 states that

> A labour contract shall be concluded in written form and contain the following clauses:
> (1) term of a labour contract;
> (2) content of work;

(3) labour protection and working conditions;
(4) labour remuneration;
(5) labour discipline;
(6) conditions for the termination of a labour contract; and
(7) responsibility for the violation of a labour contract.

Apart from the required clauses specified in the preceding paragraph, additional content in a labour contract may be agreed upon through consultation by the parties involved. (Labour Law, 1994)

This provides a series of headings, but it offers little guidance to what should be included under each heading (or what should be added). Certainly, the terms and conditions in such contracts cannot be lower than specified elsewhere in the Labour Law. Though patchy in many areas, the Labour Law deals in detail with some of these headings. In particular, it contains an extended discussion of the termination of a labour contract (e.g. Arts. 23–32). A labour contract 'may be revoked upon agreement reached between the parties involved … ' (Art. 24). The rights of management to terminate employment include cases of misconduct (Art. 25). In addition, management can – with 30 days' notice – terminate under circumstances of redundancy (Art. 27) as well as under more vague circumstances such as lack of qualification of the worker, change of objective circumstances, and the consequences of illness or injury not suffered at work (Art. 26). The individual worker can terminate the contract immediately under certain circumstances (e.g. during a probationary period, when suffering violence or intimidation, or when the employing unit fails to provide the agreed wages and working conditions) or with 30 days' written notice (Arts. 31 and 32).

This regulation of the termination of a contract resembles the regulatory provisions currently found in most OECD countries. The rights given to the individual worker are a major advance on the administrative regulations in the pre-reform system, which had allowed managers to refuse permission for a transfer to another work unit. However, there are still some points that seem to reflect a restricted notion of the rights of the individual worker to free labour mobility. Thus Art. 102 suggests that labourers are liable to pay compensation for economic losses when they 'revoke labour contracts in violation of the conditions specified in this Law'.[5] Similarly, Article 99 suggests that an employing unit is liable to pay compensation for economic losses to another employing unit when they 'recruit labourers whose labour contracts have not yet been revoked'. These are curious items, which seem out of kilter with principles of contemporary employment law, based on recognition of the peculiar nature of the employment contract and the inequality of power between the contracting parties. They seem more powerfully to reflect the operation of general principles derived from commercial contracts and tort law, in which the parties are seen as equivalent and their

---

5. It is common practice for workers to have to pay a sum of money when leaving a position. However, the 1994 Labour Law did not provide the detailed provision on such matter. It is a sphere of management initiatives (Zhu and Campbell, 2001).

rights are carefully balanced. In so far as they have a parallel, it is with the provisions of the nineteenth century Master and Servant Acts, which sought to prevent servants being enticed away from their current Master or from leaving their employment before the end of their term of hiring (see Zhu and Campbell, 2001).

In addition to its provisions for mandatory individual labour contracts, the Labour Law also allows for optional, enterprise-level *collective contracts* (Arts. 33–35, see more detailed discussion under the section of *Trade Unions* below). These are agreements between employees and management (on matters such as labour remuneration, working hours, rest and holidays, occupational health and safety, and insurance and welfare), negotiated either by the labour union or – in enterprises without a union – representatives elected by the employees. When such collective contracts are established, they lay down a new floor for all individual contracts within that enterprise.

It could be argued that the provision for collective contracts establishes a framework similar to most OECD countries, in which statutory protection for employees is supplemented by voluntary collective bargaining. It should be noted, however, that the process in China is called CNCA rather than collective bargaining, in order to suggest a difference from the adversarial system associated with most OECD countries (Zhu, 2000). Though trade unions are widespread in Chinese enterprises, they have traditionally played a distinctive role as the 'transmission belt' for the Party. The government has been reluctant to allow room for independent trade union action, and it continues to insist that industrial relations in China are fundamentally based on co-operation (*Worker*, 1/1995, pp. 4–10). Thus in the Labour Law, the right of negotiation is not accompanied by any of the conditions that would render it effective, including in particular a right to strike. In this sense, the provision for collective contracts is less meaningful than it may first appear (Josephs, 1995, p. 571; Warner and Ng, 1999).

In the wake of the proclamation of the Labour Law, an extensive campaign was launched to implement the provisions relating to labour contracts. The central task was to extend the labour contract system to all employees, first in urban enterprises. Sample labour contracts and handbooks of sample labour contracts, adapted to conform not only to the Labour Law but also to local regulations, were made widely available through the local Labour Bureaux and local employment agencies. The recent study by Zhu and Campbell (2001) confirms that the system has indeed been generalized around the whole country. However, investigation of the practice in case studies suggests that labour contracts remain largely uniform and lacking in detail. It seems to go beyond what could be expected as a result of management desire to preserve flexibility, and it suggests that the criticism that management are merely responding to an administrative campaign may have some validity.

It seems that there is a widening gap between state regulation and a sphere of management initiatives. Employment practice at enterprise level is largely characterized by unilateral management decision-making. Many central features of employment practice unfold outside the provisions of the Labour Law and the provisions set down in individual labour contracts. Even when individual labour contracts do depart from the standard template and acquire more specificity, the new detail often includes curious features such as financial penalties for employees who terminate their contract before the expiry of its term. As such, the new detail serves to buttress management authority (Zhu and Campbell, 2001).

The Labour Law undoubtedly has an impact at the enterprise level. Though problems of enforcement persist, a system of dispute settlement is in place and appears to growing in effectiveness. But the labour contract system itself appears largely ineffective. It is not serving as an effective tool for the state, management or individual workers. From the point of view of state regulation, the labour contracts provide little purchase (beyond what was already in the basic regulations). When disputes arise between employees and the employer, labour contracts are of little use in helping to resolve the dispute. They are of little help in consolidating a new sphere of effective employment law. They tend to be treated in a similar way to previous state regulations under the pre-reform system (Zhu and Campbell, 2001).

B. Trade unions

Several issues arise relating to the role and function of trade unions. Art. 7 of the Labour Law claims that 'Trade unions shall represent and safeguard the legitimate rights and interests of labourers, and independently conduct their activities in accordance with the law'. Certainly, past and contemporary empirical evidence hardly supports a notion of trade union independence and/or autonomy, no matter if we look at the position of unions in the large SOEs or in other types of enterprises, both private domestic and foreign firms. What the workers confront in the latter may not be the State-employer, but a new 'class' of 'bosses' not directly related to the State, unconstrained in many cases by any trade unions at all; or if working in the SOEs, they may in fact be unions which still function as the branch of the State-employer (see Chan, 1993).

The Act tries to give the unions a bigger role in workplace governance. One example is in the case of workplace redundancies. Art. 27 indicates that if a work unit wishes to declare workers redundant, the trade union or all of its staff and workers shall be notified 30 days in advance. Previously, the issue of redundancy, which seldom occurred, was dealt with by the local Labour Bureaux. Now, the most important parties are the employing unit (manager under the manager-responsibility system) with the trade union next most important. When management decides that redundancy is inevitable, it must negotiate with union on the number and identity of those being made redundant, and union must be involved in the final decision-making. Thus, whilst the union now has a key role in determining who will be made redundant, the Bureaux will merely receive a report and carry out the paper-work.

Other rights which are exercisable by the trade union include the right to consultation and to enter into collective agreements. Trade unions in Chinese enterprises formerly had a production role but had no representative function (see Warner, 1993). Art. 30 of the new Labour Law permits the trade union to give its opinion on, and request the work unit to reconsider, decisions on workplace rules and regulations, the content of labour contracts, and the termination of contracts. Thus, strengthening its ties with its members. However, the ability of trade union in China takes advantage of these legal rights depends upon the extent of effective organization. This is a difficulty in DPEs and FOEs where unions are quite 'thin on the ground', compared with SOEs where the role of trade unions has long been institutionalized. Moreover, even in the SOEs, management – still largely integrated into political networks – has increased its power at the expense of workers within the enterprise, and the unions' voice has been somewhat undermined by the substantially enhanced managerial power (see Zhu and Campbell, 1996, p. 41).

The new Labour Law also opens the way for an element of collective bargaining as mentioned before. However, collective contracts (in Chinese, the so-called 'collective negotiation and collective agreement – CNCA') have been used as one mechanism to promote the union's participation at enterprise level. Art. 35 provides that 'the collective contract signed according to the law is legally binding on both the enterprise and the workers of the enterprise…'.[6] One of the most important aspects of the Labour Law is to oblige business and unions to enter into collective contract and to adhere to them. There are two important issues related to the implementation of collective contract. One is that the concept of the so-called 'CNCA' is designed to promote a less confrontational system of industrial relations than the adversarial collective bargaining of the West system. This is in keeping with the Party/State's view that industrial relations in China is still fundamentally based on cooperation (see Zhu, 2000, p. 21). Second, the implementation of the collective contract regulation has been carried out as a political campaign, and State's design of the collective contract under the socialist ideology which insists that trade unions are the safeguard of the legitimate rights and interests of workers. As a result most enterprises have tended to adopt similar agreements based on the sample provided by the labour administration. Hence, the system of CNCA demonstrates a high degree of state intervention and control. This can probably be seen as one of the Chinese characteristics.

A noteworthy omission from the new Labour Law is any mention of a 'right to strike' (Zhu and Campbell, 1996, p. 44). As we noted before, 'the right to strike' was removed from the PRC Constitution during the 1982 constitutional revision. Even during the process of formulating the new Labour Law, two different opinions emerged about restoring the right to strike into the new law. Eventually, the

---

6. At the closing ceremony of the 12th ACFTU Executive Committee, the Chairman Wei Jian-xing said: 'In implementing the Labour Law, we should make overall plans while stressing key areas and tackling key contradictions. For trade unions, the important link and crucial issue is the signing of collective contracts with enterprises by trade unions on behalf of workers and staff members. To keep a firm hold on collective contracts is the crux of implementing the Labour Law, with the result that a slight move in one part will affect the situation as a whole; and the various endeavours carried out by trade unions in implementing the Labour Law will be promoted. The signing of collective contracts should be carried out gradually and in stages. At present, we should first carry out experiments in some FOEs, in enterprises that implement the modern enterprise system on a trial basis and in some SOEs that are in fairly good shape' (*Workers' Daily*, 16 December 1994).

argument which favoured maintaining consistency between the Labour Law and the PRC Constitution gained the support at the NPC and 'the right to strike' disappeared in the final version of the 1994 Law (Zhu and Fahey, 1999). From the political point of view, the paramountcy of the 1982 Constitution remains unchallenged under the Deng's leadership.

VI. REMUNERATION, BENEFITS AND WORKING CONDITIONS

Under the new Labour Law, remuneration and benefits are also subject to new scrutiny. In the light of new economic realities as China moves to a market-oriented economy, some autonomy is now permitted in wage distribution. Art. 47 endorses such an approach by providing that 'employing units can autonomously decide their own wage distribution and wage level according to the law, production levels, management characteristics and economic efficiency of the unit…'. In addition, local governments are expected, with an eye to prevailing local standards, to prepare minimum pay provisions. Another concession to market economic imperatives are new provisions for the establishment of social insurance system (Arts. 70 and 71), which a universal system covering both domestic and foreign enterprises has been developed for the insurance of retirement, illness, injury, work-related disability, occupational disease, unemployment and child-bearing. In addition, supplementary insurance for workers is also supposed to be maintained by each enterprise.

New rules also appear in the new Labour Law about maximum hours (Arts. 36 and 37), establishing an 8-h day and a 44-h week as the national standard. In keeping with China's constitution, every Chinese worker is guaranteed one day of rest per week (changed into two days under the new policy of the State Council, see below). Overtime work hours are ordinarily limited to one hour per day; in special circumstances, overtime may amount to a maximum of three hours per day or 36 h per month. Overtime pay is required to be paid at 150 per cent of normal pay rates, and at higher rates of 200 per cent on rest days and 300 per cent on holidays (Arts. 41–45) (see Yang, 1995; Zhu and Fahey, 1999, 2000).

Training has become an important concern of both government and enterprises in terms of improving employees' skills and productivity, eventually leading to high quality of products and competitiveness in the market. Chapter VIII of the Labour Law emphases the role of national and local governments and enterprises to engage various measures and channels to expand vocational training to 'develop professional skills of labourers, improve their qualities, and raise their employment capability and work ability'. The State shall 'determine occupational classification, set up professional skill standards for the occupations classified, and practise a system of vocational qualification certificates'. In addition, 'examination and verification organizations authorized by the government are in charge of the examination and verification of the professional skills of labourers. Certainly, human resource development has been seen as one of the most important issues in China's drive to become competitive in the global economy. This pressure has become more profound with China's membership of the WTO due to the further opening up the market for foreign competition (see Zhu and Warner, 2001).

A further serious problem for China's workplaces is its very poor occupational safety and health record (Feinerman, 1996) and this has also been addressed in Chinese laws and regulations, including the Law of the PRC Regarding Safety of Mines, the State Council Regulation on Prevention from Dust and Poison, Regulations on Casualties of Workers and Staff in Enterprises, and the 1994 Labour Law (Yuan, 1997, pp. 215–216).

In fact, worker protection has always been a difficult issue in China and covering up the problem of labour rights abuses by governments has been common phenomena. In recent years, however, several publications have made a serious attack upon labour rights abuse such as the lack of facilities for basic hygiene in work and living places, frequent industrial accidents, the overcrowded working environments, exposure to pollution, high temperatures and noise without protection, and so on (Zhang, 1994; Yang, 1994; Zhu, 1995, 2000; Chan, 1998, 2000).

The 1994 legislation attempts to establish and to 'perfect' protective systems with adequate process, worker education, and appropriate governmental checks on compliance (Labour Law: Chapter VI). Under the Labour Law, this new responsibility for worker health and safety appears to be a significant challenge for both work unit and trade unions, in particular for those organizations which have financial difficulties to improve their working environment and safety standards. The reality is that the situation of safety and health in certain industries such as mining, textiles and chemicals is deteriorating in recent years.

VII. LABOUR DISPUTES, MEDIATION AND ARBITRATION

The Labour Law, in keeping with other national legal systems, provides various mechanisms for the resolution of labour related disputes, including consultation, mediation, arbitration and adjudication. Art. 77 stipulates that 'Labour disputes between employing units and workers shall be resolved through conciliation, arbitration and litigation according to the law or through consultation'. Labour disputes have been defined in the 1994 Labour Law as the disputes of labour rights and liabilities between work units and labourers, including disputes caused by dismissal and resignation; by the implementation of state regulations on wages, insurance, welfare, training and so on; and by implementing a labour contract with different interpretation.

The range of possibilities begins with mediation at the level of the initial employing unit, then proceeds to arbitration at the higher levels of the Labour Bureaux. The recognition of the need for clearly defined formal ways of dealing with labour disputes is a novel feature of the new law. A very subtle innovation is the way in which the role of the Chairperson of the enterprise Mediation Committees is assigned to the trade unions, and that of the Arbitration

Committee to the Labour Bureaux. It is clear that the final decision on the outcomes of disputes remains in the hands of the State.

VIII. THE TRANSFORMATION OF LABOUR MARKET REGULATION

Several issues present themselves for investigation in the context of the new programme of labour market regulation in China. Whilst China has made great progress in labour legislation and regulation, there are evidently many remaining weaknesses and deficiencies in the legal framework as it stands. In particular, the legal framework requires more detailed legislation, and law enforcement mechanisms need to be improved so as to protect both workers and work units' legitimate rights and benefits under the social transformation and economic reform policies. It is possible to identify three major areas which need to be addressed.

First, following the successful implementation of the 1994 Labour Law, there is an urgent need to develop other supporting legislation in the form of Employment Contract Laws, Social Security Laws and so on. The reason is that in most respects the Labour Law provides only abstract principles to which it is difficult to give practical implementation. To overcome the defects of the Labour Law, further detailed regulations and legislation are needed. In this area, the Labour and Social Security Ministry has made and promulgated 14 supporting administrative regulations so far, but these are still inadequate to fulfil the needs of both employers and employees in terms of handling disputes and coping with the changes in the labour market. For example, Art. 45 of the Labour Law provides for a paid vacation system. If a labourer has worked more than 1 year without interruption, he/she will be entitled to enjoy paid vacation. But there is no further provision on how to implement this requirement. The State Council was expressly authorized to make a detailed regulation on paid vacation by the Labour Law. But 6 years has passed since then and the detailed regulation still remains in draft form. Likewise, there are also serious 'legislative inadequacies' or 'implementation difficulties' in the areas such as labour contracts, collective bargaining, wages, settlement of labour disputes, and so on. Without specific legislation in these areas, the rights of workers founded in the Constitution and the principles of the Labour Law cannot be guaranteed to have affect.

Second, rationalization is needed among the various provisions regulating the labour market and employment provisions. As noted earlier, under the current legal culture and legal framework a great deal of administrative regulation, made by the State Council and labour administration, plays a major role as well as the 1994 national Labour Law. There are some serious conflicts between these various administrative regulations which have been made in different periods of economic development. Many are directly contradictory to the 1994 Labour Law. For example, the Labour Law provides that state carries out a working hour system that labourers should work no more than 8 h a day and 44 h a week. But the State Council's Decision on Amendment of the Staff and Workers' Working

Hour Regulation, which came into effect two months later than the Labour Law, provides in its Section 3 that staff and workers should work 8 h a day and 40 h a week. Thus, the new provision conflicts with the Labour Law: if a labourer works more than 40 h but below 44 h, should the employer pay him/her an overtime wage? Lack of harmonization within the current labour legal framework appears to be one of the most serious weaknesses of the present Chinese labour law regime, creating great difficulty for implementation and enforcement of the law. The confusion and inconsistency of Chinese legal environment is also one of the major complaints of foreign investors.

Third, a full implementation of the Labour Law depends upon the foundation and improvement of the social security system. At the present time the core of labour legislation in China is the labour contract system. The contract system has not been able to be thoroughly implemented in China because of the slow development of the social security system. For example, many staff and workers have been laid off by SOEs. Their labour relations have ceased according to the Labour Law. However, the government cannot allow the laid-off workers to be treated as unemployed because of the insufficiency of social security. Thus the enterprises have to take the responsibility to arrange special programmes for the laid-off staff and workers through the so-called Re-employment Centres (*zai jiouyi zhongxin*). Under this arrangement, enterprises are obliged to conclude an agreement on basic living security, re-training and re-employment with the laid-off staff and workers and pay them living allowance for 2 to 3 years. As a result the relationship between SOEs and their staff and workers are not purely based on the labour contract. The institutionalisation of a free labour market will be hard to realise in China until the social insurance system can be improved, thus liberating enterprises from such social obligation.

Leaving to one side the problems associated with the legal framework *per se*, there are also continuing problems which arise from the Chinese legal tradition, its historical path, and the impact of the political system on Chinese legal culture. Again there are several issues to be considered. First, in China, the most important overriding legal issue is that the law and regulations be 'ideologically correct' in order for them to be passed and implemented. However, this 'correctness' is decided by the central leadership. As might be expected 'ideological correctness' changes from time to time depending on the political climate, changing leadership and the need for the regime to control society. Hence, it is not surprising to see policy and regulation shift between a 'conservative-orientated' approach and an 'open-minded' reformist-orientated approach. The fundamental issues at work in these cases are those to do with legitimating the current leadership and maintaining social stability.

Second, the modernization of the Chinese legal system is occurring under the influence of many factors. For example, the traditional philosophy and culture which the regime can draw upon for the introduction of reforms embodying 'Chinese characteristics', and abjuring 'Western' domination, have had a profound influence on the current legal system. Another is the historical influences of the concept of 'rule of law' (*fazhi*), and some colonial and Republic of China (*minguo*) legacies in contemporary history before 1949, and in Marxist and

Communist ideology under the interpretation of the CCP since 1949. The most important factor is the response of the Party/State towards the reality of global and internal economic transformation and its effects on the Chinese labour markets, such as internal pressures caused by the laying off of workers from SOEs, the floating population of internal migration between rural and urban areas, and the external pressures of globalization (e.g. China's joining the WTO and the consequences for its domestic political economy).

Third, the outlook of the ruling elite towards legal reform, stability and development may be quite opposed to that of the general populations, due to their different position and interests. The CCP still dominates the political scene and the legal framework can be used as a means for the legitimacy of the CCP's leadership, in other words, maintaining 'control'. However, compromises are made from time to time by the Party/State under the pressure of popular opinion. There are several examples of the State acting under these sorts of pressures for labour regulation reform. These include the introduction of several schemes such as a lay-off scheme and establishing re-employment centres, developing insurance systems, wage increase the urban area, and so on.

At the same time, these relatively popular policies and regulations might also be seen as a strategy for maintaining social stability. On the one hand the Party/State wants to maintain its leadership over the masses; on the other hand, the Party/State needs popular support for maintaining power and thus compromises have to be made from time to time. These outcomes are thus related to the relative bargaining strength of both sides in different political, social and economic circumstances.

Finally, the Chinese economic reform and development is based on a gradualist approach, and the process of legal reform is also following such an approach in order to maintain the legitimacy of the Party/State and political–social stability. China has the largest labour market in the world and there is no existing model can be adopted by the Chinese government to establish a 'socialist market economy'. Any extreme action taken by the government may lead to drastic social and economic disruption.

IX. CONCLUSION

Great progress has been made in labour market legislation in China since 1978. A labour law system with 'Chinese characteristics' has been developed but it is still in the early stages of development and has many defects. China is a relatively late developer in the field of labour market regulation compared with other Asian States. Most of these States were previously under full Western colonization, and this legacy has led to the development of quite sophisticated legal frameworks in those societies.

China is also different from other Asian States in several other respects. In China, the major shift in its labour market regulation system derives from the pre-economic reform era when labour laws were part of a system of political control and indoctrination. Subsequent economic liberalization has not removed the importance of this ideological aspect of labour law. China is thus in an early transitional stage with a hybrid system made up of market-oriented policies and Party/State-control mechanisms.

The combination of traditional cultures represented by Confucianism and 'Marxism, Mao Ze-dong's thought, Deng Xiao-ping's theory and Jiang Ze-min's (the current President of PRC) speech', and the interactive interpretation of those ideologies by the CCP have had a profound impact on the social structure and the relationships within the social hierarchy. As a result, the concept of the 'rule of law' (*fazhi*) has a different meaning from that in the 'West' and the interpretation and intervention of the Party/State over and above 'the law' still exists. These many issues constitute a challenge both to the regime and the masses in China to re-examine the purpose and direction of the so-called 'legal reform'.

APPENDIX: CHAPTER I: GENERAL PROVISIONS OF THE 1994 LABOUR LAW

Article 1. This law is formulated in accordance with the Constitution in order to protect the legitimate rights and interests of labourers, readjust labour relationship, establish and safeguard a labour system suited to the socialist market economy, and promote economic development and social progress.

Article 2. This Law applies to all enterprises and individual economic organizations (as employing units) within the boundary of the PRC and labourers who form a labour relationship therewith.

State organs, institutional organizations and societies as well as labourers who form a labour contract relationship therewith shall follow this Law.

Article 3. Labourers shall have the right to be employed on an equal basis, choose occupations, obtain remuneration for their labour, take rest, have holidays and leaves, obtain protection of occupational safety and health, receive training in vocational skills, enjoy social insurance and welfare, and submit applications for settlement of labour disputes, and other rights relating to labour as stipulated by law.

Labourers shall fulfil their labour tasks, improve their vocational skills, follow rules on occupational safety and health, and observe labour discipline and professional ethics.

Article 4. The employing units shall establish and perfect rules and regulations in accordance with the law so as to ensure that labourers enjoy the right to work and fulfil labour obligations.

Article 5. The State shall take various measures to promote employment, develop vocational education, lay down labour standards, regulate social incomes, perfect social insurance system, coordinate labour relationship, and gradually raise the living standard of labourers.

Article 6. The State shall advocate the participation of labourers in social voluntary labour and the development of their labour competitions and activities of forwarding rational proposals, encourage and protect the scientific research and technical renovation engaged by labourers, as well as their inventions and creations, and commend and award labour models and advanced workers.

Article 7. Labourers shall have the right to participate in and organize trade unions in accordance with the law.

Trade unions shall represent and safeguard the legitimate rights and interests of labourers, and independently conduct their activities in accordance with the law.

Article 8. Labourers shall, through the assembly of staff and workers or their congress, or other forms in accordance with the provisions of laws, rules and regulations, take part in democratic management or consult with the employing units on an equal footing about protection of the legitimate rights and interests of labourers.

Article 9. The labour administrative department of the State Council shall be in charge of the management of labour of the whole country.

The labour administrative departments of the local people's governments at or above the county level shall be in charge of the management of labour in the administrative areas under their respective jurisdiction.

Source: Labour Law of the PRC, Beijing: the Ministry of Labour of the PRC, 1994.

REFERENCES

Alford W.P. (1990), 'Seek truth from fact – especially when they are unpleasant: America's understanding of China's efforts at law reform', *Pacific Basin Law Journal* Vol. 8, pp. 177–196.

Bell M., Khor H. and Kochhar K. (1993), *China at the threshold of a market economy*, International Monetary Fund, Occasional Paper No. 107, Washington.

Benson J. and Zhu Y. (1999), 'Markets, firms and workers: The transformation of HRM in Chinese state-owned enterprises', *Human Resource Management Journal* Vol. 9, No. 4, pp. 58–74.

Biffl G. (1999), 'Unemployment, underemployment and migration: A challenge for labour market policy in China', in: Proceedings of the Workshop, the Melbourne Institute of Applied Economic and Social Research, The University of Melbourne, 8 March.

Chan P. (1992), Central Committee of the CCP and State Council, "Provisional Regulations on Congresses of Workers and Staff Members in State-Owned Industrial Enterprises" (1981 regulation, restating and amending 1950s provisions). Reprinted and translated on pp. 282–292 in *China Modernisation and Its Economic Laws*, Hong Kong Economist Newspaper, Hong Kong.

Chan A. (1993), 'Revolution of corporatism? Workers and unions in post-Mao China', *Australian Journal of Chinese Affairs* Vol. January, No. 29, pp. 31–61.

Chan A. (1998), 'Labour Standards and Human Rights: The Case of Chinese Workers under Market Socialism', *Human Rights Quarterly* Vol. 20, No. 4, pp. 886–904.
Chan A. (2000), 'Globalization, China's Free (Read Bonded), Labour Market, and the Chinese Trade Unions', in: Rowley C. and Benson J. (eds.), *Globalization and Labour in the Asia Pacific Region*. Frank Cass, London, pp. 260–281.
Child J. (1994), *Management in China During the Era of Reform*. Cambridge University Press, Cambridge.
Clarke D.C. (1991), 'What's law got to do with it? Legal institutions and economic reform in China', *Pacific Basin Law Journal* Vol. 10, pp. 1–76.
CNSB (1999), *Chinese 1999 Statistical Gazette on National Economy and Social Development*. China National Statistic Bureau, Beijing.
CSP (1999), *China Labour Statistical Yearbook 1999*. China Statistics Press, Beijing.
Feinerman J.V. (1996), 'The past – and future – of labor law in China', in: US Department of Labor (ed.), *Changes in China's Labor Market: Implications for the Future*. US Department of Labor, Washington D.C., pp. 119–134.
Hu T.W. and Li E. (1993), 'The labour market', in: Galenson W. (ed.) *China's Economic Reform*. 1990 Institute, San Francisco, pp. 147–76.
ILO (1996), *China: Employment and Training Policies for Transition to a Market Economy*. International Labour Office, Geneva.
Ip O. (1995), 'Changing employment systems in China: Some evidence from the Shenzhen Special Economic Zone', *Work, Employment and Society* Vol. 9, No. 2, pp. 269–285.
Ip O. (1999), 'A case study of human resource management practices in the PRC: Convergence or Non-convergence?', *International Journal of Employment Studies* Vol. 7, No. 2, pp. 61–79.
Josephs H. (1995), 'Labor law in a "socialist market economy": The Case of China', *Colombia Journal of Transnational Law* Vol. 33, No. 3, pp. 559–581.
Korzec M. (1992), *Labour and the Failure of Reform in China*. St. Martin's Press, New York.
Kuruvilla S.C. (1995), 'Economic development strategies, industrial relations policies and workplace IR/HR practices in Southeast Asia', in: Wever K.S. and Turner L. (eds.), *The Comparative Political Economy of Industrial Relations*, Industrial Relations Research Association, Madison, WI.
Li J.S. and Jia J.L. (1995), *Laodong Faxue (The Study of Labour Law)*. Peking University Press, Beijing.
Liang Z.P. (1989), 'Explicating "law": A comparative perspective of Chinese and Western legal culture', *Journal of Chinese Law* Vol. 3, pp. 55–91.
Lo V.I. (1999), *Law and Industrial Relations: China and Japan after World War II*. Kluwer Law International, The Hague.
LSSM (2000), *Laodong He Shihui Baozhang Bu Tongji Nianbo 2000 (Labour and Social Security Ministry Statistical Report, 2000)*. The Ministry of Labour and Social Security, PRC, Beijing.
Lubman S. (1991), 'Studying contemporary Chinese law: Limits, possibilities and strategy', *The American Journal of Comparative Law* Vol. 39, pp. 293–341.

Naughton B. (1995), *Growing out of the Plan: Chinese Economic Reform 1978–1993*. Cambridge University Press, Cambridge.
Ng S.H. and Warner M. (1998), *China's Trade Unions and Management*, Macmillan, London.
Potter P.B. (1994), 'Riding the Tiger: Legitimacy and Legal Culture in Post-Mao China', *The China Quarterly* Vol. 138, pp. 325–358.
Sharma B. (1986), 'Stages of economic development and industrial relations patterns: The ASEAN case', in: International Industrial Relations Association 7th World Congress, September 1986, Hamburg.
Unger R.M. (1976), *Law in Modern Society*. Free Press, New York.
Unger J. and Chan A. (1995), 'China, corporatism, and the East Asian model', *The Australian Journal of Chinese Affairs* Vol. 33, pp. 29–53.
Verma A., Kochan T.A. and Lansbury R.D. (1995), *Employment Relations in the Growing Asian Economies*. Routledge, London.
Wang J.E. (ed.), (1976), 'Labor Insurance Regulations of the PRC, Feb. 26, 1951 (amended Jan. 2, 1953)', in *Selected Legal Documents of the PRC*, University Publications of America, Arlington, VA. p. 301 (translation).
Warner M. (1993), 'Human resource management with Chinese characteristics', *International Journal of Human Resource Management* Vol. 4, pp. 45–65.
Warner M. (1996), 'Chinese enterprise reform, human resources and the 1994 labour law', *International Journal of Human Resource Management* Vol. 7, No. 1, pp. 776–796.
Warner M. and Ng S.H. (1999), 'Collective contracts in Chinese enterprises: A new brand of collective bargaining under "market socialism" ', *British Journal of Industrial Relations* Vol. 37, No. 2, pp. 295–314.
Warner M. and Zhu Y. (2000), 'The origins of Chinese "industrial relations" ', in: Warner M. (ed.), *Beyond the Iron-Rice-Bowl: Changing Workplace Relations in Chinese Economy*. Macmillan, London: pp. 15–33.
White G. (1987), 'The Politics of Economic reform in Chinese industry: The introduction of the labour contract system', *The China Quarterly* Vol. 111, pp. 365–389.
Wilnelm K. (1999), 'Cover Story: China', *Far Eastern Economic Review*, 18 February.
Yang F. (1994), 'Laozi Maoduen: Zhongguo Shihui Weilai Maoduen Jiaodan' (The labour-capital contradiction: Focus of social conflict in China in the future), *Viewpoint* (Beijing: China News Service), May, pp. 6–10.
Yang J. (1995), 'China adopts minimum wage system', *Beijing Review* (May 1–7), p. 24.
Yuan L.Q. (1990), *Zhongguo Laodong Jingji Shi (The History of Chinese Labour Economy)*. Beijing Economic Institute Press, Beijing.
Yuan S.Q. (1997), 'Legislation on occupational health and safety in China improves and approaches perfection day by day', in: Mitchell R. and Wu J. (eds.), *Facing the Challenge in the Asia-Pacific Region: Contemporary Themes and Issues in Labour Law*. Centre for Employment and Labour Relations Law occasional Monograph, the University of Melbourne, Melbourne, pp. 215–218.

Zhu Y. (1992), The Role of Export Processing Zones in East Asian Development: South Korea, Taiwan, China and Thailand, PhD thesis, The University of Melbourne, Melbourne.

Zhu Y. (1995), 'Major changes under way in China's industrial relations', *International Labour Review* Vol. 124, pp. 36–49.

Zhu Y. (2000), 'Globalization, foreign direct investment and the impact on labour relations and regulations: The case of China', *The International Journal of Comparative Labour Law and Industrial Relations* Vol. 16, No. 1, pp. 5–24.

Zhu Y. and Campbell I. (1996), 'Economic reform and the challenge of transforming labour regulation in China', *Labour and Industry* Vol. 7, pp. 29–49.

Zhu Y. and Fahey S. (1999), 'The impact of economic reform on industrial labour relations in China and Vietnam', *Post-Communist Economies* Vol. 11, No. 2, pp. 173–192.

Zhu Y. and Fahey S. (2000), 'The challenges and opportunities for the trade union movement in the transition era: Two socialist market economies – China and Vietnam', in: Rowley C. and Benson J. (eds.), *Globalization and Labour in the Asia Pacific Region*. Frank Cass, London, pp. 282–299.

Zhu Y. and Warner M. (2000a), 'Changing approaches to employment relations in the People's Republic of China', in: Bamber G.J. *et al.* (eds.), *Employment Relations in the Asia-Pacific: Changing Approaches*. Allen & Unwin, Sydney, pp. 117–128.

Zhu Y. and Warner M. (2000b), 'An emerging model of employment relations in China: A divergent path from the Japanese', *International Business Review* Vol. 9, pp. 345–361.

Zhu Y. and Campbell I. (2001), 'Individual labour contract in Chinese enterprises', *International Journal of Comparative Law and Industrial Relations*, Vol. 18, No. 1, pp. 5–35.

Zhu Y. and Warner M. (2001), 'Human resource management in China's "frontier" special economic zone: Selected case studies of domestic and foreign-owned enterprises on Hainan Island', *International Journal of Employment Studies*, Vol. 10, No. 1, pp. 75–104.

5. The Labour Situation in Japan (2001)

*Yutaka Asao**

I. THE ECONOMY AND THE LABOUR MARKETS: CURRENT SITUATION

The Japanese economy has remained sluggish since the bubble economy collapsed in early 1990s, and has been in so-called 'the lost decade'.

GDP increased by 0.4 per cent in real terms in 2001 shifting to a decrease from the relatively high growth of 2.8 per cent in the previous year. A major factor behind this was listless private investment, together with sluggish final private consumption expenditure: the growth of private fixed investment, which had recorded a substantial increase of 9.7 per cent in the previous year, increased by 1.3 per cent in 2001, and private housing investment shifted from an increase of 0.8 per cent to a substantial decline of 5.5 per cent. Moreover, external demand made a substantial negative contribution to GDP due to a decline in exports (6.1 per cent in real terms) against a backdrop of the slowdown in the world economy, etc. On the other hand, in the midst of sluggish domestic private demand and external demand, official fixed capital formation (public investment), a variable policy of the Government, which had declined by 9.9 per cent in the previous year, also declined by 3.6 per cent in 2001.

Last year we reported that a distinctive characteristic of recent years has been the continued decline in price levels. Even corrected for the GDP deflator (an indicator of inflation for the whole economy over one or more years, derived by dividing total GDP at current prices by total GDP at constant prices), prices continued to decline by 1.6 per cent in 2001, after declining by 1.5 per cent and 1.9 per cent in 1999 and 2000, respectively. In these circumstances, several senior government officials were of the opinion that the economy was on a moderate deflationary trend.

Reflecting this economic trend, the unemployment situation has become even more severe, with the decline in the number of employed becoming larger. The unemployment rate in 2001 was 5.0 per cent, 0.3 point higher than the previous year, hitting the 5 per cent mark on a yearly basis.

With poor economic conditions continuing, the number of companies engaged in restructuring, including personnel retrenchment, is increasing and even those companies which formerly gave strong support to employment stability for

---

*   Director of the Research Planning Department of the Japan Institute of Labour.

R. Blanpain (ed.),
Labour Relations in the Asia-Pacific Countries, 65–70.
© 2004 Kluwer Law International. Printed in Great Britain.

regular workers are beginning to show signs of a change in direction. In particular, a succession of plans were announced for personnel reduction in the immediate aftermath of the terrorist attacks which occurred on 11 September 2001, when the outlook for the world economy appeared extremely bleak. In response to the IT recession, the scale of personnel reduction plans announced by major Japanese electrical manufacturers were particularly remarkable with some tens of thousands of workers slated for redundancy. In terms of the contents of such plans, many of the personnel reductions were to be effected with respect to overseas establishments and, even when they were effected domestically, there were many cases of opting for non-replenishment for natural retirement, so the portion of personnel reduction through recruitment of voluntary retirees, etc., was not so great. However, it cannot be denied, even before the contents of these measures is discussed, that such plans constituted a factor underpinning the bleakness of the employment environment. In such circumstances, the unemployment rate (it should be noted that Japan's unemployment rate is derived based on the situation of the week at the end of each month), which was 5.0 per cent for August 2001, rose to 5.3 per cent for September, and was 5.3 per cent for October, 5.4 per cent for November and 5.5 per cent for December.

The following is a more detailed discussion of the unemployment rate, which is announced in the Labour Force Survey by the Statistics Bureau of the Ministry of Public Management, Home Affairs, Posts and Telecommunications (which covers about 40,000 households). Among the wholly unemployed, in the first half of 2001, the number of those who were involuntarily unemployed was smaller than the previous year, it began to increase in August, and the margin of increase became greater in ensuing months; that is, an increase by 100,000 in September over the corresponding month of the previous year, by 160,000 in October, by 290,000 in November and by 310,000 in December.

II. DEVELOPMENTS OF INDUSTRIAL RELATIONS

A. Historical overview of industrial relations

Until the end of the Second World War in 1945, there were no legalized trade unions in Japan. However, the labour movement became very active in the economic chaos after the war, and when the Trade Union Law was enacted in 1946, three national centers were organized. Labour movements in that period had a political or social tinge, and under the influence of occupation forces, union activities, viewed as a revolutionary movement, was forced to experience a setback. In order to overcome the weakness, the movement needed to be reviewed, and as that result, Sohyo (General Council of Trade Unions of Japan) was formed in 1950, and a number of trade unions became affiliated with it.

Soon after that, due to ideological conflict, the labour movement went into the years of break ups and reorganizations. As a result, came the era of 'four major national centers' with the formations of new national centers, *Sodomei* (Japanese Federation of Trade Unions) in 1951, *Shin-sanbetsu*

(National Federation of Industrial Organization) in 1952 and *Churitsu Roren* (Federation of Independent Unions of Japan) in 1956. This situation prevailed until late 1980s.

Meanwhile, in those turbulent days, *Nikkeiren* (the Japan Federation of Employers' Associations) was established as an employers' federation in 1948, with the slogan 'Employers must be right and strong'. Since then it has carried out its activities for half a century, putting up its three slogans: (1) higher business moral, (2) sound human relations within enterprises, and (3) enterprises' contribution to society. *Nikkeiren* merged at the end of May 2002 with Keidanren (the Japan Federation of Economic Organizations) into *Nippon Keidanren* (the Japan Business Federation), which represented employers in terms of political and economic aspects for a long time.

It was not until late 1970s that labour unions began to make their steps towards reunification. After many twists and turns, in 1987 these four private-sector national centers merged and *Rengo* (Japan Trade Union Confederation) was formed. Also unions of public sector and government employees affiliated with *Rengo* in 1989, which means that the former four national centers practically dissolved themselves. Certain groups with different lines or critical of *Rengo* refused to affiliate with it and established *Zenroren* (National Confederation of Trade Unions) and *Zenrokyo* (National Union Trade Council) – a situation which prevails until today.

B. Shunto: spring wage offensive

From 1950s to early 1960s when the labour movement had abandoned its closed political- and social-oriented line, labour disputes were very active in the major private-sector industries especially in the coal mining industry. It used to be a star business and enjoyed its prosperity for a certain period, but it later became forced to face a severe structural change due to the subsequent energy transformation. The labour disputes involving coal miners in the industry remains like a legend in the history of industrial relations.

After going through those years of active labour disputes and also based on reflection in the past, '*shunto*' became an annual custom in mid-1960s. The shunto system is a wage determination practice where labour and management have negotiations for major labour conditions by collectively bargaining annually in spring. In line with the cycle of Japanese fiscal year as well as the accounting period of industries that begins in April and ends in March in the next year, this negotiation practice, generally called 'spring wage offensive', has become well established and is still prevalent. It was in the economic background of the improving labour conditions in the high-growth period that the labour disputes in the private sector became calmed. On the other hand, disputes in the governmental and public sector, especially in the railway transportation began to increase at that time. Having reached its peak in the middle of 1975, however, such movement also became less active, because Recommendation by the National Personnel Authority began to function well and also because labour could no more get support for their dispute acts from the general public. Since 1980s labour dispute have disappeared from the scenes of labour movement.

C. Recent trend of union organization

The Ministry of Health, Labour and Welfare's Basic Survey of Labour Unions gives an overview of the situation of union organization. As of June 2001, there were 11,212,000 union members in Japan, a decline of 326,000 or 2.8 per cent from the previous year. These figures reveal a continuing, gradual decline in union membership over the long term. The proportion of union members among the total number of employed persons, or estimated unionization rate, was 20.7 per cent, a 0.8 point decrease from the previous year.

One of the reasons often given for the decline in the unionization rate is that unions formerly concentrated their attention on 'regular' employees and have failed to adjust to the diversification of employment patterns toward more part-time and other 'non-regular' forms of employment. For example, if we look at the organization of part-time workers, there are 280,000 union members (260,000 in the previous year) with an estimated unionization rate of 2.7 per cent (2.6 per cent in the previous year), representing a gradual increase, however, the rate is still quite low.

Turning to the membership of the major trade union federations:[1] in 2001, Rengo had 7,120,000 members (a decrease of 195,000 from the previous year); the National Confederation of Trade Unions (Zenroren) had 1,012,000 (a decrease of 24,000); and the National Trade Union Council (Zenrokyo) had 250,000 (a decrease of 11,000).

III. SOCIAL DIALOGUE

In Japan there is no definite system or table of negotiation of national- or regional-level that determines or affects employees' labour conditions. The two most influential national centers in the Japanese collective industrial relation are Rengo (Japanese Trade Union Confederation) representing labour and Nikkeiren (Japan Federation of Employers' Associations) representing management. It is not so often that these two organizations have meetings for a mutual exchange of opinions and claims of their respective positions. In most cases agreement on concrete labour conditions is made as the result of collective bargaining at the negotiation table in individual companies.

Rengo and Nikkeiren, as the national centers representing labour and management respectively, are conducting variety of research activities as well as public relations, compiling opinions from their members and giving information

---

1. Numbers of union members include not only those of industrial organizations but also direct local members.

to the public, in order to theoretically support their policies. Among other things, Rengo White Paper and Nikkeiren Committee Report on the Study of Labour Issues, both of which summarize their theoretical policies and activities for the spring offensive of the year, attract attention widely.

At the same time, it must be noted that in Japan when a law is enacted or revised, or when there is an important policy change, a certain level of agreement is made beforehand based on the discussion made at the table of tripartite council of government, management and labour. In that sense, it can be said that labour policies of Japanese government reflect the result of discussions between labour and management

One of the latest trends attracting attention is that the orientation among Japanese enterprises toward avoidance of unemployment and employment stability has begun to weaken. For this reason, vigorous discussion has been taking place within Rengo and Nikkeiren, national centers, on the importance of measures to sustain employment, and in August 2001, agreement was reached to continue discussions along these lines. In these circumstances, approaches for so-called work-sharing were adopted for debate. Omitting detailed description of the discussion, the conclusion was that while the management side should endeavour to maintain/secure employment, the labour side should respond flexibly to the reductions in working hours, as well as to the wage situation resulting therefrom. The Government subsequently joined the continuing debate on work-sharing, and a certain level of consensus was reached, with the argument for work-sharing becoming one of the core demands in the spring-time negotiations of 2002 in the form of 'a demand for sustainable employment'.

IV. LABOUR COST

Under the minimum wages system, employers are obliged to pay to their employees the amounts more than the minimum standards established by the Minimum Wages Law. 'Labour cost' is in many cases understood as a reciprocal number of labour productivity. With the background of stagnant economic situations, the labour cost has been increasing, while the labour productivity has been decreasing inversely. That explains why many enterprises take corporate measures including 'employment restructuring' to reduce their labour cost.

V. SOCIAL SECURITY SYSTEMS

Japan's social security system embraces five social insurance (pensions, medical insurance, long-term care insurance, employment insurance and workers' accident compensation insurance) and social assistance.

All Japanese citizens aged 20 and older subscribe to Japan's public pension plan. The public pension plan consists of national pensions which pay basic benefits, and employee pension insurance and mutual aid pensions, which pays proportional benefits in addition to national pension benefits. Private sector employees subscribe to employee pension insurance, while government employees subscribe to mutual aid associations.

The age for commencement of payments of basic benefits is 61 at present, and will be raised gradually to 65. Finally, it will be raised to 65 in 2013, however, it will be five years behind for women in the private sector.

The medical system in Japan is characterized by the fact that it is administered according to the principle of universal medical insurance, under which all citizens are insured and all citizens can receive medical services should they become ill or injured. There have been notable insurance in medical expenses especially for senior citizens recently, and there is an urgent need to reform the system.

Long-term care insurance came into effect from April 2000. It was created with the aim of lightening the care burden for families of the bedridden elderly and other aged people. Citizens aged 40 and older pay long-term care insurance premiums. And, if needed, from age 65 are eligible to receive benefits for care services at home or nursing and personal care facilities through certification of long-term care need.

Japan's employment insurance system provides the following remedies:
1. *Unemployment benefits.* There are benefits for job-seekers which is equivalent to jobless insurance in Europe and the United States, and other personal benefits for jobless workers or workers. The insurance premiums are paid by employees and employees equally.
2. Employment stabilization, still development and welfare programs. The insurance premiums are paid by employers.

Social assistances include livelihood protection with a means test, child benefit and so on.

6. 2001 Annual Review for Japan

*Tadashi Hanami**

I. ECONOMIC DEVELOPMENTS

GDP declined by 0.5 per cent in real terms in 2001 shifting to a decrease from the relatively high growth of 2.4 per cent in the previous year. A major factor behind this was listless private investment, together with sluggish final private consumption expenditure: the growth of private fixed investment, which had recorded a substantial increase of 10.4 per cent in the previous year, increased by a mere 0.4 per cent in 2001, and private housing investment shifted from an increase of 1.6 per cent to a substantial decline of 7.9 per cent. Moreover, external demand made a substantial negative contribution to GDP due to a decline in exports (6.6 per cent in real terms) against a backdrop of the slowdown in the world economy, etc. On the other hand, in the midst of sluggish domestic private demand and external demand, official fixed capital formation (public investment), a variable policy of the Government, which had declined by 9.8 per cent in the previous year, also declined by 3.4 per cent in 2001.

Reflecting this economic trend, the unemployment situation has become even more severe, with the decline in the number of employed becoming larger. The unemployment rate in 2001 was 5.0 per cent, 0.3 point higher than the previous year, hitting the 5 per cent mark on a yearly basis. Last year we reported that a distinctive characteristic of recent years has been the continued decline in price levels. Even corrected for the GDP deflator (an indicator of inflation for the whole economy over one or more years, derived by dividing total GDP at current prices by total GDP at constant prices), prices continued to decline by 1.4 per cent in 2001, after declining by 1.4 per cent and 2.0 per cent in 1999 and 2000, respectively. In these circumstances, several senior government officials were of the opinion that the economy was on a moderate deflationary trend.

II. POLITICAL DEVELOPMENTS

In January 2001, central government reforms were implemented as part of administrative reform with the result that the system of 1 office and 20 ministries and

---

* President of the Japan Institute of Labour, Professor at the Sofia University, Ex-president of the International Industrial Relations Association.

R. Blanpain (ed.),
Labour Relations in the Asia-Pacific Countries, 71–81.
© 2004 Kluwer Law International. Printed in Great Britain.

agencies was reorganized to a system of 1 office and 12 ministries and agencies. In conjunction with the establishment of the Cabinet Office for the purpose of strengthening Cabinet functions, a system has been established under which a vice minister and at least one parliamentary secretary are appointed to each ministry or agency and participate in the planning of important policies, targeting politician-led policy planning. The Ministry of Labour was formerly in charge of labour issues, but such issues are now handled by the Ministry of Health, Labour and Welfare, under which the Ministry of Health and Welfare and the Ministry of Labour were unified.

At the beginning of 2001, the Mori government was still in power, however its approval rate remained low due to the ignominious labeling Mori as the 'secretly elected Prime Minister' which had attached itself to him since the inauguration of the Cabinet, as well as to the Prime Minister's imprudent speech and behaviour. In particular, the Prime Minister's clumsy handling of the unfortunate sinking of the training ship of a fisheries senior high school by a United States nuclear submarine off the Hawaiian Islands in February 2001, led to considerable doubt being cast on Mr. Mori's aptitude for crisis management.

In these circumstances, Prime Minister Mori announced his intention to step down in April 2001 after the approval of the budget for fiscal 2001 and after witnessing the adoption of important bills necessary for the execution of the budget. Thus, the Mori Cabinet resigned en masse without being able to eliminate the unpopularity that had existed since its inception, although it achieved some results, including the enactment of the IT Basic Law enacted, setting the target of the 'regenesis of Japan'.

After Mori, Junichiro Koizumi took office as the 87th Prime Minister. Since he was elected President of the Liberal Democratic Party via an election process in which the collective opinion of party members was represented and then elected Prime Minister in an election at the Diet, he is free from the dubiousness that surrounded the birth of the previous administration. Moreover, the subsequent cabinet formation process was vibrant, being unrestrained by past practices, and the Koizumi administration enjoyed a high approval rate for a considerable period after its inauguration in April 2001 maintaining a warm relationship with public opinion. The policy stance of the administration is pro-reform as demonstrated by the slogan 'structural reform with no sacred cows'. Reform is accompanied by pain. While it is necessary to enhance the safety net to cope with the pain, Koizumi's basic philosophy is that the implementation of reform in the face of such pain will, as is implied in the slogan 'no growth without reform', eventually generate desirable results.

In June 2001, the Koizumi Cabinet formulated 'muscular policies' for economic and financial management of bad debts, making the most of advisory organs, such as the 'Council on Economic and Fiscal Policy' established under the Cabinet Office as a result of the previous central government reform. Starting with this measure, the Cabinet put forward a 'reform work schedule', a plan concerning the process for implementing those policies. Moreover, the Koizumi administration actively proceeded to examine the reform of special public corporations, with regulatory reform, and had formulated a succession of plans concerning their directions by the end of 2001.

While various plans have been presented in this way, the disposition of bad debts, which is regarded as the most important agenda item, is far from progressing satisfactorily. The Koizumi administration marked its first anniversary in April 2002. While the sluggishness of the economy and the severity of the employment situation continue, criticism and a sense of irritation that although plans are made, they are not carried through are increasing, not only among opposition parties but also among the general public.

III. COLLECTIVE BARGAINING

A. General

As was explained in the 2000 edition, in Japan, there is no practice of labour–management negotiations to determine working conditions at a national or regional level. However, it should be noted that enactment or amendment of labour legislation or major labour policy changes are, in most cases, first discussed in tripartite (public authorities, unions and employers) deliberative councils and a certain level of consensus between the parties is reached in advance. In this sense, the government's labour policy can be regarded as the result of mutual agreement between labour and management (see the 2000 edition).

Negotiations between labour and management about key working conditions, and wages and salaries in particular, are predominantly held in spring each year; thus, such negotiations are generally called Shunto, or the 'spring labor offensive'. Although the Japanese Trade Union Confederation (Rengo), a national centre, sometimes plays the role of a general 'mood maker', actual bargaining and agreements are conducted and effected between labour and management in individual companies. Moreover, the general pattern for spring-time negotiations is that major manufacturers in leading industries, such as electrical goods or auto manufacturers, take the lead followed by other large companies and finally by small and medium-sized enterprises.

In this spring-time negotiations, since the economic situation was relatively favourable, despite general sluggishness, and corporate profits were improving, Rengo adopted a policy targeting the stimulation of the economy and the stabilization of national life through a substantial wage increase, including upholding the basic demand for a 1 per cent increase in the wage level in addition to periodic wage increases.[1] Moreover, upholding the basic demand for a wage increase for part-time workers, Rengo clarified its stance of making efforts to improve the treatment of part-time workers. Faced with this posture, management countered by arguing that a wage increase was unnecessary. Their position was that companies could not afford to agree to a basic wage increase taking into account the continued harsh economic situation, progress in globalization, and so forth, and that if any offer were to be made it would be more appropriate to

---

1. See the 2000 edition for 'periodic wage increases', etc.

offer lump sums, such as bonuses, based on improvement, if any, in corporate earnings.

If the results achieved in accordance with these basic arguments are examined in terms of the results of agreements reached in major enterprises announced by the Ministry of Health, Labour and Welfare every year, the average wage increase rate was 2.01 per cent for the spring-time negotiations in 2001, which was lower than the 2.06 per cent for the preceding year, recording the lowest level since the survey began.

According to another survey by the Ministry of Health, Labour and Welfare (Survey on Wage Increase); covering enterprises employing 100 persons or more), 21.3 per cent of enterprises did not make any wage revisions in 2001, which was 19.1 per cent higher than for the preceding year, recording the lowest level since the survey began. The low wage increase rate can be said to be due both to the fact that the rates agreed to were low and to the fact that the number of enterprises that eschewed wage increases, including periodic wage increases, increased.

On the other hand, an examination of the situation of agreements on lump-sum payments that account for a substantial portion of employee income in major enterprises (assumed to be about 25 per cent on average) in Japan, reveal that those for the summer of 2001 increased by 2.86 per cent over the preceding year, shifting to an increase from a decline (0.54 per cent) in the preceding year. Year-end lump-sum payments, increased by 1.76 per cent compared with the preceding year (an increase by 0.76 per cent). Thus, lump-sum payouts in 2001 held firm. This means that, at least in major enterprises, efforts were made to increase lump sum payouts to some extent, against the backdrop of some improvement in corporate performance in the preceding year, while basic wages were restrained.

The timing of lump-sum payment negotiations vary widely: for example, they are conducted at the same time as spring-time pay raise negotiations, between spring and summer separately from spring-time pay raise negotiations, or between autumn and winter. Moreover, negotiations are conducted with respect to both summer and year-end lump-sum payments for the year, or each time for summer and year-end lump-sum payments.

B. Pay

Workers whose wages are determined by the spring-time negotiations do not necessarily constitute the majority of the workforce in Japan in the light of the unionization rate; nevertheless, it was mentioned in the 2000 edition that it is necessary to note that the wage increases which result from labour–management bargaining in this sector have a major influence on general wage levels and that the wage increases that result from the spring-time negotiations are not directly reflected in the trend in average wages.

Looking at the trend in average wages based on the Ministry of Health, Labour and Welfare's Monthly Labour Survey (which covers establishments with five or more employees), total cash earnings in 2001 were 351,335 yen per month, which represented a 1.2 per cent decline over the previous year (compared with a 0.5 per cent increase in the previous year) – a shift to a decrease from an increase in the previous year. This increase was composed of a 0.5 per cent decline in the regular wage component (compared with a 0.7 per cent increase in the preceding year), a 4.2 per cent decline in the non-regular wage component (compared with a 4.4 per cent increase in the preceding year) and a 3.0 per cent decrease in bonuses and other special payments (compared with a 1.1 per cent decrease in the preceding year); this reflected the severe economic conditions, including the substantial decline in the non-regular wage component due to further deterioration in the economic situation in the latter half of the year. Real wages declined by 0.5 per cent despite the fall in prices.

As indicated, a slight decline in workers' wages, together with the sluggish employment situation in 2001, constituted one of the major factors which account for the absence of an upsurge in personal consumption as a whole.

C. Working time

Apart from the minimum working hours standards laid down in the Labour Standards Law (in principle, 40 h per week, 8 h per day), no other national standards have been agreed between labour and management. In general, working hours are decided on the basis of negotiations between labour and management at the individual enterprise level.

According to the results of a survey by the Ministry of Health, Labour and Welfare (General Survey on Wages and Working Hours System) as of January 2001, average scheduled weekly working hours actually adopted by enterprises were 39 h and 14 min on average. This was the same as the result of the previous survey (as of the end of December 1999). However, there is a fairly substantial disparity according to the scale of the enterprise, with scheduled weekly working hours ranging from 38 h and 34 min for companies with 1,000 employees or more, to 38 h and 35 min for companies with 300–999 employees, 38 h and 57 min for those with 100–299 employees, and 39 h and 24 min for those with 30–99 employees; that is, smaller enterprises have longer scheduled weekly working hours. Scheduled working hours are determined by labour agreements or working regulations, with the minimum condition that such conform to the minimum standard laid down by the Labour Standards Law. Although scheduled working hours are on the decrease on a long-term basis, in the short term, the changes are small except for the periods before and after a change in the minimum standard laid down by the Labour Standards Law.

On the other hand, substantial changes in the hours actually worked occur from time to time, referred to as 'total actual hours worked'. Of these, the hours worked within the scheduled working hours laid down by the company are referred to as 'scheduled working hours' and any additional hours worked are referred to as 'non-scheduled working hours'. These hours are also covered by the above-mentioned Monthly Labour Survey. According to this survey, the monthly average for 'total actual hours worked' in 2001 was 153.0 h (12 months = 1,836 h), a decrease of 0.8 per cent over the preceding year (compared with an increase of 0.7 per cent in the preceding year). Of these, the 'scheduled working hours' accounted for an average of 143.6 h per month, a decrease of 0.7 per cent over the preceding year (compared with an increase of 0.5 per cent in the preceding year). Average monthly 'non-scheduled working hours' were 9.4 h, a decrease of 4.4 per cent over the preceding year (compared with an increase of 3.6 per cent in the preceding year), recording a substantial decline, mainly in the latter half of the year when the economy deteriorated further.

According to the calculations of the Ministry of Health, Labour and Welfare, in 1999 the annual total actual hours worked (for manufacturing industry production-line workers) were almost the same in Japan, the United States and the United Kingdom (1,942 h, 1,991 h and 1,902 h, respectively) but showed considerable disparity with France (1,672 h (1998)) and Germany (1,517 h (1997)).

IV. JOB SECURITY, TRAINING AND SKILL DEVELOPMENT

Employment stability and skills development are important issues for both labour and management, however, in terms of collective labour–management relations, since they are subject to discussion at the individual company level, there is no systematic data available. Nonetheless, the results of the Survey of Labour–Management Communication by the Ministry of Health, Labour and Welfare were introduced in the 2000 edition as related data. However, since new results have not yet been announced on the basis of this survey, they cannot be provided in this 2001 edition. Since discussions are held between labour and management on various matters in Japanese enterprises, those of you who are interested are encouraged to refer to the 2000 edition.

Regarding employment stability, employer-instigated dismissals cause problems, but no formal regulations exist within Japanese labour law restricting this type of dismissal; even so, the accumulation of legal precedents has seen the establishment of the legal principle that dismissal without a rational reason is invalid. Due to the high priority assigned to employment stability among enterprises, together with the influence of that legal principle based on precedents, it can be said that dismissals are generally handled with caution.

With poor economic conditions continuing, the number of companies engaged in restructuring, including personnel retrenchment, is increasing and even those companies which formerly gave strong support to employment stability for regular workers are beginning to show signs of a change in direction. In particular, a succession of plans were announced for personnel reduction in the immediate aftermath of the terrorist attacks which occurred on 11 September 2001, when the outlook for the world economy appeared extremely bleak. In response to the IT recession, the scale of personnel reduction plans announced by major Japanese electrical manufacturers were particularly remarkable with some tens of thousands of workers slated for redundancy. In terms of the contents of such plans, many of the personnel reductions were to be effected with respect to overseas establishments and, even when they were effected domestically, there were many cases of opting for non-replenishment for natural retirement, so the portion of personnel reduction through recruitment of voluntary retirees, etc., was not so great. However, it cannot be denied, even before the contents of these measures is discussed, that such plans constituted a factor underpinning the bleakness of the employment environment. In such circumstances, the unemployment rate (it should be noted that Japan's unemployment rate is derived based on the situation of the week at the end of each month), which was 5.0 per cent for August 2001, rose to 5.3 per cent for September, and was 5.3 per cent for October, 5.4 per cent for November and 5.5 per cent for December.

The following is a more detailed discussion of the unemployment rate, which is announced in the Labour Force Survey by the Statistics Bureau of the Ministry of Public Management, Home Affairs, Posts and Telecommunications (which covers about 40,000 households). Among the wholly unemployed, in the first half of 2001, the number of those who were involuntarily unemployed was smaller than the previous year, it began to increase in August, and the margin of increase became greater in ensuing months; that is, an increase by 100,000 in September over the corresponding month of the previous year, by 160,000 in October, by 290,000 in November and by 310,000 in December.

Thus, it is probably true that the orientation among Japanese enterprises towards avoidance of unemployment and employment stability has begun to weaken. For this reason, vigorous discussion has been taking place within Rengo and Nikkeiren, national centers, on the importance of measures to sustain employment, and in August 2001, agreement was reached to continue discussions along these lines. In these circumstances, approaches for so-called work-sharing were adopted for debate. Omitting detailed description of the discussion, the conclusion was that while the management side should endeavor to maintain/secure employment, the labour side should respond flexibly to the reductions in working hours, as well as to the wage situation resulting therefrom. The Government subsequently joined the continuing debate on work-sharing, and a certain level of consensus was reached, with the argument for work-sharing becoming one of the core demands in the spring-time negotiations of 2002 in the form of 'a demand for sustainable employment'.

V. LEGISLATIVE DEVELOPMENTS

There have been a number of major revisions to the law in recent years in response to changing socio-economic conditions.

Enactment of and amendments to labour-related laws enforced in 2001 included the following:
(a) Partial amendment of the Employment Insurance Law (enforced in April 2001): The period for payment of unemployment benefits varies based on the reason for resigning. That is, where a worker simply resigns for personal convenience or where the timing of old-age retirement is known and it is possible

to make preparations in advance, the period of eligibility for payment of unemployment benefits has been shortened, but where there is a valid reason for dismissal or resignation, the period of payment has been lengthened.

(b) Law concerning the Continuation of Employment Contracts Following the Division of a Company (enforcement in April 2001): In step with the amendment to the Commercial Code concerning the division of a company, this law lays down rules concerning the continuation of employment contracts on the occasion of the division of a company; this law stipulates that, in cases where the contracts of workers who are engaged in work affected by the division are not carried over, those workers can lodge an objection and have the employment contract continued.

(c) Employment Measures Law, etc. (enforcement in October 2001): For the purpose of promoting smooth reemployment in response to changing socio-economic conditions, the Employment Measures Law, and the Law Concerning the Promotion of Local Employment Development, the Human Resources Development Promotion Law, etc., were amended simultaneously. The main points of the amendment: those employers who make an employment adjustment that generates a large number of redundancies at one time are required to adopt a reemployment support plan to systematically support reemployment ahead of termination; employers are required to endeavor to give equal opportunities without, as a rule, setting an age limit at the time of recruiting/hiring workers; and so forth.

(d) Law on the Promotion of the Settlement of Individual Labour Disputes (enforcement in October 2001): The law is aimed at structuring a scheme for promoting settlement for the purpose of dealing with the not infrequent occurrence of individual disputes between employers and workers, and of promoting the smooth and simple settlement of such disputes. In concrete terms, overall counseling will be provided by (prefectural) labour bureaus which are local offices of the State established in each prefecture, or by others, and, as necessary, advice/guidance will be provided by the director of the bureau; moreover, good offices will be offered by the 'dispute adjustment committee', which is established within the labour bureau at the request of a party concerned.

VI. THE ORGANISATION AND ROLE OF THE SOCIAL PARTNERS

The Ministry of Health, Labour and Welfare's Basic Survey of Labour Unions gives an overview of the situation of union organization. As of June 2001, there were 11,212,000 union members in Japan, a decline of 326,000 or 2.8 per cent from the previous year. These figures reveal a continuing, gradual decline in union membership over the long term. The proportion of union members among the total number of employed persons, or estimated unionization rate, was 20.7 per cent, a 0.8 point decrease from the previous year.

One of the reasons often given for the decline in the unionization rate is that unions formerly concentrated their attention on 'regular' employees and have failed to adjust to the diversification of employment patterns toward more part-time and other 'non-regular' forms of employment. For example, if we look at the organization of part-time workers, there are 280,000 union members (260,000 in the previous year) with an estimated unionization rate of 2.7 per cent (2.6 per cent in the previous year), representing a gradual increase, however, the rate is still quite low.

Turning to the membership of the major trade union federations:[2] in 2001, Rengo had 7,120,000 members (a decrease of 195,000 from the previous year); the National Confederation of Trade Unions (Zenroren) had 1,012,000 (a decrease of 24,000); and the National Trade Union Council (Zenrokyo) had 250,000 (a decrease of 11,000).

As national centres, Rengo and Japan Federation of Employers' Associations (Nikkeiren) represent the interests of the workers' and employers' sides, respectively. In addition to being engaged in information dissemination and publicity activities, they endeavor to fortify their respective positions by undertaking a wide range of survey and research activities. Accordingly, the Rengo white paper and the Report of the Nikkeiren research committee on labour problems, which are issued immediately before Shunto each year, attract considerable attention as the major representations of the respective positions of the federation.

It has been agreed that Nikkeiren and Japan Federation of Economic Organizations (Keidanren) will be unified to form the Japan Business Federation on 28 May 2002. Mr. Hiroshi Okuda, currently chairman of Nikkeiren, is expected to be named the chairman of the new organization.

Since the Ministry of Health, Labour and Welfare's Survey on Labour Unions' Activities (which is conducted every 5 years) (conducted in July 2000 this time) was published in July 2001, I will introduce basic points of the survey. First of all, the percentage of labour unions which have undertaken revisions to the wages/retirement allowance system in the past three years was 56.0 per cent. Regarding the contents of the revisions, 'new establishment or expansion of payment based on job/payment according to function/payment by results' accounts for 53.0 per cent, and 'Adjustment of the calculation method for retirement allowance' for 26.5 per cent. The ratio of labour unions that participated in the revision of the wages/retirement allowance system was 94.0 per cent. The issue given highest priority by the labor unions was, 'securing transparency and fairness/impartiality' at 60.1 per cent. With respect to the fact that in recent years there has been a marked trend among employers towards the introduction of skill factors in the awarding of salaries, most labour unions, or 47.9 per cent, opted for 'It is acceptable if the method of evaluating the skills of workers is appropriate', followed by 'even if it is an unavoidable trend, measures are necessary so that workers will not be placed at a disadvantage' which accounted for 32.6 per cent. Generally speaking, while understanding management policies, labour unions are endeavoring to be cautious so as to avoid workers being disadvantaged when such policies are effected.

---

2. Numbers of union members include not only those of industrial organizations but also direct local members.

VII. INDUSTRIAL ACTION

The Statistical Survey of Labour Disputes, issued annually by the Ministry of Health, Labour and Welfare, provides an overview of trends in labour disputes. The latest edition available is the one covering 2000. Bearing in mind that 2000 was a year in which there were signs of relative economic recovery, there were 958 labour disputes, involving a total of 1.117 million workers. Compared with the previous year, the number of disputes decreased by 144 (13.1 per cent) and the total number of participants by 17,000 (1.5 per cent). In 2000, there were 305 disputes involving strike action and in which 85,000 workers participated. The number of working days lost was 35,000. Compared with the previous year, this represents a decrease of 114 strikes (27.2 per cent), 22,000 participants (20.4 per cent) and 52,000 working days lost (59.7 per cent).

Looking at the disputes in terms of the major demands made, wage increases was the largest single item at 310 cases (32.4 per cent), followed by non-regular wage payments (bonus) 224 cases (23.4 per cent), opposition to dismissal and reinstatement of dismissed workers 147 cases (15.3 per cent). A comparison of these figures with statistics for 1999 reveals that in 2000, there were 75 fewer disputes over wage increases, 12 more disputes over bonuses, and 61 fewer disputes over dismissals or reinstatement of dismissed workers. The decrease in disputes involving dismissals or reinstatements was particularly marked.

Examining the number of disputes involving strike action according to affiliation with one of the three leading union federations, we find that Rengo was involved in 118 disputes with 33,000 participants and 11,000 working days lost. The figures for Zenroren and Zenrokyo were 99 disputes, 38,000 participants, and 10,000 working days lost, and 24, 1,000 and 1,000, respectively.

VIII. NEW FORMS OF WORK

Employment patterns continue to diversify over the mid-to-long term. The Special Labour Force Survey is issued by the Statistics Bureau of the Ministry of Public Management, Home Affairs, Posts and Telecommunications in February each year. According to this survey, the percentage of employed persons (excluding those in managerial positions) who are 'regular' employees declined from 80.2 per cent to 72.8 per cent between 1991 and 2001. Conversely, the percentage of part-time workers increased from 11.5 per cent to 15.4 per cent, and the percentage of casual workers (called arubaito in Japanese) from 4.7 per cent to 7.6 per cent. Employment patterns are indeed diversifying.

With respect to part-time workers, the percentage of those who occupy important positions (e.g. restaurant managers) is increasing, and the equal treatment of part-time workers and 'full-timers' has become an issue. In the Japanese labour market, where the concepts of different types of work or of hourly wages are not clear, it is not possible to make all judgments on the basis of the principle of 'equal pay for equal work', and there is a tendency to fumble for an ideal form of equal (balanced) treatment based on Japanese traditions.

Even among regular employees, the number of employees working non-traditional schedules is increasing. For example, employees working under a flextime system have increased gradually from 4.8 per cent in 1990 to 8.7 per cent at the end of 2000. This percentage is higher (14.9 per cent) in large corporations employing 1,000 persons or more; that is, one in seven workers in such firms is working flextime.

Personnel practices are also becoming increasingly diversified. More than 90 per cent of corporations with 300 or more employees have a personnel evaluation system in place. A comparatively large proportion of companies, particularly large corporations, have introduced new personnel management systems, including self-evaluation by employees, publicizing of job openings in-house and 'multi-track' personnel systems.

On the other hand, the number of workers engaged in telecommuting is also increasing. While it is extremely difficult to collect systematic data on telecommuting, according to a report by the Japan Telework Association, the telecommuting population (total of those working at home and those working in satellite offices) was 2,464,000 at the time of the survey in 2000; this figure is expected to rise to 4.45 million in 2005.

These changes are an indication that the former 'group-based' employment contracts under which all workers shared common conditions will increasingly be replaced by contracts of an individual nature. In these circumstances, the adaptations and changes that this will necessitate in existing patterns of labour–management relations can be expected to become the subject of considerable debate.

IX. OUTLOOK

Recently, there are signs of improvement in the world economy which was on the verge of an extremely bleak situation particularly in the latter half of 2001. Signs of recovery are also evident in the IT sector, which was once overshadowed by pessimism and the view is becoming stronger that there is no need to be excessively pessimistic. While these trends basically constitute bright factors for the Japanese economy and its employment situation, which continues to be sluggish, it is difficult to anticipate a straight economic recovery if the collapse of the so-called IT bubble implies a change in the terms of industry profitability. It cannot but be said that the Japanese economy, which has not yet succeeded in solving the question of bad debts, will continue to face a number of crucial tests.

7. Industrial Relations in Korea
Recent Changes and New Challenges

Won-Duck Lee*

I. HISTORICAL BACKGROUND

Over the past 15 years, the labour relations system in Korea has shown dynamic transformation. Under new environmental conditions, such as democratization, globalization, and economic crisis, this period has witnessed profound changes in the country's industrial relations and labour standards. Democratization taking place in 1987 dismantled the authoritarian regime, characterized by the developmental state's interventionist labour policy, and led to explosive growth of labour movement in the late 1980s. Organized labour which strengthened its leverage in the industrial relations both at the firm level and the national level pressured employers and the government to improve working conditions, including wages, and labour standards through collective bargaining and institutional reforms.

From the early 1990s, a rising tide of globalization also exerted substantial influence over the government's labour policy as well as industrial relations. Under the context of growing global competition, the government and employers made efforts to control continued wage increases and promote the flexibility of labour market. Labour unions demanded to enhance labour rights up to international standards. Given diverse interests of labour unions and employers, the government established the Presidential Commission Industrial Relation Reform (PCIRR) in an effort to reform the existing labour laws in 1996. The labour law reform underwent a comprehensive revision after severe nation-wide confrontation in the early 1997.

The outbreak of the economic crisis at the end of 1997 heavily impacted Korean labour relations. In the early 1998, the government, forced to rely on a financial bail-out from the IMF, formed the Tripartite Commission to deal with a variety of national issues, such as massive unemployment, economic restructuring, and labour reforms. The Commission produced the historic 'Social Pact' in February 1998 (Table 1), which included labour law reforms for a more flexible labour market and improved labour rights. However, government-led economic restructuring, launched in mid-1998, created a series of intense confrontations

---

*   President of the Korea Labour Institute.

R. Blanpain (ed.),
Labour Relations in the Asia-Pacific Countries, 83–88.
© 2004 *Kluwer Law International. Printed in Great Britain.*

Table 1: The key contents of the social pact (February 1998)

(1) Promotion of management transparency and corporate restructuring
(2) Stabilization of consumer prices
(3) Employment stabilization and unemployment policy
   • Improvements on the employment insurance system and expansion of its coverage
   • Support for unemployed workers
   • Enlargement of job placement service
   • Expansion of vocational training
   • Job creation
(4) Extension and consolidation of social security system
   • Integration of health insurance system and expansion of its coverage
   • Enactment of Worker's Wage Claims Act
(5) Wage stabilization and the promotion of labour-management cooperation
   • Securing the effectiveness of collective agreements
(6) Enhancement of basic labour rights
   • Legalization of Teachers' unions
   • Trade unions' right to political activities
   • Establishment of works councils for government officials from January 1999
   • Recognition of the unemployed workers' right to join trade union organized on trans-enterprise level
(7) Enhancement of labour market flexibility
   • Introduction of a worker dispatch scheme
   • Deregulation of dismissals for managerial reasons

with labour unions, which opposed massive layoffs in the private and public sector. At the same time, the government instituted legislation and social programs to protect the unemployed and women workers.

II. FEATURES OF THE MAJOR ACTORS IN INDUSTRIAL RELATIONS

Labour unions in Korea are predominantly enterprise-based, although industrial unions have appeared in recent years. Enterprise unions or enterprise units affiliated with industrial unions exercise to a certain extent autonomy in their union administration and collective bargaining. This enterprise unionism has contributed to decentralized collective bargaining practices.

The number of trade unions increased almost three-fold (from 2,742 to 7,883) between 1986 and 1989. In this period, as shown in Table 2, union membership nearly doubled from 1,050,000 to 1,931,000, and union density also soared from 11.7% to 18.6%. In the 1990s, the density rate has continued to decrease and it was 11.6% in 2000.

The labour movement in Korea is now divided between two national centers: the Federation of Korean Trade Unions (FKTU) and the Korean Confederation of Trade Unions (KCTU). As of the end of 1999, the FKTU had 27 affiliates (industrial federation or industrial unions) with 4,501 unit unions and 888,500 members, while the KCTU had 16 affiliates with 1,256 unions and 564,800 members.

The KCTU, which was legally recognized in November 1999, largely inclines towards militant activism, whereas the FKTU has taken a more cooperative

Table 2: Changes in major indexes of trade unions by year

Year	No. of trade unions (E/A)	Union membership (1,000 persons)	Union density (%)
1986	2,742	1,050	11.7
1987	4,103	1,267	13.8
1989	7,883	1,932	18.6
1990	7,698	1,887	17.2
1991	7,656	1,803	15.9
1995	6,606	1,615	12.7
1999	5,637	1,481	11.8
2000	5,698	1,527	11.6

Note: Union density = (number of union members/total number of employed workers) × 100.
Source: Korea Labour Institute (2001a).

stance towards the government and employers. According to 1997 union statistics, the average size of KCTU-affiliated unions (458 members) is much larger than FKTU-affiliated unions (242 members). Many labour unions at large firms organized after 1987 are affiliated with the KTCU.

There are two national-level organizations to represent the interest of employers: the Korea Employers Federation (KEF) and the Federation of Korean Industries (FKI). While the FKI mainly consists of chaebol (conglomerate) groups and deals with issues of industrial policies, the KEF includes small firms as well as chaebol companies and focuses on industrial relations issues. The KEF, which was founded in 1970, is a nation-wide umbrella organization encompassing 13 regional employers' associations, 20 economic and trade associations, and about 4,000 major enterprises in the manufacturing, construction, transportation, banking and insurance sectors, and service industries.

The KEF has been the official voice of Korean employers in national-level negotiations and consultations regarding industrial relations issues, as demonstrated by its representative roles in the PCIRR and the Tripartite Commission. In fact, The KEF's growing role as a major player in industrial relations is attributable to the significant growth in the labour movement in the late 1980s and government-initiated tripartite efforts in the 1990s.

The Ministry of Labour is the government organ that administers labour policies. Within the Ministry, the Labour Policy Bureau are in charge of policy-making and administration regarding industrial relations issues. The Labour Policy Bureau consists of three divisions – the Labour Policy Division, Trade Unions Division, and Labour–Management Consultation Division.

The Ministry of Labour has 46 local offices including six Regional Administration Offices located in major cities and 40 Regional Offices. At these Regional Offices, labour inspectors are charged with not only supervising working conditions in accordance with the Labour Standards Act, but also with taking actions against labour disputes and resolving labour issues at firms located in their regional area.

III. INSTITUTIONALIZED STRUCTURE OF INDUSTRIAL RELATIONS

Collective bargaining at most unionized firms is primarily conducted at the firm level in accordance with the enterprise-based union structure. There are a few exceptions, such as the transportation (e.g. taxi and bus) and textiles sector, which conduct regional- or sector-level bargaining. While the Trade Union and Labour Relations Adjustment Act, enacted in 1997, stipulates that no collective agreement shall have a term of validity exceeding two years, collective bargaining takes place every year in most unionized firms. In practice, collective bargaining for a wage contract is conducted every year, while that for collective contracts determining other working conditions takes place every 2 years.

Even though the collective bargaining structure is decentralized, the influence of national centers over company-level bargaining is not negligible. The two national centers (the FKTU and the KCTU) make nation-wide bargaining demands for wage increases and other contractual changes (e.g. the reduction of working hours and employment security in recent years) at the beginning of every year, which serves as an influential guideline to enterprise-level collective bargaining. In response to these proposals by national union centers, the KEF offers its own negotiation guidelines to member companies.

In Korea, there exist labour–management councils, which function as an institutionalized channel to promote communication and cooperation between employees and management and facilitate employee involvement. The labour–management council is formed based on the Act on Promotion of Worker Participation and Cooperation (APWPC).[1] This act stipulates that all companies with more than 30 workers should form a council and hold regular meetings every quarter.

The labour–management council is composed of the same number of representatives from employees and management, usually totaling three to ten persons from each side. When a company has a labour union representing a majority of its workers, it must allow the union's leaders to participate as the employees' representatives. The APWPC also gives the labour–management council greater authority by stipulating obligatory issues requiring prior agreement in the council, such as workers' training and corporate welfare plans.

It is noteworthy that many labour unions have used council meetings as an extension of collective bargaining. Thus, the labour–management council at many organized firms has become a vehicle of quasi-bargaining in practice.

The Labour Relations Commission (LRC) plays a central role of an official organ to mediate labour disputes. It is composed of members representing labour unions, management, and public interest. The labour and management representatives of the Commission elect the public interest representatives. The LRC has local offices in 13 major cities, and the Central Labour Relations Commission

---

1. The labour–management council was introduced by the Labour–Management Council Act (LMCA) in 1980. The LMCA was replaced by the APWPC in 1997.

is charged with mediating particularly significant cases of labour disputes involving more than two cities or provinces.

The Trade Union and Labour Relations Adjustment Act stipulates a narrower scope and stricter conditions of compulsory arbitration for public services. Public services are classified into general and essential services, and only essential public services (water, electricity, gas, oil, telecommunications, railroads, and hospitals) are subject to compulsory arbitration. Compulsory arbitration can be conducted by the Labour Relations Commission only after the Special Mediation Committee composed of three public interest representatives recommends arbitration.

IV. CURRENT ISSUES OF INDUSTRIAL RELATIONS IN KOREA

The historical overview of industrial relations in Korea demonstrates that transformation from the authoritarian model of the pre-1987 period towards a new model of tripartism is still under way. However, the recent years of economic crisis witnessed confrontational industrial relations both at the national level and at the firm level in the process of economic restructuring.

In conclusion, we address several key issues concerning industrial relations and labour standards particularly sensitive for the three parties at present. First, a reduction in statutory working hours may be the most important issue. Labour unions have demanded that the current 44 working hours per week be shortened to 40 h in order to improve the quality of work life. In contrast, employers have shown resistance to a reduction in the statutory working hours because of the rising labour cost. In addition, they have argued that monthly and annual paid leaves and menstruation leaves were costly and therefore should be abolished or reduced. Given the differing opinions of labour unions and employers, the government has been seeking a compromise through the consultation process of the Tripartite Commission.

Second, the size of the irregular workforce has been rapidly growing during the recent years of economic crisis, adding another contentious issue to industrial relations. Official reports reveal that the share of irregular workers (i.e. temporary and daily workers) out of the total workforce increased from 45.9% in 1997 to 52.4% in 2000. Given the sharp increase of irregular workers, labour unions and civil activist groups have pointed out their poor working conditions and unstable employment status, demanding legislation to protect and improve their social welfare and employment conditions. Moreover, while the national labour centers – the FKTU and the KCTU – have launched organizing campaigns, irregular workers in some firms have organized their own labour unions and engaged in collective actions, constituting a new issue of its own. However, employers have opposed the legislation of social protection for the irregular workforce, insisting that these workers were their only option since the existing employment structure for organized regular workers was so rigid. At any rate, the changing composition of employment, resulting from the rapid growth in the irregular workforce, will call for continued reform in current labour standards.

Third, labour unions of several sectors have transformed their organizational structure from the enterprise union model to the industrial union model.

Along with this organizational transformation, unions such as the Metal Workers Federation, the Medical and Health Workers Union (affiliates of the KCTU) and the Banking Workers Union (an affiliate of the FKTU) have demanded industry-wide central collective bargaining in recent years. The response of employers is still negative, and, therefore, contention over bargaining structure is occurring between in unions and employers.

Finally, there still remain issues concerning unionization. Currently, the National Civil Servants' Law stipulates categories of public servicemen who are recognized as engaging in physical labour. Under current regulations those public servicemen employed in postal office, the national railway, and public hospitals are classified as labourers and allowed to form trade unions. However, the issue of granting the right to organize unions to 'general' civil servants has long been a source of debate within the Tripartite Commission. Although the government agrees in principle to expand civil servants' freedom of association, details such as coverage, recognition of the right to collective action have still to be worked out. Thus amendment of existing laws is pending concertation on the above issues.

REFERENCES

Hyun, Chun-Wook (1999), 'The Labor Standards Act System', in Korea International Labour Foundation (ed.), *Labor Relations in Korea*.

Lee, Won-Duck (1997), *Industrial Relations Reform: Choice for the Future*, KLI. (In Korean.)

Lee, Won-Duck and Byoung-Hoon Lee (1999), 'The Industrial Relations System in Korea', in Korea International Labour Foundation (ed.), *Labor Relations in Korea*.

Lee, Won-Duck and Kang-Shik Choi (1998), *Labor Market and Industrial Relations in Korea: Retrospect on the Past Decade and Policy Directions for the 21st Century*, KLI.

Ministry of Labor, *Yearbook of Labor Statistics*. (In Korean.)

Ministry of Labor, White Paper on Labor Policy (for the years 1987–1997). (In Korean.)

Park, Jong-Hee, Chun-Wook Hyun, Scott Balfour, Gyeong-Joon Yoo, and Ha-Nam Phang (1998), *Korean Labor and Employment Laws: An Ongoing Evolution*. Korea Labor Institute and Kim and Chang Law Offices.

8. PDR Systems Theory Perspective on Employment Relations in a Globalizing Asia
A Korean Case

Hyo-Soo Lee* and Jaehooni Rhee†

Abstracts This study is focused on the effects of environmental changes on the actors' values, actors' strategic choices about employment relations practices and resulting performance. Our research question is 'What kinds of strategic choices have been made in Korean employment relations since the globalization of the 1990s and the 1997 financial crisis, and will these experiments be indeed successful?' The PDR systems theory can provide the answer to this research question. According to the PDR systems theory, if Korean firms are to be adapted to the environmental changes, they have to fit their PDR systems to their changing environments. Based on a case study of Hankuk Electric Glass, the existing paternalistic HR practices should be modified gradually in the ever-changing socio-cultural climate rather than reverting to authoritarian employment relations or adopting American-style contractual employment relations. That is, while stimulating humanware mindset, such modified HR practices, established within a balanced system of rule-making, distribution, and production (PDR), can eventually generate high performance and mutual gains.

I. INTRODUCTION

Korea, like other Asian countries, has been under high pressure to modify or reinvent its traditional employment relationship practices, more specifically its so-called paternalistic HR practices, since the globalization of the 1990s and the 1997 financial crisis. Especially since the 1997 foreign currency crisis, some Korean companies are trying to modify their paternalistic HR practices. Other companies are trying to revert to authoritarian employment relations or to adopt American style contractual employment relations.

Companies such as General Electric and Microsoft have achieved notable successes while implementing layoffs, maintaining private ownership, and establishing an employment process that will seek out qualified individuals from

---

* Professor at Yeungham University, Korea.
† Associate Professor at Yeungham University, Korea.

R. Blanpain (ed.),
Labour Relations in the Asia-Pacific Countries, 89–106.
© 2004 *Kluwer Law International. Printed in Great Britain.*

both inside and outside the organization. This kind of American-style contractual employment relations has been stressed for flexibility, speed and keen competition in globalizing Asia.

Our basic research question is 'Will these experiments which have taken place in Korea since the globalization of the 1990s and the 1997 financial crisis be successful in Korea?' More specifically, we ask, 'Will the "best" bundle of HR practices which is known to be associated with superior organizational performance in US industries work in Korea?' and 'How can we promote fairness and mutual gains in changing work and employment relations in globalizing Asia?'.

In this chapter, we are trying to find the answers to the above questions especially in the perspective of the PDR Systems Theory, since the theory is actually a dynamic model and focuses on the synthesis of production, distribution and rule-making systems. Thus, after reviewing the PDR Systems Theory and its usefulness for this analysis, we discuss the nature of the currently prevalent paternalistic HR practices in Korea and the reasons for their prevalence, in terms of PDR theory. Then, we explore the essential changes in the employment relations environment and their effects on HR practices. Next, we investigate the case of Hankuk Electric Glass that modified and reinvented its employment relations systems in order to overcome its adversity. Finally, based on this case study, we discuss the strategic choices leading towards fairness of employment relations in Korea in the era of globalization and resulting high-performance organization.

II. WHY IS THE PDR SYSTEMS THEORY?

A. The PDR systems theory

Several partial theories that were focused on specific facets of employment relations were advanced after Commons (1909), but before Dunlop (1958) no one had attempted to construct a conceptual framework that integrated and systematized the disparate parts of the field into a coherent whole (Kaufman, 1993, p. 100). After Dunlop (1958), several notable theoretical attempts were made by Somers (1969), Fox (1974), Kochan, Katz, and Mckersie (1986), Adams (1993), Hyman (1994), and Lee (1996a,b). Dunlop's model was framed almost entirely in terms of unionized employment situations (Kaufman, 1993, p. 101). Thus, his model had difficulty in explaining the dynamic aspects of industrial relations (Kochan et al., 1994, p. 7) as well as non-unionized employment situations. The other theories also failed to explain the conflict mechanism of the actors' interests or the need for their cooperation for mutual gains, because they did not address the interaction of PDR systems within their frameworks. In addition, both neoclassical economics and most organizational theories either deny or minimize the legitimacy and enduring nature of conflicting interests in employment, or else they assume that market forces or appropriate managerial behaviour will obviate them (Kochan, 1992, p. 11).

To overcome these limitations, Lee (1996a,b) examined employment relations from the perspective of synthesis and interaction of the PDR systems. The PDR systems theory is deeply rooted in the work of Commons (1909, 1924, 1934, 1950), Dunlop (1958), and Kochan et al. (1986). The PDR systems model consists of four parts characterizing employment relations: (1) the environment, (2) the actors' (values and power positions), (3) the contents and interactions of the PDR systems, and (4) the resulting performances (Lee, 1996a,b). As illustrated in Figure 1, the four parts are inter-connected in a logical, real-world framework. Environmental factors have a strong effect on the actors' values and power positions, which in turn influence the actors' strategic choices involving the PDR systems. The contents of the PDR systems and their interactions determine the performance level, both workers' productivity and overall quality of life.

The PDR systems theory accepts the legitimacy and enduring nature of conflicting interests within PDR systems and suggests the need and possibility for the actors' resolution of conflicts by stressing the importance of synthesis and balance within these systems.

B. The role of the environment, actors' values, power positions, and strategies

The PDR systems theory categorizes the environment into competitive and general environments. The competitive environment includes technology, capital and product markets, the labour market, corporate governance, and firm size. The general environment is composed of the socio-cultural climate, economic status, and political status. Compared with the general environment, the competitive environment can be the target of various business strategies, and can be altered rapidly. It is, on the other hand, very similar to the general environment in that it indirectly affects the PDR systems by influencing the actors' values and their power positions.

According to the PDR systems theory, the actors' values determine the scope of strategic choices that they may consider, and their relative power positions determine the most effective strategic choices. The actors' values and strategic choices are analytical tools similar to Commons' volitional psychology, which is a creative agency looking towards the future and manipulating the external world and other people in view of expected consequences (Commons, 1950). Actors use two kinds of strategies that affect employment relations. One is to strengthen their power positions through such means as union organization strategies or competitive environment strategies, and the other is to reconstruct or renovate PDR systems. Therefore, the actors' values and power positions are crucially important in any analysis of employment relations based on the PDR systems theory.

In the context of the PDR systems theory, based on social Darwinism or institutionalism, the employment relations system must be evolutionary; it must gradually change because the actors (workers and trade unions, employers, and government) continue to develop and create strategies for PDR systems, in light of the ever-changing employment relations environment (see Commons, 1909, 1924, 1934, 1950; Bush, 1987; Lower, 1987; Mayhew, 1987; Mirowski, 1987; Neale, 1987; Stevenson, 1987; Woodbury, 1987; Kinnear, 1999 on institutionalism and institutionalist methods).

C. Significance of the human-ware system and the synthesis of the PDR systems

These institutionalist perspectives of the PDR systems theory are similar to Commons' (1909, 1950), Wilkinson's 'productive system' (1983), and Birecree and Konzelmann's (1997). However, the production system in the PDR systems theory is different from Wilkinson's productive system, in that it consists of three subsystems: (1) the human-ware system, (2) the software system (organizations and workplace practices), and (3) the hardware system. The production system, with particular emphasis on the human-ware system, is synthesized with the distribution system (compensation system and working conditions) and the rule-making system through the mindset of the human-ware system (see Figure 1).

The human-ware system converts human resources into creative resources. Human resources have intangible assets such as minds and latent abilities. The human-ware system has three subsystems to develop these intangible assets: the employment system (hiring, staffing, and discharge), the mindset, and the ability-development system (training and education). The mindset for production activities requires creative, cooperative, and learning minds. The level of these minds is determined by the contents and the fairness of the distribution and rule-making systems, as well as the employment and ability-development systems.

Within the production system, the human-ware system interacts with the software system and the hardware system. The most important point in the PDR systems theory is that the creative human resources can create the human-ware system, as well as the software and hardware systems, whereas the other production subsystems are not creative. The hardware system does just what it is

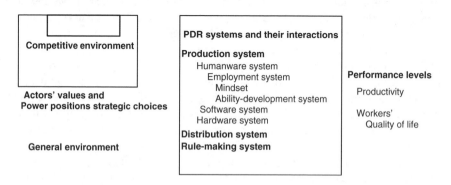

Figure 1: Theoretical framework for analyzing employment relations
Source: Adapted from Lee (1996a).

made to do and nothing more. The software system neither has flash ideas nor can find a way to improve itself, even though it may be very diverse in a given production system. However, the software and hardware systems can be continuously improved and used efficiently by workers who have learning, creative and cooperative minds. Therefore, the engine of the production system is the human-ware system that converts human resources into creative resources.

The other important thing to remember in the PDR systems theory is the operating mechanism that synthesizes and balances the PDR systems and their subsystems. Imbalance in the PDR systems generates conflicts among actors and low performance, because the production system is heavily influenced by the distribution and rule-making systems through the mindset of the human-ware system (see Figure 1).

The PDR systems theory is philosophically based on Commons' stabilized and humanized capitalism because it rejects the 'commodity' approach and accepts the possibility of reconciliation of conflicts of interest. This is quite a different approach from the neoclassical economics that treats labour as a 'commodity' or simply as another factor of production. The PDR systems theory starts from the human perspective that labour, with minds and latent abilities, does not behave like inanimate factors of production such as capital and land.

D. The message and the application of the PDR systems theory

We receive following two messages from the PDR systems theory. The first one is that the changing environments have strong effects on the actors' values and their power positions, which in turn, cause actors to take new strategic choices for PDR systems. The second is that considering the recent severe environmental changes and resulting changes in values and power positions which Korean society has faced, Korean firms are more likely to take what are called 'high-road strategies' in order to survive.

PDR systems theory has been found very useful in both analysis (science-building) and diagnosis (problem-solving) of employment relations (see Lee, 2001). Thus, we will use this theory for the following analysis of employment relations in Korea, following its unprecedented financial crisis, globalization, traditional value changes and drastic transformation of employment relations.

III. THE TRANSFORMATION OF EMPLOYMENT RELATIONS IN KOREA

A. Authoritarian to paternalistic HR practices

The interaction of three socio-cultural factors, (1) Confucian culture, (2) the extended family system, and (3) rice-agricultural society, established and strengthened Korea's patriarchism including familism, collectivism and seniority-based human resource practices. When the power relationship between employers and employees is unequal, employers are more likely to be authoritarian; on the other hand, when the power relationship between employers and employees is equal, employers are more likely to be paternalistic. That is, when employers are given the opportunity, they will take the easiest way and treat employees in an authoritarian manner. On the other hand, when workers' power position is strengthened, patriarchism changes into paternalism. In short, patriarchism may be seen in either authoritarian or paternalistic styles, depending on the actors' power positions (Lee, 2001).

Until the mid-1980s, authoritarian HRM dominated the management style in Korean companies. Employers had complete discretion in making decisions about their employees' status. The employers had never experienced stiff resistance from either workers or trade unions in building up and managing the human-ware system (hiring, staffing, promotion, training and development), the software system (organization and workplace practices), the hardware system, the distribution system (compensation and working conditions), or the rule-making system (Kim, 1988, pp. 258–329).

Authoritarian employers demanded that their employees work long hours with low wages and poor working conditions (Jeoun, 1981, pp. 105–145). They did not adequately or conscientiously invest in their workforce when it came to safety and prevention of industrial accidents. Because of this lack of safety measures and concern for the workers, the industrial accident rate was quite high during the authoritarian period (Lee, 2001). There was no shared management information and no mutual understanding or respect between management and labour.

As the workers' power position strengthened in the latter half of the 1980s, however, workers gained more of a voice and increased their labour activity in dealing with management. In spite of this, employers still attempted to maintain their PDR systems in an authoritarian style but they were faced with thousands of intense labour disputes and violent conflicts between 1987 and 1989.

After the great labour dispute period, the government and employers came to the pragmatic realization and sensible conclusion that it was impossible to maintain an authoritarian HRM style. In November of 1987, the government revised labour laws that were contrary to the authoritarian HR practices. As a result, employers moved to a more functional, humanistic, and paternalistic HRM style. The chief goal for the new paternalistic HRM was not only to maintain managerial authority, but also to heighten labour productivity by improving the workers' overall well-being via mutual understanding, shared management information, respect, better compensation and benefits, and improved working conditions. These paternalistic values and strategic choices induced spontaneous and genuine cooperation, which is quite different from forced or feigned cooperation in authoritarian HRM systems. Many Korean companies experienced this kind of transformation (Lee, 2001).

The transformation began in the middle of 1987. We can see that, since then, both workers' well-being and productivity have significantly improved. The average real wages more than doubled from 1985 to 1997, and working hours decreased from 53.8 to 46.7 hours per week during the same period. The industrial accident rate also dropped substantially from 3.15 in 1985 to 0.81 in 1997. Labour productivity has increased in proportion to the improvement of the workers' overall well-being during the same period (Lee, 2001).

Employment separations are another indicator of this transformation. The separation rate is lower in the paternalistic HRM than in the authoritarian HRM, because workers take the 'voice solution' in a paternalistic situation and the 'exit solution' in the authoritarian situation. In an authoritarian HRM, workers who are dissatisfied with an employer's unilateral decision-making and/or bad working conditions have no choice but to quit their organizations. In a paternalistic HRM, workers discuss working conditions with their employers, rather than just quitting. This is because paternalistic HR practices are based on mutual respect, understanding, and consideration. The separation rates in the authoritarian period from 1970 to 1985 ranged from 4.5 to 6.0 per cent of total manufacturing employment per month. With the diffusion of paternalistic HR practices since beginning of the 1990s, the separation rate decreased remarkably to only 2.4 per cent in 1999.

According to PDR systems theory, these paternalistic HR practices can be said to create a unique 'mind stimulation' system that cultivates paternalistic relationships between employers and employees. There is a warm and genuine human bond, not simply the impersonal 'cash' connection that exists in most western countries. Paternalistic 'mind stimulation' systems are different from incentive and motivation systems that aim at a concrete target or performance. Because job demarcations are less significant in Korea, a horizontal team spirit is likely to flourish. The resulting commitment network encourages employees to cooperate spontaneously in their work efforts. In addition, the paternalistic HRM style, based on implicit employment practice, is very flexible relative to job transfer, working hours, and wage adjustments. These actions, which benefit the company, are based on the concepts of familism, collectivism and loyalty, rather than on individualism. Managers can easily modify and rearrange human resource patterns to suit the company's work demands and job requirements. Korean companies can move a worker to a more demanding job with little concern about trade unions, since the worker will not suffer any pay cut or loss of security. Workers often feel that they are capable of carrying out any number of tasks since there are no clear-cut job demarcations. This is the opposite of work situations in many western countries, where everyone has clearly defined tasks with well-defined boundaries of responsibilities (Leibenstein, 1987).

Consequently, the PDR systems as well as the actors' values have changed to suit paternalistic patterns. Furthermore, what Bush's theory of institutional change calls 'progressive' institutional changes have occurred (Bush, 1987).

IV. NEW ENVIRONMENTAL CHANGES AND THREE OPTIONS

In the latter half of the 1990s, Korea experienced another dramatic change in the fabric of its employment relations environment with the onset of globalization and the 1997 financial crisis. The Korean economy was severely impacted by the foreign currency crisis at the end of 1997, which was initially ignited by the Southeast Asian financial crisis beginning in the middle of 1997. This crisis forced the government to agree to a rescue package from the IMF, which quickly caused the government to implement a wide range of macroeconomic and structural reforms.

The Korean economy experienced a serious and dramatic recession the year after the financial crisis. In 1998, the GDP growth rate dropped by 6.7 per cent, and the unemployment rate soared upwards to 5.6 per cent from the 2.3 per cent level of 1997. The unemployment level reached a peak of 8.6 per cent in February 1999. This was Korea's worst recession in 30 years.

With the diffusion of a new liberalism and globalization and the 1997 financial crisis, the actors' power positions have apparently changed and a new valuational process has come into action. This changing environment has shifted power from the workers and trade unions to the government and employers. The government revised labour laws in December 1996 and again in March 1997. With these revisions of the labour laws and the 1998 Tripartite Commission agreement in the wake of the economic crisis, Korean authorities and employers have adopted several institutional reforms in the area of employment relations to enhance the numerical flexibility of the labour market and spread the merit pay system.

A major concern in this chapter is whether or not these environmental changes have shifted the actors' power positions and changed their values significantly enough to affect paternalistic HR practices, so that Korean firms will shift their paternalistic HR practices to the American-style contractual HRM or some other HR practices. In other words, in this chapter, we will review three plausible options in terms of PDR systems theory, one of which Korean firms must take because of required restructuring since the 1997 financial crisis and under the increasing pressure of globalization.

A. Back to the authoritarian employment relations?

At this juncture, we are very sure that it is impossible to turn back the pages of history and return to the authoritarian HRM style because employees, since the 1987 democratic movement, have tasted 'democratic ideas' and experienced the 'voice solution'. If an employer makes authoritarian strategic choices within the PDR systems, the employer will encounter explicit and implicit resistance from the employees. During the period of serious recession and structural reform, the employees' power position weakened substantially but, beginning in 1999, it recovered considerably with the rapid, overall recovery of the economy. In such a situation, an authoritarian HRM within the PDR systems would confront explicit resistance. Even if there is no explicit resistance, the employer cannot expect high performance because the production system will not function very well with the human-ware system at a low level, due to a lowered mindset.

B. Adopting Western systems and similar alternatives

Will there be movement toward an American-style contractual HRM or another HR practice? Apparently, a new valuational process has been increasing since Korea's financial crisis and the onset of globalization, but these changes have not yet produced alternative values and HR practices to substitute for paternalistic HR practices. So far, the changes have been only modifications of former paternalistic HR practices. The numerical flexibility of the labour market has increased a fair amount since the various labour market reforms, but it should be understood that this was not caused by introduction of American-style HR practices. We will explain more specifically the reason why paternalistic HR practices are still prevalent and effective in Korean workplaces, although employment relationship practices, including labour laws, have been somewhat modified and reinvented in response to the increased pressures growing out of the globalization activities of the 1990s and the 1997 financial crisis. It should be again noted that the human resource practices of Korean firms are fundamentally grounded in paternalism, although after the 1997 foreign currency crisis some large Korean companies are trying new strategies such as a 'merit pay' system.

For example, Korean employers increased the proportion of contingent workers instead of introducing an American-style lay-off system. In other words, unlike US firms, Korean employers are hesitant about terminating employees. The strategy of most employers is to restructure rather than discharge workers who are no longer needed because of a lack of work. It is noteworthy that despite the 1997 financial crisis, the separation rate went down, not up. It was 2.4 per cent in 1999 (Lee, 2001). It was expected that layoffs increased and voluntary quits decreased to a greater extent during the crisis period, considering the swing of the business cycle. However, the rate was not very high considering the financial crisis and the separation rates prior to the paternalistic changeover in 1987. Mass unemployment in spite of low separation rate can be attributed both to job destruction due to bankruptcies and to recent graduates who were not able to find jobs, rather than to layoffs. The major reason that Korean employers have not easily introduced an American-style lay-off system is that a strong Confucian value heritage, especially familism, is still prevalent, which has created a distinctive feeling of mutual commitment between employers and employees, resulting in high performance.

As another example, although some companies revised their wage systems, they did not create an American-style system, but rather modified the paternalistic wage system to reflect workers' abilities and their efforts. In Korea, unlike in the United States, wage rates are linked to individuals rather than to job positions. The wage system is very comprehensive and is composed of three fundamental wage components: regular fixed pay, variable pay (overtime pay), and bonuses. Regular fixed pay includes a base rate plus various fixed allowances. The base rate is quite important because it is the basis for calculating various kinds of allowances, bonuses, and even retirement pay. This initial base rate is determined by a formula that takes into account the person's educational accomplishments, sex, age and work experience. Once this base rate is set, incremental pay increases and promotional advancements are based mainly on the length of company service. This kind of wage system is called '*yeun-gong*' system, which means 'seniority or length of service'.

Recently, the government and management have been actively discussing the limitations of the '*yeun-gong*' wage system. There appears to be a desire to change to a system based on evaluation of ability, monthly in the '*jik-neung*' system or annually in the '*yeun-bong*' system. These ability-based wage systems reflect a workers' perceived ability to do one or more kinds of jobs, whereas a western-style '*jik-moo*' (job-based) system is based on the specific job the worker is actually doing.

According to a 1997 Korea Labour Institute (KLI) survey, 85.1 per cent of the companies who answered the questionnaire have a '*yeun-gong*' system (34.3 per cent) or a 'modified *yeun-gong*' system (50.8 per cent). The 'modified *yeun-gong*' system incorporates some attributes of '*jik-neung*' and '*jik-moo*'. Of the remaining 14.9 per cent companies surveyed, 5.8 per cent have '*jik-neung*' (ability-based) pay systems, 2.9 per cent have '*jik-moo*' (job-based) pay systems, and 6.2 per cent have a system that combines '*jik-neung*' and '*jik-moo*'. In response to the question about desirable pay systems, 74.3 per cent of the respondents preferred a 'modified *yeun-gong*' system, although only 2.5 per cent preferred the pure '*yeun-gong*' system. Of the remaining 23.2 per cent, 11.2 per cent preferred the '*jik-neung*' system, 10.3 per cent preferred a combined '*jik-neung*' and '*jik-moo*' system, and only 1.7 per cent preferred the '*jik-moo*' system (KLI, 1998).

Since the 1997 financial crisis, the government has urged private and public sectors to adopt the '*yeun-bong*' wage system, which reflect an individual's ability, performance, and contributions based on annual evaluation. However, the system Korean firms are adopting is more of a 'modified *yeun-gong*' system than an American-style merit pay system. This modified system incorporates '*merit pay*' into the '*yeun-gong*' system.

According to a Ministry of Labour survey, 18.2 per cent of the 5,116 surveyed companies with over 100 employees had a '*yeun-bong*' wage system as of January 2000. The '*yeun-bong*' system is presently applied only to upper management and some specific jobs. Only 32.2 per cent of companies using a 'yeun-bong' system applied the system to as much as 50 per cent of their employees (Ministry of Labor, 2000b). This means that only 5.8 per cent of the surveyed companies used a '*yeun-bong*' wage system as their main wage system.

In sum, since the financial crisis, the number of companies incorporating '*yeun-bong*' systems has increased, but a paternalistic '*yeun-gong*' or a 'modified *yeun-gong*' system remains most prevalent in the workplace. The 'modified *yeun-gong*' system appears to be more functional and effective than the pure merit-pay system, and will probably continue to be the most common practice in the future. This means that age and seniority within a firm will continue to be major factors in determining an individual's wages and opportunities for promotion. This is because the compensation system is based on familism or collectivism, rather than individualism.

C. Improving paternalistic employment relations

According to the PDR systems theory, the human-ware sub-system of the production system is strongly influenced by the distribution and rule-making systems in terms of mindset (see Figure 1). The human-ware system focuses on the development of creative, cooperative and learning minds, as well as on improving employees' abilities. In this regard, paternalistic HRM has a unique 'mind stimulation' system that cultivates paternalistic relationships between employers and employees. There is a warm and genuine human bond, not simply the impersonal 'cash' connection that exists in most western countries. Paternalistic 'mind stimulation' systems are different from incentive and motivation systems that aim at a concrete target or performance.

In short, there are still many paternalistic HR practices, although new valuational processes have already commenced in the workplace. On reflection, exactly why did not the environmental shocks change paternalistic HR practices? The answer is that the socio-cultural climate was not changed sufficiently to create new common sense tendencies and new social norms, all of which take time. If an employer makes strategic choices about the PDR systems that are contrary to prevalent common sense tendencies and social norms, the strategies will cause the workers' mindset to contract. A consequence of strategies contrary to common values is that the functionality of the entire production system will decrease because of a dysfunctional human-ware system.

This does not mean that the socio-cultural climate is unchangeable or constant. The socio-cultural climate is continuously evolving through continuous movement in both the economic and political realms, and it is also influenced by foreign cultures. Paternalistic HR practices are modified gradually in the ever-changing socio-cultural climate. In that respect, a recent work by the Ministry of Labour (2001) revealed that a significant change is going on in existing Korean paternalistic employment relations. That is, what is called either transparent management or open book management, active employee participation, and fair gain-sharing are proliferating in Korean business circles, an important sign that Korean firms are seeking to improve their existing paternalistic employment relations in order to adapt to the changing environments and globalization.

V. A CASE STUDY OF HEG: MODIFIED PATERNALISTIC APPROACH TO ENHANCE HUMANWARE

We will take as a test case Hankuk Electric Glass (HEG), which is a very good firm to analyze with the PDR systems theory regarding the transformation of employment relations. HEG is a manufacturer of glass for cathode ray tubes, established as an affiliate of Hankuk Glass in 1974. HEG was faced with a crisis of bankruptcy by both the failure of competitive environment strategies and severe conflict in industrial relations. As a result, their share price plummeted to zero-value. Subsequently, HEG was taken over by the Daewoo Group after a

77 day long strike in 1997.[1] Only three years after this transfer, the company succeeded in moving from antagonistic to cooperative industrial relations and had an astonishing achievement: it ranked best among listed companies in Korea in terms of operating profit ratio, in 2000. The debt-to-equity ratio that had peaked at 1,114 per cent plunged to 37 per cent, whereas annual sales recorded a steep rise from $18 million to $55 million (Ministry of Labour, 2001, p. 50).

We have three questions about HEG: why was the company faced with the crisis of bankruptcy? why were the industrial relations aggravated before the business transfer? and how could such drastic changes happen in both industrial relations and business performance? The PDR systems theory can give answers to these questions.

According to the PDR systems theory, the actors' values determine the scope of strategic choices that they consider, and their relative power positions determine the most effective strategic choices. Actors use two kinds of strategies that affect employment relations. One is to strengthen their power positions through such means as union organization or competitive environment strategies, and the other is to reconstruct or renovate the PDR systems. Antagonistic industrial relations and mutual losses are attributable to disharmony of actors' values and imbalance of PDR systems, while shared actors' values and balanced PDR systems lead to mutual gains.

From the viewpoint of the PDR systems theory, HEG is a typical case of a clash between actors' values and imbalance among PDR systems, which led to conflicts and mutual losses. Management had resorted to the old authoritarian styles, although labour's values had moved toward democratic styles and their power position had become much stronger since the great 1987–1989 labour disputes. Thus, management's strategic choices clashed with those of the trade union, creating discord between management's authoritarian values and labour's democratic values. What made the matters worse, management did not share important information with employees, not even with general managers. That is, only a few top managers had access to important information; therefore, the prevalent mentality among employees and even managers, 'we are not interested in our organization, only top management know and do everything on their own'. This value conflict, the greater strength of labour power and asymmetric information availability generated distrust and antagonistic industrial relations.

The trade union was not interested in the production system with this serious asymmetric information, but was concerned only about distribution. The trade union asked for wage increases and working condition improvements without consideration of productivity or competitiveness. The increase of wages by strike in the absence of shared values could not stimulate the mindset of the human-ware system: learning, creative and cooperative minds. The management

---

1. HEG was taken over again by Asahi Glass of Japan in 1999. However, we will not discuss this business transfer because it did not depend on HEG's management or industrial relations problems, and because ownership was changed but the CEO and IR systems were not. It was sold because of bankruptcy of the Daewoo Group, although it had itself achieved high profits.

tried to keep exclusive rights to the production and rule-making systems, even though they yielded to trade union in wage negotiation. What was worse, management's strategic choices for production and rule making systems were not effective because of the workers' stronger power position and deep distrust between management and workers. For example, employees refused management's plan to educate and replace employees, which management thought was inevitable, because they were so concerned about job loss. The implication is that there was no shared management information exchange and no mutual understanding or respect between management and labour. This means that the distribution and rule-making systems were not balanced with production system.

According to the PDR systems theory, an improvement of distribution and rule-making systems should enhance the production system through its effect on the human-ware system (see Figure 1). An increase of labour cost with no productivity improvement must weaken the company's competitiveness, which restricts the improvement of distribution, including wages and working conditions, in the next period. Management cannot expect effective improvement of the production system without enhancement of distribution and rule-making systems, since the PDR systems must be balanced for their interactions to generate mutual gains.

HEG lost its competitiveness by conflicts between actors and imbalance of the PDR systems. Booz Allen & Hamilton, a world-renown consulting firm which undertook consulting work for HEG, reported, 'Our conclusion is that HEG cannot survive in its current position.'

According to Lee (2001), since the great labour disputes of 1987–1989 in Korea, workers' values and power positions have changed so drastically that authoritarian HRM styles came to a dead-end. That is, until the great labour disputes of 1987–1989, most workers worked very hard and took for granted authoritarian PDR systems which employers constructed alone, because an authoritarian value system was dominant in Korea. However, the democratization and great labour disputes of 1987–1989 made Korea's socio-cultural environment much more democratic, as well as making workers' power position stronger. Under these new socio-cultural environments, employers had only to move towards paternalism. If authoritarian employers did not change their values and strategic choices despite the changes in their power position, they would be faced with both direct confrontation and indirect, subtle resistance from the workers. Ultimately this could lead to serious problems or even conflict. Therefore, employers tried to take paternalistic approaches such as setting good examples for employees, sharing information and addressing employees' demands actively.

The new CEO after the transfer of HEG tried to make strategic choices consistent with employees' values and, based on these strategic choices, to renovate the PDR systems. For example, he introduced paternalistic approach such as transparent management techniques based on mutual understanding and consensus. In return, the union also shed its past practice of counter-productive and antagonistic negotiation. These changes of strategic choices led to a great transformation of employment relations in HEG.

The new CEO ended authoritarian management and began paternalistic HR practices. According to Lee (2001), paternalistic HR practices are a reciprocal, cooperative style of management in which the employer acknowledges and considers the employees' rights and feelings. This type of relationship is analogous to a father who does not forcibly control or direct the activities of his child or children, but guides them in an understanding and loving way. Basically, the paternalistic HR leadership concept is based on the values of reciprocity, consideration, and mutual respect. The employer gives respect, consideration and management information to the employees and, in response, the employees spontaneously cooperate and commit themselves wholeheartedly to the company. Paternalistic strategic choices basically depend on a family or community concept rather than contract concept. In the paternalistic HR practices, the CEO should set a good example to employees. To enhance trust, respect and authority, managers should serve as role models and act by the Korean definition of a Confucian leader.

The new CEO made strategic choices on the basis of these principles of paternalistic HR practices. First of all, he decided to set a good example to employees. For example, he quit smoking and drinking and drove himself to work at 6 o'clock every morning, encouraging workers to change themselves in similar ways. He renovated the PDR systems instead of instigating layoffs, stressing that only changing organization can survive and that they all share a common destiny.

The CEO believed it is essential to disclose important information about his organization in order to restore trust between management and labour and instill common values. Thus, he very actively introduced 'Open Book Management', going public with all kinds of financial statements and even strategic information. In this way, he encouraged employees to participate in almost all of the company's decision-making in order to renovate the existing rule-making systems.

Deeply impressed with the CEO's example and his promise of job security in spite of the crisis of bankruptcy, the workers joined the CEO, taking for themselves the slogan 'stay awake while other sleep; work while others play; and study while others rest'.

HEG renovated its organization and workplace practices, the software of the production system, on the basis of shared values and information. The hierarchical organizational structure was renovated into a team-based one, and workplace practices were broadly updated. The previous routine of 'one hour work, 30-min break' was replaced by a new practice of 'two hours work, 10-min break'. Consequently, process that had formerly taken 3 days could now be finished in only 2 h. The yield rate increased as much as 90 per cent, while the claim rate recorded a zero. The software system restructuring in the production system, with harmonious rule-making and distribution systems, stimulated the human-ware's mindset.

Especially, workers' cooperation in the distribution system was quite different from Western employment relations. In return for the CEO's promise not to reduce the headcount, employees voluntarily decided to accept a pay freeze as well as returning their bonuses. Employees voluntarily gave up summer vacations and overtime pay and started to work longer hours, both of which are characteristic of Korean paternalism. This could not have happened in Western societies where individualism and contractualism prevails. What is more important, employees perceived such a pay freeze and return of bonuses as unavoidable choices for job security and the future, and they worked even harder to get past the difficult time as soon as possible. While the CEO set a good example in person, these rule-making and distribution systems stimulated human-ware's mindset.

The lesson from the HEG case from the perspective of PDR systems theory is that actors' strategic choices were based on an implicit consensus of reciprocity through self-sacrifice between management and labour, which made a harmonious balance among rule-making, distribution, and production systems. In the end, such a balance of the PDR systems generated great cooperation and high performance. Driven by strong performance, the share price shot up to 90,000 won from almost zero-value. HEG had finally grown to be a high value-added company.

Specifically, in this case, employment relations had to be modified gradually in the ever-changing socio-cultural climate that affect actors' values. The reason is that if an actor's strategy is contrary to common sense or the standards of fairness that identify the society, it is considered to be unjust, unequal, and unfair. This causes the clash of actors' values and strategies, and imbalance of the PDR systems that generate mutual losses.

VI. CONCLUSIONS

In sum, paternalistic HR practices are presently being challenged by the environmental demand for a flexible labour market and by globalization and by the more liberal younger generation of today. In what direction will Korea's firms move in the future? Both employers and employees recognize that paternalistic HR practices are still effective in Korea mainly, because there is no viable alternative industrial relations model. It is also true that individualism and rationalism are growing and proliferating rapidly among younger workers. Therefore, to adapt to these changes, paternalistic HRM needs to be modified and restructured, rather than totally removed. While the paternalistic HRM has such weak elements as lack of rationality and transparency in management, lack of fairness and innovation, and poor communication, there are also such strong points as flexibility, stimulation mechanisms and spontaneous cooperation. What Korean companies need to do in today's changing employment environment is to reinvent PDR systems to minimize the weak points and maximize the strong points of current paternalistic HR practices. To maximize such strong points as commitment, flexibility and risk sharing, the concept of trust is extremely important. Commitment without trust is likely to be fragile; the commitment is likely to disappear if the trust proves to have been unfounded (Leibenstein, 1987, p. 170). Essentially, trust, faithfulness and employee loyalty can be ensured by employers' concern for their employees, a transparent and rational management style, a good example set by employers in person, and a creative human-ware system.

Especially considering the fact that environmental changes caused by the onset of globalization and the economic crisis and resulting demands for a more flexible labour market are unavoidable, Korean companies have to be prepared to modify their paternalistic HR practices. Of course, as discussed above, such environmental changes cannot easily change Korean actors' values and PDR systems. It should, however, be noted that the socio-cultural climate is not unchangeable or constant, but continuously evolving through continuous movement in both the economic and political realms. Therefore, if Korea is to adapt to the environmental changes, it has to fit its PDR systems to its changing values and environmental factors. That is, paternalistic HR practices should be modified gradually in the ever-changing socio-cultural climate. The reason is that if an actor's strategy is contrary to common sense or the standards of fairness that identify the society, it is considered to be unjust, unequal, and unfair. According to PDR systems theory, when employees perceive unfairness in their PDR systems, even the best rule-making and distribution systems cannot stimulate the human-ware's mindset. The successful HEG case suggests 'fusion management', a merging of the American management style of transparent management and the Korean mind-set placing more emphasis on moral duty than on immediate gain a lot to Korean business circles.

We can draw two important theoretical ideas from this case study. One is a theoretical framework guiding the analysis of HR practices and industrial relations, and the other is an issue of convergence/divergence in industrial relations systems.

The PDR systems theory is very useful in analyzing the transformation of industrial relations. This study shows how we should consider socio-cultural factors, locus of actors' power positions and evolutionary dynamics in explaining changing patterns of industrial relations. We cannot explain the emergence and transformation of industrial relations patterns, such as paternalistic HR practices in Korea, without considering these factors. Neo-classical theory has a basic limitation in analyzing these transformations because it disregards socio-cultural factors and power positions. In contrast to the neoclassical paradigm, the analytical tools of the PDR system theory includes environmental factors such as socio-cultural factors, actors' power positions and values, and also evolutionary dynamics, in that actors make new strategic choices about PDR systems in light of their ever-changing environment within the institutionalist paradigm.

Are industrial relations evolving into one-dimensional homogenized systems in the world market? This study predicts that convergence will go on, but that divergence will still exist in industrial relations systems. According to the PDR systems theory, actors' strategic choices about industrial relations depend on those actors' values and their power positions, which are in turn influenced by socio-cultural and other environmental factors. These factors will converge by frequent interchanges and severe competition in the global market, but will not become homogeneous because there will be divergence in actors' values and their power positions. This study concludes that paternalistic HR practices are being modified and transformed in changing environments as in the case of HEG, but that convergence to a neoliberal system based on a pure contractual relationships is unlikely to occur because of cultural diversity and, thus, that there is unlikely to be one single best set or bundle of HR practices among all global corporations.

REFERENCES

Adams, Roy. (1993), 'All Aspects of People at Work: Unity and Division in the Study of Labor and Labor Management', in Adams, Roy and Melz, Noah (eds.), *Industrial Relations Theory: Its Nature, Scope and Pedagogy*, Longman Cheshire, Melbourne: pp. 119–60.

Birecree, Adrienne M. and Suzanne Konzelmann. (1997), 'A comparative analysis of cases of conflictual labor relations in the corn processing, steel, paper, and coal industries', *Journal of Economic Issues* Vol. 31, No.1, pp. 129–144.

Bush, Paul D. (1981–1982), 'The Normative Implications of Institutional Analysis', *Economic Forum* Vol. 12; 'Theory of Institutional Change', *Journal of Economic Issues* Vol. 21, pp. 1075–1116.

Commons, John R. (1909), 'American Shoemakers, 1848–1895: A sketch of industrial evolution', *Quarterly Journal of Economics* Vol. 24, pp. 39–84.

Commons, John R. (1924) *Legal Foundations of Capitalism*, Macmillan, New York.

Commons, John R. (1934) *Institutional Economics: Its Place in the Political Economy*, Macmillan, New York.

Commons, John R. (1950) *The Economics of Collective Action*, Macmillan, New York.

Dunlop, John T. (1958), *Industrial Relations Systems*. Holt, Rinehart, and Winston, New York.

Fox, Alan. (1974), *Beyond Contract: Work, Power, and Trust Relations*. Faber, London.

Freeman, Richard B. and James L. Medoff. (1984), *What Do Unions Do?* Basic Books, Inc.

Hyman, Richard. (1994), 'Theory and Industrial Relations', *British Journal of Industrial Relations* Vol. 32, No. 2, pp. 165–80.

Jeoun, Ki H. (1981), 'Wage and working conditions', Lim, Jong C. and Bai, Moo K. (eds.), *Korean Labor Economy*. Moonhak and Giseung Press, Seoul, pp. 105–145.

Kaufman, Bruce E. (1993), *The Origins and Evolution of the Field of Industrial Relations in the United States*. ILR Press, Ithaca.

Kim, Hyung K. (1988), *Monopoly Capital and Labor in Korea*. Kachi Press, Seoul.

Kinnear, Douglas. (1999), 'The Compulsive Shift to Institutional Concerns in Recent Labor Economics', *Journal of Economic Issues* Vol. 33, pp. 169–181.

Kochan, Thomas A. (1992), 'Teaching and Building Middle Range Industrial Relations Theory', MIT, mimeo.

Kochan, Thomas A. 'Industrial relations and human resource policy in Korea: Options for continued reform' in: Cho, Lee J. and Kim, Yoon H. (eds.), *Korea's Political Economy-An Institutional Perspective*. Westview Press, Boulder, pp. 663–697.

Kochan, Thomas A, Harry Katz, and Robert B. McKersie. (1986), *The Transformation of American Industrial Relations*. ILR Press, Ithaca.

Korea Labor Institute (KLI). (1988), *A Fact-Finding Survey of 1997 Wage Bargaining Activities*.
Lee, Hyo-Soo. 'A Comparative Analysis of Industrial Relations: Korea and Japan'. *The Korean Economic Review* Vol. 4, pp. 227–256.
Lee, Hyo-Soo. (1996a), 'Theory construction in industrial relations: A synthesis of PDR systems'. *The Korean Economic Review*, Vol. 12, No. 2, pp. 199–218.
Lee, Hyo-Soo. (1996b), 'The interaction of production, distribution, and rule-making systems in industrial relations'. *Relations Industrielles/Industrial Relations* Vol. 51, No. 2, pp. 302–332.
Lee, Hyo-Soo. (1997), *The Economics of Mutual Gains* The Korean Labor Education Institute, (in Korean).
Lee, Hyo-Soo. (2001), 'Paternalistic human resource practices: Their emergence and characteristics'. *Journal of Economic Issues* Vol. 35, pp. 841–869.
Leibenstein, Harvey. (1987), *Inside The Firmæ The Inefficiencies of Hierarchy*. Harvard University Press.
Lower, Milton D. (1987), 'The concept of technology within the institutional perspective', *Journal of Economic Issues* Vol. 21, pp. 1147–1176.
Mayhew, Anne. (1987), 'The beginnings of institutionalism'. *Journal of Economic Issues* Vol. 21, pp. 971–998.
Ministry of Labor, Republic of Korea (2000a), *Best Company Practices in Korea*.
Ministry of Labor (2000b), *Report on the "Yeun-Bong" Wage and Gain Sharing Systems Survey*.
Ministry of Labor (2001), *Transparent Management, Sound Cooperation – Best Practices of Cooperative Labor Relations*.
Ministry of Labor (1995), *Report on the Enterprise Labor Cost Survey*, Relevant Issues. *The labor News* (December 18).
Mirowski, Philip. (1987), 'The philosophical bases of institutional economics', *Journal of Economic Issues* Vol. 21, pp. 1001–1038.
Neale, Walter C. (1987), 'Institutions', *Journal of Economic Issues* Vol. 21, pp. 1177–1206.
Somers, Gerald G. (1969), 'Bargaining power and industrial relations theory', in Gerald G. Somers (ed.), *Essays in Industrial Relations Theory*, Iowa State University Press, pp. 39–53.
Stevenson, Rodney E. (1987), 'Institutional economics and the theory of production', *Journal of Economic Issues* Vol. 21, pp. 1471–1493.
Wilkinson, Frank. (1983), 'Productive systems', *Cambridge Journal of Economics* Vol. 7, pp. 413–429.
Woodbury, Stephen A. (1987), 'Power in the labor market: institutionalist approaches to labor problems', *Journal of Economic Issues* Vol. 21, pp. 1781–1807.

9. Social Security in México
An Overview

*Angel G. Ruiz Moreno**

A product of the revolutionary movement at the beginning of the twentieth Century, social rights in Mexico were enshrined in the Constitution in force since 1917.

When a new Social Security Law was passed in 1973 – preceded by the Federal Labour Law, considered at the time to be progressive and taken as paradigm for all of Latin America – we confidently expected an enviable future, a bright destiny which, sadly, never materialized because, as nearly always happens, reality turned out to be wiser than law. Despite the good intentions of the legal measures and of the government of the day, the Mexican Institute of Social Security (IMSS) soon suffered a crisis that threatened its very existence.

After unexpected successes between 1960 and 1980, this decentralized public agency of the federal government had become Mexico's 'great doctor', casing for more than half of the eligible citizens, and described in its prime as the institution which was 'the pride of the republic', in the 1990s fell victim to its own successes.

The pronounced rising curve in the demographic and epidemiological variables of Mexico leapt upwards: the expectation of life rose dramatically from 49 years in the initial year of the IMSS to almost 79 years at the present, converting Mexico from a youthful nation to a rapidly-aging one. The worst aspect for social security is that there is no real social culture with regard to this phenomenon, which will inexorably take its toll of systems designed for conditions very different from those of to-day.

The present outlook is gloomy owing to the high cost of medicines – which had been the IMSS's greatest weakness – and to the greater life expectancy of the insured population and the consequently longer period of pension payments. It is now evident that pensions are becoming an extinct species, not only in Mexico but also in the world as a whole.

We cannot omit to mention the phenomenon of the noticeable 'delaborization' of social security – inseparably linked to labour relations, and already a reality of which there is general consciousness. The idea was to extend cover to other, diverse social group of formal employment in total transformation due to the use of contemporary technologies.

---

* Academic and national researcher of Mexico.

However, it seems that all that has been achieved with this populist (or some right say, demagogic) policy is the lowering of the quality of the service rendered to the principal recipients, the workers who, together with the employers, with their respective contributions, continue to sustain, and in fact to subsidize, the rendering of this public service to others. For this reason, the State has found it necessary to materially increase its, previously symbolic, contributions, so as not to raise even further the cost of social insurance which already lies between 25 per cent and 30 per cent of basic wage including the item for operatives' housing.

Notwithstanding the view, still widely held, that social security is a public service originally provided by the State steps are already being taken to transfer it to private hands. In Mexico, the process began with the implementation of the 'previsional model of individualized capitalization' applicable to pensions, based on the 1997 Social Security Law. The latter was modified in December 2001 – two-thirds of the original text was changed – with the object of reinforcing the character of an autonomous fiscal organism, which the IMSS possessed. But this is not the only sign that the States intends to throw in the towel with respect to this public service, although in some areas of compulsory insurance the model of shared, common fund – for example, in work accident insurance – all of which shows that it is a 'legal hybrid' without an identity of its own and with evident signs of unconstitutionality in its design.

Another essential fact to be borne in mind is the formal implementation of the Retirements Funds Administration (AFORE). This agency is charged with managing privately the technical reserves for financing pensions, for which it charges the approximately 12 million permanently insured persons an amount equal to almost 25 per cent of the daily amount charged for a retirement pension by a private insurance company. Of course, the pensions market offers enormous potential for stock exchange business, as witness the fact that, in 5 years' operation they have succeeded in accumulating more than US$50,000 millions and by the year 2030 it is forecast that the enforced savings of the insures will be equal to half of Mexico's Gross National Product.

The Specialized Health Insurance Institutions, or ISES, which are privately owned, seek to fill the gaps in the attention of millions of entitled persons who are permanently dissatisfied with the services of the IMSS.

Another example of the trend is the recent reform of the Retirement Savings Systems Law, which reinforces the privatizing tendency in the Mexican social security system. Contrary to some opinions, this is not merely a question of management, since there are evidently underlying profit motives in these activities. In fact, every day there is more encroachment of private enterprise in public business and, despite the time-worn official denials, it is now plain that not even items like oil and electric power – historically so sensitive for the Mexican – can escape the ferocious assault of the 'market without a human face'.

To sum up, Mexico today lives in the same state of uncertainty, which affects the other countries in its geographical area. Can Mexican social security resist the colossal challengers of the twenty-first century?

The answer to such a fundamental question for our country is yet to be given, so any opinion on the subject cannot be more than more conjecture.

10. Employment and Work Culture in Mexico under the Shadow of NAFTA, 1994–2002

*Arturo Vásquez Párraga**

Mexico is the 11th most populated country in the world. Fifty-six per cent of its more than 100 million inhabitants, 51.2 per cent women and 48.8 per cent men, belong to the economically active population (INEGI, 2002b). It is also one of the world's largest recipients of foreign direct investment (United Nations, 2000), and one of the world's largest exporters of products (WTO, 2001). And, as if that is not enough, Mexico now has its first indigenous saint, San Juan Diego, canonized in August 2002.

Mexico's privileged position in the world, however, is supported but weakly by less than solid economic structures, and the country's ability to strengthen and further develop its position is hampered by problems with employment and in labour relations. North American Free Trade Agreement (NAFTA) has been in effect since January 1994 and has accentuated the ambivalent character of Mexico's efforts to provide effective, integrative solutions for the country's economic, occupational and labour problems.

What follows is a succinct analysis of Mexico's occupational and labour situation from the year of NAFTA's implementation to the present. The period under study has been selected because of the need to check new results against conclusions published earlier, some of which do not seem to be guided by analysis and/or objective evaluation. More important, we need to evaluate NAFTA's impact on these situations, as NAFTA is considered one of the major factors – if not the major factor – in Mexico's trade and its related economic activities. Our analysis raises questions about how much impact NAFTA can be expected to have on Mexico's economic problems.

I. EMPLOYMENT AND OCCUPATIONAL PROFILE

Mexico is a developing country that seeks to accelerate its development in order to reduce the distance that separates it from its trade partners, the United States and Canada. Seven of the 10 Mexican men and 4 of the 10 Mexican women

---

*   University of Texas-Pan American, Texas, USA, Director of Latin American Companies in the USA Project, ex-researcher of Analisis Laboral (1977–1980), Peru.

actively participate in such development. On average, the 56 per cent of the population that is economically active constitute slightly more than 40 million people. However, only 98 per cent of those workers are employed. Of those employed, only 87 per cent earns a paycheck equal to or greater than a minimum wage (around $120) (INEGI, 2002a). Ironically, about 12 per cent of the 40 million labourers work more than 48 h per week but earn less than a minimum wage. Of the remaining 60 million who do not work, some (27 per cent) are under age, and a larger group (32 per cent) is economically inactive (32 per cent) (INEGI, 20021). This latter group is comprised of housewives (49 per cent), students (38 per cent), retirees and pension holders (6 per cent), and others (7 per cent) (INEGI, 2002b).

We are focused on the 30 million employed who earn an income. Because 10 million of the 40 million of Mexico's employed do not earn an income, the distribution by sector of economic activity – (primary = 18 per cent, secondary = 27 per cent, tertiary = 55 per cent) – does not accurately reflect Mexico's employment structure. These non-earning 10 million labourers work mainly in the primary and tertiary sectors. The focus of the analysis that follows is the 30 million people who are employed and also earn an income. Forty-three per cent of this population works in firms of 1–5 people (INEGI, 2002b).

As in most countries, the large majority of the employed works in the private sector (85 per cent), whereas a small minority works in the public sector (15 per cent). Of the latter group, 90 per cent work in the government (28 per cent in the central government, 52 per cent in the local government, and 10 per cent in the social security system), and 10 per cent work in the control, direct or indirect, of public companies (INEGI, 2002c). The labour force in the private sector quantitatively dominates Mexico's labour pool.

The 85 per cent who work in the private sector are employed primarily in services (37.2 per cent), trade (21.9 per cent), and manufacturing (21.1 per cent), an aggregate representing 80 per cent of the total. The remaining 20 per cent are employed in construction (5.9 per cent); communications and transportation (5.9 per cent); extractive industries and electricity (0.9 per cent); and agriculture, livestock, forestry, and fishery (0.8 per cent) (INEGI, 2002a). We should remember that the latter two industries employ greater numbers of people, but they compensate workers with wages and salaries much lower than the other industries, if they compensate them at all.

The size of the labour force in the service, trade, and manufacturing industries has not changed overall, but it has experienced internal shifts over the long-term, which is to say that the labour force in services and trade has grown almost constantly while the number of people working in most manufacturing industries during the last 10 years has been shrinking (INEGI, 2002b). This trend can also be observed in the distribution of jobs by type of occupation. The proportion of industrial workers – high-level administrators and management personnel – is decreasing while the proportion of people in trade and related administrative positions is increasing. In contrast, the percentage of workers in services, professional and technical, and agriculture is remaining constant (INEGI, 2002b).

Manufacturing industries employ about 1.4 million people (INEGI, 2002d). This figure is about the same as it was in 1994, when NAFTA was implemented, but it is smaller when compared to the rest of the employed population. This statistic has been interpreted by some observers as indicative of NAFTA's negative effect in Mexico; it failed to create jobs (Juraidini, 1993). Nevertheless, another statistical source shows that the number of people employed in the *maquiladora* industry, an employment sector directly linked to the objectives of NAFTA, grew 120 per cent between 1994 and 2000, even though it experienced a set back between 2000 and 2002, which limited total growth to 83 per cent between 1994 and 2002 (INEGI, 2002e). In fact, the rapid generation of jobs in the cities on the Mexico–United States border is directly attributable to the opening of *maquiladora* plants in Northern Mexico (Jimenez, 2000).

Moreover, labour efficiency has remained relatively constant in the manufacturing industry during the period under study, as shown by the number of man-hours changing slightly from 45.7 in 1994 to 45.9 in 2002. But labour efficiency significantly improved in the *maquiladora* export industry, where the number of man-hours decreased from 44.7 in 1994 to 43.1 in 2002. This improvement in labour efficiency is more pronounced in some industrial categories as shown by the points of difference in the improvement: canned food (4.1), chemical products (3.9), tools and equipment (2.5), shoes and leather products (2.2), and transportation equipment (1.9).

The evaluation of NAFTA as an employment factor must be circumscribed by the purposes of the agreement, that is, it must measure the achievement (though in stages) of a freer trade of goods and services between Mexico, the United States, and Canada. Any evaluation must also take note of the fact that NAFTA involved side agreements regarding the environment and labour relations, protecting areas that Mexico and the United States considered in need of protection. Other than the areas, which we have discussed, NAFTA is not part of any economic, labour, or cultural policy as established by the general agreement. NAFTA is not like the European Union (EU), a more advanced integration project where common policies will be adopted soon by the participating countries. The EU started operating with the EURO, a common currency in most countries joining this economic bloc. NAFTA is not even a customs union, an agreement that sets common tariffs to third countries, as MERCOSUR aims at but is unable to implement now. Thus there is no justification for praising or blaming NAFTA for nearly everything that happens in Mexico's occupational and employment arenas.

II. UNEMPLOYMENT: RATES, MOTIVATIONS AND CHARACTERISTICS

When we look at the distribution of the employed population by the hours worked in June 2002 (INEGI, 2002b), we see that 83.4 per cent of the employed population is fully employed; employees work 35 h or more per week. The remaining percentage includes the unemployed and under-employed. Twelve per cent of this group works from 15 to 34 h weekly, and 3.3 per cent works less than 15 h, which is the reason why this population is considered under-employed. Finally, 2.1 per cent does not work, and thus is part of the open unemployment. The percentages vary month by month, but the numbers shown seem to be typical (see INEGI, 2002b).

Estimated open unemployment rates in Mexico fluctuate between 2 per cent and 6 per cent. The statistics show a general decline in those rates (INEGI, 2002f), even though they fluctuated between 1994 (3.7 per cent) and 2002 (2.6 per cent), and peaked in 1995 at 6.2 per cent, a spike explained by the financial crisis that affected the country that year. However, the above rates do not seem indicative of actual unemployment in Mexico. Remember that about 10 million employed persons do not receive income. This number alone represents 25 per cent of the employed population (INEGI, 2002f). Another 27 per cent of the employed do not earn wages, salaries, commissions or bonuses because they are self-employed, entrepreneurs, or work without pay (INEGI, 2002b). Moreover, according to the Partial Occupation Rate (TOPD2), which includes the unemployed and those employed less than 35 h weekly, the rates reported fluctuated between 17 per cent and 28 per cent during the period 1994–2002 (INEGI, 2002f). Therefore, we must conclude that hidden unemployment is much greater than open unemployment in Mexico. Because we lack statistics on hidden unemployment, we are limiting our examination to open unemployment, where nine of 10 unemployed people have work experience (INEGI, 2002b).

The reasons for losing employment have to do more with involuntary causes such as dismissals (40 per cent in June 2002) and temporary work ending (13 per cent) than with voluntary ones such as job dissatisfaction (39 per cent) and other reasons (7 per cent). These percentages have been changing since 1994, the last year in which the voluntary and involuntary causes of unemployment were equal, until 2002, when involuntary causes surpassed voluntary ones, though the gap was considerably widened in some months when involuntary layoffs jumped to 65 per cent (December 2001) and 62 per cent (January 2002), as reported in INEGI's (2002f) periodic survey. The reasons that 14.5 per cent of the employed work less than 35 h a week include: work schedule limitations (58 per cent); reduced production due to market conditions (10 per cent); personal reasons (23 per cent); and vacations, holidays, and leaves (8 per cent) (INEGI, 2002b).

The principal location of unemployment is the service sector, followed by manufacturing and trade. In the past, manufacturing was the area with the highest unemployment, followed by the service sector and, at a distance, trade (INEGI, 2002b). This new trend affirms once more the assertion that NAFTA is not a major cause of unemployment in the Mexican economy. On the contrary, manufacturing, even if the *maquiladora* industry is taken into account, continued laying off employed personnel at the rates it did before 1994, which shows that NAFTA had minimal, if any, impact.

For obvious reasons, the highest rate of open unemployment is among the younger age groups, with rates fluctuating between 4.3 per cent and 7.3 per cent in the last years, while the groups with older members are less affected. Their rates fluctuated between 1.0 per cent and 3.2 per cent over the same period. Around 55 per cent of the unemployed are reported to be sons or daughters living in households, while a third is reported to be household heads, and about 7 per cent spouses (INEGI, 2002b). The connection between unemployment and education is unclear. Fifty-five per cent of the unemployed reported having only a basic education (elementary and/or secondary at best); 45 per cent reported having higher levels of education. What does not seem obvious is the fact that the rates of open unemployment among women are increasing while open unemployment rates for men did not increase overall despite short-term fluctuations (INEGI, 2002b). The increase of unemployment rates among women might be attributed to a significantly greater participation of women in the Mexican labour force (see Nauman and Hutchinson, 1997).

If we look at unemployment trends by region, some trends can be observed in the fluctuation of open unemployment rates between 1994 and 2002: (1) The *maquiladora*-hosting cities on the US border started with relatively high unemployment rates in 1994, saw reductions in those rates between 1994 and 2000, and slight increases between 2000 and 2002. The jobs generated by the *maquiladora* plants may have caused the reductions, and their recent layoffs may have increased the more recent unemployment rates. (2) Trends in the interior cities went in the opposite direction. Many cities reduced their unemployment rates over the last 2 years by transferring their unemployed to the border areas, where unemployment produced by cyclical layoffs was already in place. In contrast, a prolonged scarcity of qualified workers has been observed in Northern Mexico since 1997, despite substantial increases in wages and salaries offered for jobs requiring highly qualified personnel (Malkin, 2000).

III. COMPENSATION

Thirty million employed people receive compensation, but the compensation received by most of them is not enough to live comfortably. Fifteen per cent earned more than five minimum wages, the reason why this small segment may be in a comfortable situation, whereas 45 per cent of the work force obtained between two and five minimum wages, 23 per cent received between one and two, and 6 per cent received less than a minimum wage (INEGI, 2002b). A minimum wage is calculated by dividing the total wages and salaries earned by the total earning population. The result is divided by the number of days in the corresponding month, which yields the average daily wage in each geographic area (three in total). A Christmas bonus is included for the month of December (CONASAMI, 2002).

The minimum wage almost tripled between 1994 and 2002. It grew 2.84 times, rising from 13.97 to 39.74 pesos a day (almost $4 daily), an amount similar to the annual median compensation, which also tripled over the same period (INEGI, 2002d). This growth in wages was stimulated by an increase in the manufacturing mean compensation (3.25 times), which was directly impacted by a four-fold increase (4.03 times) in *maquiladora* industry compensation.

Similarly, the annual median compensation in construction and trade more than tripled (increased 3.16 and 3.08 times, respectively).

Compensation includes wages, salaries, and employee benefits, all of which are reported as means. In the manufacturing industry, where those means grew 3.25 times between 1994 and 2002, the mean compensation grew more rapidly in those industries that paid above the median such as chemical, non-metallic minerals, metal products, paper and paper products. The same kind of growth was also experienced in food, beverages, and tobacco, industries that pay below the median. Compensation rates in other industries paying below the median – wood, textiles and clothing, basic metals – also grew, but at rates below the general average (INEGI, 2002d).

The above observations are consonant with the compensation levels and increases we see in the *maquiladora* industry, where the median compensation grew more rapidly in the industries that pay above the median (INEGI, 2002e). For example, among the industries that pay more than the median, the average growth was 4.13 times, while the average growth in the *maquiladora* industry in the period 1994–2002 was 4.03 times. So far there has been no attempt to establish a cause–effect relationship between the compensation changes in the *maquiladora* industry and those that occurred in manufacturing, but there are similar trends underscoring their association. And we should not forget that the *maquiladoras* are part of the manufacturing sector. It is not in the *maquiladora* industry, as some observers have argued, that Mexican workers have made little gains (Zapata, 2002).

IV. SOCIAL SECURITY

The *Instituto Mexicano del Seguro Social* (IMSS) recently reported that more than 12 million workers (12,281,018 in July 2002) are covered by Mexico's social security system (IMSS, 2002). Eighty-six per cent are covered permanently and 14 per cent are covered temporarily. This figure registers a growth of 21 per cent between 1994 and 2002, which contrasts sharply with the limited growth in the labour force and lack of growth in the work force employed in manufacturing industries over the same period. If we multiply the size of this work force by 4.5 family members, we find that slightly more than 55 million people can claim benefits from the national health system (IMSS, 2002).

The population entitled to benefits is served by the IMSS (79 per cent), the ISSSTE (17 per cent), PEMEX (1 per cent), SDN (0.8 per cent), SM (0.3 per cent), and the government (2.2 per cent). But the population effectively served by these social welfare organizations is only one-sixth of the covered population, and mainly includes minors between 0 and 19 years of age (43 per cent), families (12 per cent), women between 20 and 49 years of age (3 per cent), the elderly (3 per cent), the handicapped (0.3 per cent), and beneficiaries of government programs (36 per cent).

The 86 per cent of the workers covered permanently by social security are concentrated in the three larger economic sectors: manufacturing (33 per cent), services (32 per cent), and trade (21 per cent). This percentage is greater than the percentage of the people employed in those three sectors. Conversely, the proportion is lower than the corresponding participation in the employment structure of the remaining sectors: agriculture (3.3 per cent), extractive industries (0.6 per cent), electricity and water (1.1 per cent), transportation and communications (5.6 per cent), and independent workers (0.1 per cent).

The earning population that contributed to social security was 12.4 million in 2000 (the last number available), and the contribution rates were greatly influenced by the compensation level, the company size, type of economic activity, and geographic location. The higher the compensation, the greater the contribution. For example, 53 per cent of contributors earn more than two minimum wages. The bigger the organization, the greater the number of contributors and the higher the mean daily wage of contribution. For instance, companies with 301 or more workers (the largest) generate 41 per cent of the contributors and offer 18 per cent more in mean wages of contribution (167.97 pesos) than the immediately lower level (101–300 workers).

The 12.4 million contributors earning wages and salaries worked in 738,115 organizations and contributed, on the basis of a mean compensation, 127.20 pesos (IMSS, 2002). This average was higher in some industries such as electricity and water, transportation and communications, business services and personal services, and extractive industries. It was lower in other industries. Finally, the average contribution was higher in *Mexico D.F.*, the *state of Mexico*, and the states of *Nuevo Leon* and *Queretaro*, and lower in the other states. Similarly, the number of organizations with contributing employees was relatively greater in *Mexico D.F.*, the *states of Mexico, Monterrey*, and *Guadalajara*, and lower in other states (IMSS, 2002).

V. COLLECTIVE BARGAINING AND UNIONISM

Revisions of wages, salaries, and contracts between employers and workers are requested by a union or its associative body (federation or confederation), but not all unions are affiliated with the *Congreso del Trabajo* (CT), the complex national entity comprised of: the *Confederacion de Trabajadores de Mexico* (CTM), the *Confederacion Revolucionaria Obrera y Campesina* (CROC), and the *Confederacion Regional Obrera de Mexico* (CROM). Other confederations such as COR, CGT, CRT, COCEM, CTC, the *Sindicatos Nacionales Autonomos* (SNA), the *Asociaciones Sindicales Autonomas* (ASA), and other independent unions such as FAO, FROT, FORET, and FOR negotiate on behalf of workers.

In the past, these unions and federations represented traditional unionism, which in Mexico means pro-employer, and it is because of this lingering association that they were often accused of favouring employers over workers in labour negotiations (*Multinational Monitor*, 2000). The confederations that were affiliated generally with the *Partido Revolucionario Institucional* (PRI) and the CTM became known as 'dinosaurs' because they were always perceived to be affiliated with the governing party (*Multinational Monitor*, 1991).

Outside the CT are about 20 independent unions and union associations such as the UNT, FAT, CNI, COM, ASPA, and others, all of whose memberships grew between 1994 and 2002. Mexican workers have had the right to form independent unions since May 1999, when the Mexican Supreme Court granted it to them (*Multinational Monitor*, 1999). The most visible indication of the conflict that exists between labour organizations associated with traditional unionism and the new independent unions who are clearly trying to establish themselves as pro-worker can be seen in the appearance of the *Union Nacional de Trabajadores* (UNT) in 1997 and its subsequent positioning as an alternative to traditional unionism (La Botz, 2000). The following event is indicative of its recently acquired importance. In August 2000, the leaders of the CTM and UNT were invited to a meeting with then President-elect Vicente Fox so that each could deliver its demands. The CTM requested wage increases; more jobs; the creation of training programs; the establishment of a single minimum wage; more opportunities for women; and an end to child labour (as in the old times), but the UNT demanded the elimination of state-controlled unions (such as the CTM, CT, and FSTSE); an end to 'protection contracts' that gave workers only the legal minimum wages and required only minimal working conditions while protecting employers from organizing campaigns; and labour-union freedom that gives workers the right to form, join, or leave unions as they choose. The UNT clearly represents an essential departure from the traditional unionism of the CTM. However, the UNT's achievements have been limited by labour policies the government already has in place (Bensusan, 2000), policies that favour CTM's agenda (La Botz, 2000).

In the period 1994–2002, the number of revisions in compensation and contracts increased at an annual rate of 12 per cent. The average wage increases obtained as a result of these revisions grew from 5.3 per cent to 9.1 per cent, and the number of workers who benefited increased 13 per cent. However, most successful revisions (92 per cent) were not the result of mediation. Most of the successes were presented by the parties directly to the *Jurisdiccion Federal de Conciliacion y Arbitraje* (JFCA); only 8 per cent of the improvements were obtained by mediation. Curiously enough, the wage increases obtained through mediation were not always higher than those obtained without mediation; in fact, such increases were lower in 5 of the 9 years examined.

As expected, the leadership of the larger confederations and unions was able to obtain a large number of revisions. In the period January–June 2002, for example, the three largest confederations obtained 78 per cent of the revisions, the independent unions 19 per cent of the changes, the other confederations 5.6 per cent, and the SNA and ASA each obtained 2.8 per cent of the revisions. However, the results did not always favour the largest confederations, even though, on average, they obtained 6.7 per cent of the wage increases and benefited 52 per cent of the workers involved. The independent unions, on the other hand, achieved 6.1 per cent of the revisions and benefited 28 per cent of the workers. The SNA and ASA obtained 5.6 per cent of the compensation and contract revisions to benefit 15 per cent of the workers (JFCA, 2002).

The CTM is responsible for 57 per cent of the collective bargaining agreements in Mexico, and it has been negotiating agreements at similar rates,

53–60 per cent, since 1994. The CROC, on average, negotiated 12 per cent of the agreements, and the CROM 5 per cent of the agreements, on average. The other confederations have increased their influence, from negotiating about 2 per cent of the agreements in 1994 to 6 per cent of the agreements in 2002. Their example was followed by the SNA and ASA, both of which increased the number of agreements negotiated from 6 to 8 per cent, and by the independent unions, which negotiated 12 per cent of the agreements in 1994 and 16 per cent in 2002 (JFCA, 2002).

Perhaps because the number of wage revisions grew at an annual rate of 12 per cent and the number of collective bargaining agreements grew at a rate of 1.8 per cent per year, the number of work stoppages announced did not increase overall even though they fluctuated significantly between 1994 and 2002 (STPS, 2002a). The registered work stoppages that did occur often took place in the economic sectors with higher employment figures such as manufacturing (25 per cent), services (24 per cent), trade (21 per cent), and construction (17 per cent), and they occurred in only three states: *Baja California, Jalisco*, and *Mexico D.F.* (INEGI, 2002g). Moreover, the monthly number of actual strikes was drastically reduced from 166 strikes in 1994 to 31 in 2002. The number of workers participating in strikes decreased by 25 per cent, and the number of working days lost per month was reduced in 2002 to 20 per cent of the corresponding number in 1994 (STPS, 2002a).

The above observations do not mean that there are no reasons or that there are fewer reasons today for work stoppages, nor do they mean that foreign firms can trust Mexican unions more. In fact, with the advent of NAFTA in 1994, both American unions and American firms have become intensely interested in knowing more about the structure and functioning of Mexican unions (Greer and Stephens, 1996). In the past, conflicts between some multinational corporations and their unions were common (Alvarez, 1991), which is why it was hoped that NAFTA could operate as a moderating factor. But NAFTA did not acquire any such role either in the establishment of norms or in the enforcement of labour policies in any of the signature parties' countries, except for the possibility it might have assisted in the interpretation of some norms, a task given to the National Administrative Office (NAO) in each country by the North American Agreement on Labour Cooperation (NAALC), an agreement accompanying NAFTA.

The NAO has provided opinions on some cases such as those of Honeywell, General Electric, and Sony, but its role has been primarily consultative (Perez-Lopez, 1995). It is probable that the NAO's role evolved in this direction because cross-border labour relations are becoming more difficult due to growing competitiveness, economic liberalization, increasing privatization of industries, and the periodic changes in each country's labour policies. Changes such as these can increase employer resistance to unionization because the ties between government and labour organizations are weakening, because the role of the government as employer is diminishing, and because of the independent unions' greater resolve to secure economic gains for their members.

VI. NEW WORK CULTURE

The results obtained in wage revisions, collective bargaining agreements, and work stoppages seem to be indicators of labour peace and the prevalence of negotiation over conflict in Mexican labour relations. The Mexican government expressly believes that such results are due to this 'new work culture' spreading through the work force (STPS, 2002b). In July 1995, the CTM, represented by its then-famous leader Fidel Velasquez, and the *Confederacion Patronal de la Republica Mexicana* (COPERMEX), represented by Carlos Abascal, signed the document *'Por una Nueva Cultura Laboral'* (For a New Work Culture), which was endorsed by the CT and the *Consejo Coordinador Empresarial* (CCE) in August 1995. A year later, government representatives, workers, and employers signed the document *'Principios de la Nueva Cultura Laboral'* (Principles of the New Work Culture) in the presence of President Ernesto Zedillo. Since then, the representatives of the three sectors have been meeting periodically in the Council for a Dialogue with the Productive Sectors to find solutions to Mexico's labour problems.

Critics of the new work culture not only believe that it has failed to produce any change, but also that it is just another thread of continuity woven into Mexico's labour policies (Bensusan, 2000; Carrillo, 2001). I do not think that this debate is of great use to readers of this article because the labor environment in Mexico is far more favourable to negotiation than it is to conflict. In fact, the number of collective bargaining agreements has increased almost as much as the number of wage revisions and contracts. The number of work stoppages and their consequences have been reduced significantly. The efficiency in some plants, particularly the *maquiladoras*, is gradually improving. However, the absorption of labour has been concentrated dangerously in three economic sectors – manufacturing, services, and trade – which pay the highest wages and make the highest contributions to social security.

More specifically, the role of the *maquiladora* industry in this panorama is multi-faceted. It has generated employment, it has improved wages and salaries in the involved industries, and it has increased exports. But in bringing about these improvements, it has also concentrated production in the manufacturing sector, a result that may not be desirable in a country of 100 million inhabitants where only 1.4 million are actually employed in manufacturing. Mexico cannot depend on NAFTA to solve its national problems. Curiously, even critics of the current situation become skeptical about NAFTA's potential when they criticize its role not so much as a driver of trade and production but as a motor of development and generator of employment in the country (Conchello, 1992; Hernandez, 2000). To think that NAFTA is the last chance for Mexico to solve its economic problems, as some believe it is, not only involves a disproportion in the problem–solution relationship, it also obscures the reality of Mexico's economic situation, which seems to involve difficulties considerably more complex than an analysis of only the country's trade and production problems would suggest. Mexico lacks a national strategy that can simultaneously use and benefit from its social and economic structures. A successful national strategy could effectively utilize NAFTA as a factor of development instead of, in the absence of a national strategy, relying on NAFTA to generate, *motu propio*, a development that would also require an accompanying miracle.

• *Director's note*: In an article published in ANALISIS LABORAL, Néstor de Buen made the next comments about the labour relations in Mexico: 'With respect to the degree of trade unionism in the country, that is a difficult question to answer. Our LFT recognizes the right of the unions to incorporate in what are inappropriately called 'collective labour contracts' clauses which prohibit entry and those concerning separation. The large corporative organizations include these clauses in their contracts with the result at unionism, by sheer force, expresses nothing. Neither are the so-called independent unions averse to eliminating the entry-prohibition clauses, which enable them to maintain the majority which they must have in order to enter on terms of equality into their collective labour agreements.

The clauses, which provide for expulsion on termination of employment, have been declared unconstitutional by the Mexican Supreme Court (2001) – in my opinion erroneously. I am one of the few who consider that they are constitutional buy that, at the same time, they are a disgrace. To quote figures, with all the risks of error involved in such estimates. I would say that about 3 1/2 million workers in Group 'A' (private enterprise) and around 2 millions in Group 'B' (public sector workers), are union members, but that this does not means sincere devotion to trade unionism but, rather, a simple requirement in order to obtain and retain a job. All the sectors have collective labour contracts and some industries have what are called 'law contracts', an ambiguous and misleading expression. But the more existence of collective agreements or contracts should not be trusted too implicitly. In its Article 386, the LFT provides that a collective contract is signed by the union representative and by the employer, without the need for confirmation by the workers. This has led to the signing of the so-called 'protection contracts' which are signed without the knowledge of the workers and which practically reproduce the legal disposition without improvements. Such contracts are legally binding because their deposition before a conciliation and arbitration board is sufficient to render them mandatory.

The problem is that when workers take courage to undertake the venture of forming a trade union and, exercising a legal right, challenge the company with a strike, it is sufficient that the authorities certify that there already exists a recognized contract in order to prevent the strike from going ahead. This would require a court action to establish title, with all the problems this would bring – among others, the ceremony of counting heads in orders to determine which union has the majority; the use of open voting, in the presence of authorities, employers' representatives and delegates of the 'mother-union', with all the possibilities of repression that this would imply.

REFERENCES

Alvarez Bejar, A. (1991), 'Economic Crisis in the Labor Movement in México', in K.J. Middlebrook (ed.), *Unions, Workers, and the State in México*. Center for U.S.-Mexican Studies, University of California, San Diego, CA.

Bensusán, Graciela (2000), *El Modelo Mexicano de Regulación Laboral.* UAM/FEC/FLACSO y P y V, México.
Carrillo, Patricia (2001), 'La libertad sindical en la agenda de los 20 compromisos', in José A. Bouzas (ed.), *Democracia Sindical.* AFL-CIO/FAT/UNAM/UAM México.
CONASAMI, Comisión Nacional de los Salarios Mínimos (2002), *Salarios Mínimos.* CONASAMI, México.
Conchello, José Ángel (1992), *El TLC: Un Callejón Sin Salida.* Grijalbo, México.
Greer, Charles y Gregory Stephens (1996), 'Employee relations for U.S. companies in Mexico', *California Management Review* Vol. 38, No. 3, pp. 121–145.
Hernández, Enrique (2000), 'Distribución del Ingreso y Pobreza en México', in Graciela Basusán y Teresa Rendón (eds.), *Trabajo y Trabajadores en el México Contemporáneo.* Porrúa, México.
IMSS (Instituto Mexicano del Seguro Social) (2002), *Informe Mensual de la Población Derechohabiente.* IMSS, México.
INEGI (Instituto Nacional de Estadística, Geografía e Informática) (2002a), *XII Censo General de Población y Vivienda, 2000.* Base de Datos y Tabulados de la Muestra Censal. INEGI, México.
INEGI (2002b), *Encuesta Nacional de Empleo Urbano.* INEGI, México.
INEGI (2002c), *Indicadores Macroeconómicos del Sector Publico, 1988–2000.* INEGI, México.
INEGI (2002d), *Encuesta Industrial Mensual.* INEGI, México.
INEGI (2002e), *Estadística de la Industria Maquiladora de Exportación.* INEGI, México.
INEGI (2002f), *Encuesta Nacional de Empleo Urbano e Indicadores de Empleo y Desempleo.* INEGI, México.
INEGI (2002g), *Estadísticas Sociodemográficas.* INEGI, México.
JFCA, Jurisdicción Federal de Conciliación y Arbitraje (2002), *Coordinación General de Funcionarios Conciliados, empresas y sindicatos.* JFCA, México.
Jimenez, Miguel (2000), 'Global change, economic restructuring and labour market issues in Mexico City', *International Journal of Manpower* Vol. 21, No. 6, pp. 464–481.
Juraidini, Jorge (1993), 'NAFTA's effects: A Mexican analysis', in A.R. Riggs y Tom Velk (ed.), *Beyond NAFTA: An Economic, Political, and Sociological Perspective.* The Fraser Institute, Vancouver, Canada.
La Botz, Dan (2000), 'Into the frying pan: Mexican labor faces its greatest crisis', *Dollars & Sense* Vol. 232 (Nov/Dec), pp. 29–30.
Malkin, Elisabeth (2000), 'Desperately seeking skilled labor', *Business Week* Vol. 3673, p. 60.
Multinational Monitor (1991), 'Labor Mexican Labor: The Old, The New and The Democratic' (January), 1–4.
Multinational Monitor (1999), 'Mexico's New Labor Rules' (May), 4.
Multinational Monitor (2000), 'Double Standards', 21, 11 (November), 24–29.
Nauman, A.K. y Mireille Hutchinson (1997), 'The Integration of Women into the Mexican Labor Force since NAFTA'. *American Behavioral Scientist* Vol. 40, No. 7 (Jun/Jul), pp. 950–957.

Perez-Lopez, J.F. (1995), 'The institutional framework of the North American agreement on labor cooperation', *U.S.–México Law Journal* Vol. 3, p. 133.

STPS, Secretaría del Trabajo y Previsión Social (2002a), *Negociaciones Colectivas de Jurisdicción Federal.* STPS, México.

STPS (2002b), *La Nueva Cultura Laboral en México.* STPS, México.

United Nations (2000), *World Investment Report 2000.* United Nations, New York.

WTO, World Trade Organization (2001), *Annual Report.* WTO, Geneva.

Zapata, Francisco (2002), 'NAFTA: Pocas Ganancias para los Trabajadores de México', *Análisis Laboral* Vol. XXVI, No. 301, pp. 47–48.

11. Labour in New Zealand

*Alan J. Geare**

I. INTRODUCTION

Since the 1890s the strength of the labour movement in New Zealand has been significantly influenced by the State – primarily through industrial relations legislation, which has had a major impact on unions, unionization rates and collective bargaining and also through general policies which help determine employment levels.

Given that this special edition is celebrating 25 years of publication, it seems appropriate to consider the major influences on New Zealand labour over the same period.

II. ARBITRATION ERA

In 1977 the Industrial Relations Act 1973 was in force. This was the last few years of the Arbitration era, which began back in 1894. During this time unionism was encouraged by the legislation. Once registered, a union enjoyed monopoly bargaining rights and protection against any other union trying to 'poach' members. From 1936 there was also compulsory union membership by law. This was replaced in 1961 with compulsory membership 'by agreement'. (If the union and employer agreed, then the collective document required union membership.) This encouragement and protection of unions meant that there were large numbers of small unions at this time. Using data from the 1981 Census (Geare, 2000, pp. 404–405) suggests that around 63.7 per cent of wage and salary earners were in unions at that time. However this protection could be removed by 'de-registration' which in effect could destroy the union. This sanction, although infrequently applied, could in law be used against any union involved in strike action.

This era was so named because, although most collective arrangements were reached by either informal collective bargaining or formalized collective bargaining ('conciliation'), compulsory arbitration of interest disputes was available through the Arbitration Court. Although it has been shown (Geare, 2000, p. 510) that less than two percentage of collective arrangements made between 1975 and 1987 involved arbitration, the few Arbitration Court rulings clearly influenced many other settlements.

---

*   Professor of Management, University of Otago, Dunedin, New Zealand.

R. Blanpain (ed.),
Labour Relations in the Asia-Pacific Countries, 123–130.
© 2004 *Kluwer Law International. Printed in Great Britain.*

Informal collective bargaining resulted in 'industrial agreements' and applied to a single employer and union. Both formalized collective bargaining and arbitration resulted in 'awards' which sometimes applied to a single employer but most often to a number of employers and a union. These awards ensured minimum conditions to workers in an industry or occupation on a regional or national basis.

A further feature of this period was that the principal legislation applied only to the private sector, with the public sector being governed by totally separate legislation and systems. There were two central union bodies – the Federation of Labour and the Combined State Services Organizations (which became the Combined State Unions in 1978).

III. COLLECTIVE BARGAINING ERA

In the mid 1980s labour in New Zealand was affected very significantly by the policies of the 1984 Labour Government which introduced major New Right reforms to the economy. While the new administration initially had no major agenda for reform.

Very quickly, however, Treasury thinking and corporate influence (in particular from the New Zealand Business Roundtable[1]) converted core personalities in the Cabinet to the view that there was no alternative to a programme – an ideology – of fundamental change. The objective was to transform the architecture of the State on the foundation of economic rationalism ... In a blitzrieg of change, financial and foreign exchange markets were liberalized, factor and product markets were largely deregulated, incentives and supports were removed, public entities were corporatized and often privatized, and substantial revamping of provision for health education and welfare took place (Kelly, 1995, pp. 334–335).

One area of reform, which did receive careful consideration and lengthy consultation not only with all major interest groups but also with the general public, was industrial relations legislation. The Labour Government introduced both the Labour Relations Act 1987 (LR Act 1987), which made significant changes to private sector industrial relations (see Geare, 1989), and the State Sector Act 1988 which brought the public and the private sectors together. The LR Act introduced the 'collective bargaining' era. Unions still received protection, having monopoly bargaining rights, but had to have a minimum size of 1,000 members (compared to the original seven) to remain registered. Union membership remained compulsory by agreement and national and regional awards remained, providing basic minimum conditions. Major changes were that interest arbitration was no longer provided by the State, and strikes and lockouts were legalized under certain conditions. Collective bargaining, free from an overarching arbitral body, was encouraged.

---

1. An informal, but very influential organization consisting primarily of Chief Executives of major organizations.

Not only did the legislation bring together the private and public sectors, but also the central union organizations merged. In October 1987 the New Zealand Council of Trade Unions (CTU) had its first conference, combining the Federation of Labour and the Combined State Unions.

These reforms did not meet the approval of the proponents of the New Right, namely the Treasury in the Government, and in the private sector the New Zealand Employers Federation (NZEF) and the New Zealand Business Roundtable (NZBR). In a series of publications the two latter organizations attacked unions and union officials (NZEF, 1990; NZBR, 1991), compulsory union-membership (NZEF, 1986, NZBR, 1989, 1991), and the system of wide coverage union–management documents (NZBR, 1989, 1990). The over-riding call was for flexibility in the labour market in order to achieve efficiency,

The 'blitzkrieg type' reforms mentioned earlier created an economic environment conducive to the changes proposed by the New Right. Public servants, who had traditionally enjoyed job security, saw their job numbers slashed from 90,000 to 50,000 between 1986 and 1990 (Kelly, 1995) and in the country as a whole unemployment rose dramatically from near zero in 1976, to 115,000 in 1987, and then to 280,000 in 1992. Notwithstanding that union membership was still compulsory, restructuring and redundancies caused a significant drop in union membership from 680,000 in 1985 down to 600,000 in 1992 (Harbridge and Hince, 1993).

Unions were weak, the workforce as a whole badly shaken and apprehensive, and so when the Employment Contracts Act 1991 (EC Act) was introduced by the new National Government opposition to the legislation was minimal and ineffective.

IV. LAISSEZ-FAIRE ERA

The EC Act was seen by most observers as clearly benefiting employers over both employees and unions. A visiting American scholar stated that many of the provisions of the Act 'match with great precision those advanced by employer associations' (Dannin, 1992, p. 3). Technically the Act was not overtly biased against unions – it simply ignored them. However, given that over the past century New Zealand legislation had supported unions, and in more recent years ensured compulsory unionism – the total revival of any support appeared anti-union and by extension anti-labour.

Unions lost all the benefits that had been afforded them by legislation in the past. They lost sole bargaining rights, and compulsory unionism was made illegal. The EC Act also allowed for individual bargaining resulting in individual employment contracts. While strikes remained legal when negotiating for a collective contract, it was illegal to strike to obtain a multi-employer contract. So while the EC Act did not explicitly make multi-employer contracts illegal, given that employers at that time favoured site agreements, the EC Act effectively brought about their demise. McAndrew (1992) has shown that just prior to the EC Act, nearly 80 per cent of union management agreements were national or regional multi-employer awards. A year later, the Department of Labour (1993) reported that only three per cent of union–management agreements were multi-employer.

The Council of Trade Unions (CTU) suffered during this period as it was seen as weak and ineffectual. In 1993 a number of traditional blue-collar unions withdrew from the CTU and formed an alternate central union body, the Trade Union Federation (TUF).

To some extent the pro-employer bias of the EC Act was lessened by Employment Court decisions which many observers felt tended to favour unions and employees. Somewhat ironically, those liberal interpretations may have reduced the probability the National Government would have amended the legislation. Over mounting criticisms, the Government could point to the Court decisions which appeared to favour employees and collective bargaining, and could then claim there was no problem with the EC Act itself. In February 1993, the CTU laid a complaint against the Government of New Zealand with the International Labour Organization (ILO) alleging the Act violated ILO conventions 87 (on Freedom of Association and Right to Organize) and 98 (Right to Organize and Collective Bargaining). The Committee on Freedom of Association of the ILO made an interim decision in March 1994 which was very critical, but submitted 'a much revised and more muted' Anderson (1996, p. 105), Final Decision in November 1994. As Anderson (1996, p. 108) rightly suggests, the change in position was 'heavily influenced by judicial decisions during the period'.

It is of course possible that the previous Government would have totally ignored strong criticism from the ILO. It certainly demonstrated a willingness to ignore muted criticism. However, it is also possible that strong criticism would have led to some amendments to the EC Act in the early 1990s. As argued in full elsewhere, Geare (2001), Court decisions made possibly in an effort to ameliorate the statute, could well be the reason why the statute was not amended until after a change of government.

V. LABOUR IN NEW ZEALAND TODAY

In 1999, there was a new Government, a Labour–Alliance coalition. In 2000, they repealed the EC Act replacing it with the Employment Relations Act 2000 (ER Act). Although this Act is more favourably disposed towards unions and collective bargaining, it left a number of the significant features of the EC Act reasonably intact, and it is reasonable to suggest that the 'Laissez-faire' era is still continuing.

According to government rhetoric, the ER Act is supposed to foster 'good faith' relations between all groups, to encourage collective bargaining and unions. However, the ER Act does not give anything like the support to unions and collective bargaining that occurred in the 'arbitration', or 'collective bargaining' eras, described above.

VI. UNIONS AND COLLECTIVE BARGAINING

The major strengths afforded unions by legislation, prior to the EC Act 1991, were:
- sole bargaining rights,
- compulsory union membership,
- collective bargaining for all employees.

These major benefits to unions have *not* been returned by the ER Act 2000. Compulsory union membership is illegal and the de-emphasis on collective bargaining introduced by the EC Act remains as the ER Act still allows employers and employees to 'choose' whether they want collective bargaining (resulting in a 'collective agreement') or individual bargaining (resulting in an 'individual agreement'). Clearly the stronger party (usually the employer) can significantly influence the 'choice' of the weaker party.

One change introduced by the ER Act is that where there is to be collective bargaining, then only a registered union can negotiate on behalf of the employees. However, there is considerable difference between the past practice of giving a registered union sole bargaining rights for all employees in that industry and region, and the current practice. For example, previously the New Zealand Printers Union would negotiate for all employees in the printing industry everywhere in New Zealand. Now if a small printing employer originally wanted to negotiate a collective agreement with his/her employees he/she may agree that they ask a national union to represent them. Alternatively, he/she may decide either to push for individual bargaining and ensure the union had nothing to do with his/her enterprise, or alternatively encourage his/her employees to register themselves as a new 'union'.

Table 1 shows that subsequent to the passing of the ER Act a large number of small unions were created. These new small unions may operate effectively as unions, but there is concern that some may be 'paper' unions only, there to sign whatever the employer puts before them.

Table 1: Trade Unions, membership and union density 1985–2000 (selected years)

	Union membership (1)	Number of unions (2)	Potential union membership		Union density	
			Total employed labour force (3)	Wage and salary earners (4)	(1) / (3) % (5)	(1) / (4) % (6)
Dec 1985	683,006	259	1,569,100	*1,287,400*	43.5	53.1
Sep 1989	684,825	112	1,457,900	*1,164,600*	47	55.7
May 1991	603,118	80	1,426,500	*1,166,200*	42.3	51.7
Dec 1991	514,325	66	1,467,500	*1,153,200*	35.1	44.6
Dec 1992	428,160	58	1,492,900	*1,165,700*	28.7	36.7
Dec 1993	409,112	67	1,545,400	*1,208,900*	26.5	33.8
Dec 1994	375,906	82	1,629,400	*1,284,900*	23.1	29.3
Dec 1995	362,200	82	1,705,200	*1,337,800*	21.2	27.1
Dec 1996	338,967	83	1,744,300	*1,389,500*	19.9	24.4

Table 1: (Continued)

	Union membership (1)	Number of unions (2)	Potential union membership		Union density	
			Total employed labour force (3)	Wage and salary earners (4)	(1)/(3) % (5)	(1)/(4) % (6)
Dec 1997	327,800	80	1,747,800	*1,404,100*	18.8	23.3
Dec 1998	306,687	83	1,735,200	*1,379,200*	17.7	22.2
Dec 1999	302,405	82	1,781,800	*1,414,000*	17	21.4
Dec 2000	318,519	134	1,818,400	*1,454,500*	17.5	21.9

Source: May *et al.* (2001).
Notes: Total employed labour force includes self-employed, employers and unpaid family workers. Column 5 figures in italics are different to those previously reported due to a revision of Labour force figures in 1997 by Statistics New Zealand.

Overall, however, most workers who are in unions, are in large unions. May *et al.* (2001) show that 77 per cent of union members belong to one of the 10 largest unions.

VII. CENTRAL UNION ORGANIZATION

The Council of Trade Unions is experiencing a slight resurgence in influence and status. As stated above, during the period of the EC Act it lost considerable status and in 1993 had a rival body. In 2000 the rival body, the Trade Union Federation merged, or rejoined the CTU. In 2000 May *et al.* (2001) report that 86 per cent of all union members are in the 26 unions affiliated with the CTU.

VIII. MULTI-EMPLOYER AGREEMENTS

The ER Act has introduced a change with respect to multi-employer documents in that it is no longer illegal for a union to strike to try to obtain such an agreement. It is likely that some multi-employer agreements will appear, but given the 10 year period when they were illegal and given the emphasis on enterprise bargaining encouraged by the previous EC Act and given that the ER Act gives no direct encouragement – they will never regain the significance that national and regional awards had in the past.

Obviously the employer organizations which argued against awards in the late 1980s and early 1990s will be pleased they are unlikely to re-emerge. However, other observers see a growing problem of non-core workers who are in a very weak position. Allan *et al.* (2001, p. 270) point out that the 'growth of a non-core segmented labour market has often resulted in greater job insecurity, lower organizational commitment, and declining work satisfaction'. In a similar vein Anderson (2001, p. 116) considers:

> The experience of the last decade and current rates of union membership clearly indicate that collective bargaining will not benefit the great majority of employees, and the reality is that many of those employees need some of the protection previously provided through the national award system ... in general such employees have made few positive gains from the ERA and that in some respects at least the deterioration in their legal position during the period of the ECA has been consolidated by the failure of the ERA to clearly reverse some of changes that occurred over the last decade.

IX. STRIKE ACTIVITY

From a peak in 1986, when there were 1,329,000 person-days of work lost, strike activity has been low in New Zealand. In the 1990s the New Zealand Employers Federation and the National Government attributed this to the EC Act 1991, ignoring the fact that strike activity had dropped markedly two years before the EC Act was introduced.

As mentioned earlier, the reason that the EC Act was able to be introduced with little effective opposition was because restructuring and redundancies had weakened the resolve of employees and unions. These same factors were the primary reason why strike action has been so low since the late 1980s.

As the economy improves, and employment picks up, employees will be more prepared to take strike action to improve wages and conditions than in the recent past when they faced possible loss of job.

X. CONCLUSION

The New Zealand economy has been improving over the last few years and employment is picking up. Unemployment levels are down to 5 per cent (but still nearly 5 per cent *higher* than the virtually zero unemployment of the 1950s–1970s). This increase in levels of demand should ameliorate to some extent the problems faced by non-core workers mentioned above. Ironically, these conditions will also result in higher strike activity amongst the relatively better off employees who will also be seeking to regain a standard of living which has dropped back for most people over the past decade or so.

REFERENCES

Allan, C., Brosnan, P., Horwitz F. and Walsh P. (2001), 'Casualisation and outsourcing: A comparative study', *New Zealand Journal of Industrial Relations* Vol. 26, No. 3, pp. 253–272.

Anderson, G. (1996), 'Collective bargaining and the law: New Zealand's employment contracts act five years on', *Australian Journal of Labor Law* Vol. 9, pp. 103–134.

Anderson, G. (2001), 'The individual and the employment relations Act', *New Zealand Journal of Industrial Relations* Vol. 26, No. 1, pp. 103–118.

Dannin, E.J. (1992), 'Labor law reform in New Zealand', *New York Law School Journal of International and Comparative Law* Vol. 13, pp. 1–39.

Geare, A.J. (1989), 'New directions in New Zealand labour legislation: The Labour Relations Act 1987', *International Labour Review* Vol. 128, No. 2, pp. 213–229.

Geare, A.J. (2000), *Industrial Relations: A General Introduction and the New Zealand System.* Fourth edn. FIRRE, Dunedin.

Geare, A.J. (2001), 'The Employment Contracts Act 1991–2000: A decade of change', *New Zealand Journal of Industrial Relations* Vol. 26, No. 3, pp. 287–306.

Harbridge, R. and Hince, K. (1993), 'Unions and union membership in New Zealand', *New Zealand Journal of Industrial Relations* Vol. 18, No. 3, pp. 352–361.

Kelly, G.M. (1995), 'Structural Change in New Zealand: Some implications for the labor market regime', *International Labor Review* Vol. 134, No. 3, pp. 333–359.

May, R., Walsh, P., Thickett, G. and Harbridge, R. (2001), 'Unions and Union Membership in New Zealand: Annual Review for 2000', *New Zealand Journal of Industrial Relations* Vol. 26, No. 3, pp. 317–328.

New Zealand Business Roundtable (1989), Review of the Operation of the Labour Relations Act in the 1988/9 Wage Round. NZBR, Wellington.

New Zealand Business Roundtable (1990), Submission to the Select Committee on the Labour Relations Amendment Bill. NZBR, Wellington.

New Zealand Business Roundtable (1991), Submission to the Select Committee on the Labour Relations Amendment Bill. NZBR, Wellington.

New Zealand Business Roundtable and New Zealand Employers' Federation (1992), A Study of the Labour/Employment Court. NZBR and NZEF, Wellington.

New Zealand Employers' Federation (1986), Response to Government Green Paper on Industrial Relations. NZEF, Wellington.

New Zealand Employers' Federation (1990), The Benefits of Bargaining Reform. NZEF, Wellington.

12. 2002: The Peruvian Labour Field

*Jorge Bernedo Alvarado**

I. AN ONEROUS HERITAGE

In order to understand fully the present, one needs a clear awareness of the past. It is especially needful to reiterate this truism at the present time. On viewing the reality of the Peruvian labour field, characterized by widespread unemployment, under-employment, low wages, increasing informality, little dialogue and no national policy, we should remember that not all of these problems can be blamed on present errors – which of course there are – but that they have origins deeply rooted in the past.

For a long time Peru has been suffering from the impact of a population 'boom'. Since before the mid-1900s we have had a population explosion, due to a more drastic reduction in the death-rate than in the birth-rate. And we shall have to wait another 20–30 years to see a period of decline in population growth and of demographic stability.

It is a fact that, in 1940, Peru's population re-attained its early sixteenth century, pre-conquest level of around 7 millions. From that time on, the population fell to little more than 2 millions before the end of the sixteenth century and started to grow slowly in the nineteenth century. But from 1940 onwards it took off exponentially, quadrupling in only six decades.

In more expressive terms, we grew only 5 millions in almost 4 centuries and more than 20 millions in 70 years.

Highest birth-rates in Peru occurred in the 10 years from 1960. Of course, this growth is not a peak which appears in one particular year, disappearing in the next. Rather, it is a kind of wave which started one generation earlier and declined the generation after. In other words, the population 'boom' occurred between 1940 and 1980 and then began to increase in time. Fifteen years later, in 1975 – precisely at the outset of Peru's economic crisis – the crest of the wave reached the labour market. In the year 2000, this wave will have its peak at 40 years of age and only in the year 2025 will its peak have left the normal working age-groups.

Likewise, since the mid-1900s, together with the changes in population and in its distribution, marked by increasing concentration in the coastal region and in cities – especially in Lima – we find, more and more clearly defined, the

---

* Researcher of Análisis Laboral, Peru.

R. Blanpain (ed.),
Labour Relations in the Asia-Pacific Countries, 131–145.
© 2004 *Kluwer Law International. Printed in Great Britain.*

pattern of economic development which has put a strangle-hold on Peru. Chances of autonomous industrial development have been snuffed out, the agrarian sector lacks a coherent policy and the services sector has expanded, based on the rapid expansion of subsistence employment in jobs of low or zero productivity. But between 1975 and 1990, Peru has its worst years as regards foreign and national investment and moreover began to service – on increasingly onerous and arbitrary terms – its foreign debt.

Also in this period, trade and financial currents were re-defined, with concentration in the industrialized countries and the progressive exclusion of the Peruvian market. This was a long period of recession and inflation in Peruvian history.

Thus the figures portray, for Peru's critical 1975–1990 period, in the first place, a striking deterioration in all the indicators and, second, that this deterioration was worse for Peru than for the other countries of the region. Finally, it can be understood that recovery – given the huge backlog – is bound to be slow and fraught with risks.

External financial pressures cannot be ignored. Foreign debt between 1975 and 1990 had grown sixfold – and fourfold in per capita terms. In that period Peru paid 26 billions of dollars in this respect, an amount greater than the debt outstanding in 1990 and greater than the sum owed at present. The export products price index fell 40 per cent, while foreign investment was almost non-existant. The accumulated adverse balance of payments exceeded 12 billion dollars, despite a favourable trade balance of some US$3.134 billions in the same period, more due to the effect of the recession in imports than to the effects of healthy growth. When we consider that the 1990s was the worst decade socially, we can, and should, criticize the inadequacy of the solutions still pending, but we should not forget the huge proportions of the challenge.

GDP growth from beginning to end of this period was zero at constant prices and fell to 70 per cent of its original value in per capita terms. If GDP had continued the trend of the 15 years prior to the crisis, it would have more than double instead of suffering this decline, while gross capital formation in its equipment and machinery component would have increased sixfold.

Total liquidity of the economy and cash in hands of the public dropped likewise to one-sixth of their former value. Of course, this reduction was induced by successive restrictive measures in order to contain inflation, a highly intensive process towards the end of the 1980s. From December 1975 to December 1990 consumer prices increased 14.8 million times, while the currency was devalued 11.5 million times. Nor were these Peru's only troubles: of unhappy memory between 1980 and the mid-1990s the country suffered the depredatory effects of the terrorism scourge which, in addition to its heavy toll of human life, inflicted very costly destruction on infrastructure, especially in the power generation, transport and production sectors, comparable to Peru's foreign debt, taking into consideration not only the destruction but also the loss of production potential, international isolation and loss of national image. It is a fact that Peru has had to face a double debt: the foreign one and that generated by the noxious effects of terrorism.

This is the scenario Peru has had to face since 1990. Given that the 1990s was the worst decade socially, one may in fact, must criticize the inadequacy of the solutions applied, but we should not overlook the enormous dimensions of the challenge. A hitherto undreamt of flow of capital would have been needed to counteract the effects of the populations 'boom' on the labour market. Who can say whether this hypothetical flow of capital would have avoided terrorism or have helped to combat it more promptly and effectively. But none of this happened rather, the contrary occurred.

II. A DEPRESSED LABOUR MARKET

The government of the 1990s and its liberal model tried to deal with the situation. A prolonged and drastic process of demand austerity permitted the control of hyperinflation, but with heavy social costs. Peru achieved reinsertion in the international financial community but, in spite of the effort made, the price of reinsertion proved very onerous. The pattern of freer trade, floating currency and sale of public assets was attractive to foreign capital, but the latter confined its interventions to key sectors for its own interest (financial, mining, telecommunications), giving rise to a novel phenomenon: investments without benefit to employment, at least in the short term.

Between 1990 and 1992 poor productive performance reflected the effects of the stabilization programme. Between 1993 and 1997, with a 'freeze' in 1996, it seemed that a period of sustained growth had begun but, from 1996 to the present time, we have had negative per capita growth, recession-due, in part, to the effect of the successive international financial crisis: Mexican, Asiatic, Brazilian, Russian, Argentine, and to the depredatory effects of the 'El Niño' phenomenon in 1998. The last 3 years too, brought a serious fiscal problem and, at the same time, a generalized political crisis which cannot be considered to have been overcome, despite the transitional administration of Don Valentín Paniagua – in fact it has been re-fuelled by the government sworn-in on 28th July 2001.

The main constant in Peru's social history in recent decades is the progressive deterioration of the quality of employment, and the growing lack of stable jobs and of acceptable wages. The negative inertia of informality and the growth of a tertiary unproductive sector, as well as the extension of 'wage underemployment' are the characteristics of a chronically depressed labour market. What is the fundamental reason for this uncontrollable depression in employment volume and wages, almost independent of production and investment?

There seem to us to be three sources of the problem: the first, which we may call structural, is the contradiction between the evolution of the trade balance and the provision of better jobs. At most, the recent depressions have been able to reduce the trade gap, but not the endemic ill of Peru's underdevelopment in which growth turns out to be adverse because it is dependent and the country's way of balancing the economy is pitted with successive sacrifices of popular well-being. With growth, Peru has had to import more than it exports and this is the seed of a future monetary and financial crisis. In the growth years of the 1990s the sale of public assets, concessions and attractive interest rate in the financial market, warded-off this crisis by momentarily attracting capital, but this situation had its limit. A production system that imports more than it exports cannot accumulate wealth – it has insufficient internal savings – and less still pay off its obligation to labour. It generates more employment abroad than well-being for Peruvian families. A second source could be identified as the neo-liberal model 'a la peruana'. Its structures of macroeconomic prices, import duties, exchange-rates, interest-rates, faxes, public charges and wages appear to have been synchoonised in order to favour the export of capital. To a great extent, this situation is the result of conditions imposed by the program of austerity and stabilization, but international experience shows that, even within these limitations, it is possible to impose more pragmatic criteria in defense of the internal market, especially as regards a better combination between exchange-rate and interest levels, to use the expression of Victor Tockman of the ILO.

The third source should be sought in our very limited progress in the relations which link the economy with social progress. There are at least four elements in these relations which transmit economic to social progress (i) A pattern of labour relations of an equitative, consensus-seeking, participatory and with wide fields of representation and negotiation. (ii) A tax policy that favours just distribution, based on taxation of income rather than of consumption. (iii) A de-centralization of expenditure and of public decisions in favour of the non-metropolitan areas. (iv) Much wider access to credit than at present, under conditions of greater transparency and equity. In all these scenarios political performance in the last decade has been very poor, with the result that the effects of the little growth achieved did not seep down to the mass of the population.

III. THE OUSTANDING CHARACTERISTICS OF THE NEW EMPLOYMENT SITUATION

At national level, unemployment in the year 2000 affected 5.4 per cent of the economically-active population, but in urban areas this figure was between 7 and 9 per cent while sub-employment fluctuated around 42–45 per cent in recent years, applying the new methods of measurement which came into force in 1995. And only in the period of recession between 1998 and March 2002, employment in companies with more than 100 employees in the city of Lima decreased 5 to 6 per cent (about 15,000 workers), even though this is the most dynamic sector in the country.

In order to get closer to a general evaluation of the labour situation, we must make mention of the most recent – and certainly the best known-problems in the employment field, which are the result of the profound crisis in the Peruvian labour market, and which have been aggravated by restrictive fiscal measures and the recent reappearance of the recession in production.

These adverse characteristics are principally:
(i) Loss of dynamism in job creation in the formal market, especially through failures or reductions in output in the manufacturing sector which is not competitive in present international conditions.

(ii) Similarly the expansion of informality and the overall decline in national productivity. At the present time, 80 per cent of the employed population is in micro-enterprises with fewer than 10 employees, or are unskilled independent workers, unpaid family workers (mainly in agriculture) or domestic employment.
(iii) Substitution of workers – we expressly avoid saying 'reduction' – in the public sector, as part of fiscal restrictions and reorganization of the State, while increasing its ability in terms of terminated and retired employees.
(iv) More recently, wider employment in agriculture. This is mainly female, but with wage levels similar to those of men.
(v) Shorter job duration, associated with faster alternation between employment and unemployment. Nine out of ten urban unemployed have had former work experience. This practice is preferable to a rigid hiring regime with widening open unemployment.
(vi) The decline of wage levels to an all time low in 1990 and their subsequent partial recovery, also the increasing differentiation of wages and of salaries. In this area, that of incomes, we also are nearer to understanding that declining wages are an alternative to more widespread unemployment, within limits, of course.

We are, thus, facing a very complex problem, to which no solution may be found in the short term, nor will there be easy answers for they will involve nation-wide approaches that are difficult to achieve, especially in today's political environment. None of which precludes a hopeful outlook or frank discussion of alternatives such as we are now attempting.

IV. WAGES AND INCOMES, DECLINE AND INEQUALITY

The last decade will go down to history as the one with the lowest incomes and wages for the Peruvian people. Nor does the new decade show any sign of a reversal of the trend. In the final analysis, it is always the people who have to shoulder the burden. As we have indicated earlier, wage behaviour in the 1990s started out from the lowest-ever lever of purchasing-power in Peru's statistical history, due to the adjustment of prices and wages with which the stabilization process began in 1990. That 'shock' was inflicted upon a population already manifestly impoverished by another turn of the economic adjustment (1988) and by the process of hyperinflation.

An orderly policy of redistribution of income, therefore, is not simply a social need or a question of justice. More than this, it is a condition for the efficiency of the whole productive system, towards which it should proceed harmoniously, systematically and with common accord, laying the basis for its sustainability in time.

Between 1991 and 1994, due as much to government policy as to 'deflation' and the limited presence of collective bargaining, overall wage income recovered to about the 1989 level. This recovery was more visible in the sectors with a greater measure of training and bargaining power, being stronger for executives and office-workers and scarcely noticeable at unskilled worker level.

From 1997 onward, the wage situation worsened, reflecting the recession in the economy. The mechanisms of collective bargaining weakened and the process of differentiation seen in the period before was accentuated. This time, executives still have margins of recovery, the office-workers experience no improvement in their purchasing power and the unskilled workers suffered a 20 per cent cut in their already insufficient remuneration. To the extent that wage-incomes were transferred to a considerable degree towards the informal and peasant sectors, the lot of these latter sectors also suffered and, in general, the market shrinks, complicating the performance of the economy above all if it is not just a brake on excessive consumption but hits people who are at subsistence level. With regard to the 'inequality process', this should exist between the major income groups: companies, wage-earners, independent workers, financial incomes, but, at the same time, for the great mass of the population, there will be greater 'equality' due to the crushing of the income pyramid, as is confirmed by recent standard-of-living polls.

This inequality between the different sectors that participate in national income, and this general depression of incomes have come to appear as critical points which impede a recovery of the market as a motor of development. For sustained production growth, especially internal, which is what generates employment most quickly, there needs to be a 'critical mass' of resources in the hands of the people. It is very likely that Peru has already descended to that critical level – half of its workers have wages less than 100 dollars a month – which could sustain growth, and we should not cease to worry about it. Such low incomes force a more intensive participation of families in the labour market, enlarging the labour supply and entering the vicious circle of a falling standard of living, for the decline in income as well as reducing the productivity of the group, also reduces the possibilities of training the work force.

An orderly policy of redistribution of incomes, therefore, not only is a social necessity and a question of justice. It is a condition for the efficiency of the whole system of production, towards which we should strive harmoniously, systematically and with common accord, forming the basis for its sustainability over time.

V. THE LABOUR MODEL IN CRISIS

Having seen this state of affairs, one turns necessarily towards the modern, private sector of the economy. That 'privileged' 10 per cent of the population which work in companies that have at least 20 employees and which account for the greater part of Peru's production, exports, credits, taxes and technological innovation. Also, this is the sector that is compelled to comply with labour regulations, a sector in which trade unions are frequently active and in which the technical and commercial changes brought by globalization are most acutely felt.

What has happened in this sector? Was it able to adapt to conditions of competition and competivity and so lead the march towards progress? Is it the standard-bearer of national unity?

We all know this was not so. This relatively modern sector has suffered contraction of its sales in an environment economically unfavourable in particular, it has been unable to give an example of collaboration based on common interests between capital and labour, or to assume a role of promoter or leader.

A new body of labour has been tried out, with negative results despite the possibly good intentions with which it was initially defended. With regard to employment by contract the rules were made more flexible, similarly those governing dismissals and reductions in personnel, seeking to favour labour mobility in order to increase productivity. With reference to collective labour relations, it was hoped to increase the autonomy of the parties to collective bargaining, do away with state intervention, favour union liberty and democratize the exercise of the right to strike.

The labour law reform, however, distorted considerably these laudable initial intentions, as we can now appreciate. Flexibilizing recruitment and dismissal procedures, although it overcame the evils of absolute job security – especially its resistance to technological change, its adverse effect on productivity and the increase in the cost of working-time – it diversified needlessly the systems of recruitment, creating for the young worker forms of labour relations without obligations and encouraging the role of intermediary performed by bogus 'labour cooperatives' and 'services' companies which, in any case, signify unnecessary costs. Moreover, the weakness of the resources for labour administration has meant that freedom to recruit and dismiss workers, in many cases, has resulted in arbitrary and unfair treatment of workers, with accompanying deleterious effects on productivity.

In the area of collective labour relations, the legislation has reached a dead point – in which the employer will not accept arbitration, nor are the workers in a position to go on strike – often leading to the paralyzation of collective bargaining. Likewise, limitative conditions and administrative intervention have come about in matters of unionism and strike action which have provoked adverse comment by the International Labour Office with respect to the legislation in force at present. The net result, according to the almost unanimous opinion of Peruvian labour relations specialists, is that the legal model has become inequitable, creating limitations to individual and collective labour rights, which impede normal development of labour relations with few benefits for employees – which was the initial intention – and still less in terms of productivity.

At the present time, as has been stated above, the private sector has lost its capacity to generate employment, although this result is due rather to the difficulties in the economic environment than to labour legislation, while the weakening of labour in the system of recruitment has significantly weakened collective defense.

Trade union organization in Peru now consists formally of four trade union centers, which participate in the National Labour Council, and which represent the traditional international alignments (the CGTP Marxist; the CNT social democratics; the CATP Christian Social and the CTP Aprista, linked to the Social Democratic movement). The degree of unionism is very limited, covering only 6–7 per cent of the potential union population (some 60,000 workers in firms with 20 or more workers); the number of cases of collective agreements does not reach 500 per year, in a context of decentralized collective bargaining. Thus, trade unionism in Peru has reached its lowest historical level, with a higher incidence of cancelation of union memberships than of new enrolments. Likewise, in collective bargaining, federative negotiation has disappeared, and the number of agreements has also declined drastically, to levels comparable with those of several decades ago, possibly around the 1960s. The incidence of strike actions also is very low, at insignificant levels and at the bottom end of the statistical series, not so much to a desirable atmosphere of peace on the labour front as to a lack of the trade unions' inability to defend themselves in the companies. The democratization in the political scene since the year 2000 has revived union protest, but the same capital laws concerning individual and collective rights remain in force. The characteristics of the present labour situation unfavourable to the workers are, in large measure, an onerous heritage of the past. But a tradition of state intervention, internal conflicts within companies, 'politization' of labour relations and antagonism between capital and labour, has been laid to rest.

In its place, however, we have yet to see established an industrial relations system based upon identification of common interests, a horizontal plane of administration or participation in or development of production and productivity targets. Rather, there has been a swing of the pendulum towards another, equally traditional position of labour relation based on unfairness and abuse, with adverse effects on the possibility of creating social progress and, particularly, of directing the production system towards competitiveness based on modern concepts.

Therefore, there is an urgent need for a re-formulation of labour relations in the 'relatively modern' production sector. This re-formulation should restore the original concept of greater flexibility in systems of recruitment, autonomy of the negotiating parties and democratization of the exercise of trade union activities. However, this should be done with sincere respect for the total freedom of the labour market – avoiding the 'threat' of job stability as a counterpart to hiring by means of 'dodges' or of intermediary action – and restoring the exercise of collective rights in a framework of productivity promotion within the company.

Of course, this objective cannot be achieved simply by modernizing the legal structure. Its definitive success rests rather on the possibility of a very significant change of attitude on the part of the actors in labour relations. Both employers and workers, and their representative bodies, will really have to accept a set of responsibilities related to improvement in the quantity and quality of production and a juster distribution of the benefits of employment and of the risks of investments.

Likewise, the state should significantly reinforce labour administration so as to operate a system of prevention and of training in development of labour relations based on mutual recognition and respect, the exercise of dialogue, transparency and the security of an equitable and independent system for the solution of individual and collective disputes in the area of labour law. All this is yet to be achieved, but it can be done. There are very positive signs of an increase in company responsibility and in employer's understanding of the merits of a system of shared benefits and dialogue. The traditional system, which oscillated between paternalism and conflict, is being replaced by a more exacting view, limited on the one hand by the failure of production and on the other by its success in the difficult scenario of present competition, which calls for a set of capabilities, both of workers and of employers within the productive units. More recently, the creation of the National Labour Council – a nation-wide labour forum for tripartite discussion – has created an encouraging possibility of interchange and process.

VI. PROTECTION AND SOCIAL SECURITY

Nevertheless, it will also be realized that overall social well-being is not limited to the world of those few private sector companies that operate in the realm of labour legislation, despite their significant importance for the formal economy – and the economy in general.

Both for the creation of a new system of labour relations, and for the extension of its benefits to the population at large, there still remains pending the possibility of developing a system of extended social protection – naturally, within the measure of national possibilities.

In the area of social security, we have had an important change, with the introduction, in 1993, of the Private Pensions System (SPP). This system now has 2.8 million members (of which it quotes approximately one half), however, around a million workers have stayed in the Public Pensions System, at present administered by the Previsional Normalization Office (ONP). With the private pension system, Peru is seeking to exploit the possibility of establishing a private administration of pension funds – but, above all, the association of the use of these funds with the behaviour of individual savings and the profitability of the national capital market.

The present situation in the labour market evidently works against the improvement of the social security systems, above all, against the extension of their coverage and risks, especially in the field of pensions, despite the fact that demands tend to increase very significantly with the 'ageing' of the population.

As we know, this new approach to pensions – inspired by the Chilean experience initiated in 1981, but with very significant differences as regards the economic environment, the State's responsibilities for contributions previously received, and mechanisms for protecting pension funds – is still too new to be judged, in the sense of proven efficiency in the long run, when a significant proportion of affiliated workers are receiving their pensions under the new provisions.

This does not mean that one should not point out risks and limitations in the existing SPP. In the decisive terrain of financing, impelled by the anxiety to make the SPP 'attractive' compared with its whittled-down public competitor, the IPSS – now, for these purposes, the ONP – the contributions – 100 per cent by the worker – have been reduced to 8 per cent, the lowest figure in the region. If we compare this low contribution with the, also low, profitability of the system in the last few years – which no doubt finds its explanation in the financial crisis, although we should not consider these to be exceptional – with the instability of the labour market, low wages and the State's diminished recognition of the contributions of the former IPSS, one may foresee if there are no significant changes in the near future, that the system will yield inadequate pensions for its present members, and even will be unable to compete with the public system, if the latter succeeds in recovering its funds or, at least, avoid they being squandered by the State as in the past. The SPP is not to blame for the behaviour of the market, but it will be responsible for fixing the contribution rate, for the efficiency of collection, for the transparency and competence of the investments and, above all, for the existence of suitable mechanisms for protecting the accumulated funds of the pensioners. The method of calculating the compensation of the funds for significant variations in the market, has, however, been much relaxed by the legislation, creating a serious risk of extreme weakening of the system, a risk that does not appear to have been correctly measured.

Health is the area of social policy with the most urgent needs. There have been advances in terms of coverage, both through the social security system – of which the capacity for attention to new demands should be evaluated technically – and in the public health system. But, given the enormous deficits there is evidently a long road to travel.

The presence of the SPP and its present pre-eminence over the public system, stem in great measure from the squandering of the funds of the latter, resulting in its virtual insolvency at the close of the 1980s. The public system in turn, which has under its case almost all the pensions, deprived of funds and hard-pressed by fiscal urgencies, in practice abandoned its charge and proceeded to award absurdly low pensions, which, to a large degree, have been maintained or have risen slowly, sustained by a contribution rate of 13 per cent of wages. In fairness it should be mentioned that the ONP's pension-fund is in recovery; it has a larger contribution rate (13 per cent against SPP's 8 per cent) and has been able to order a twice-yearly payment of about US$100 to its pensioners. Known by the acronym FONAHPU, this money comes from the capitalization of a fund obtained from State enterprises. This payment, despite its small proportion, is significant for those at the bottom end of the pensioner class and evidently in a state of extreme poverty.

On the other hand, the ONP has shown little initiative – even we might say disinterest in face of the problem of the minute pensions it pays. For instance, a suggestion by the People's Defense Office (Ombudsman) in 1998, with funding provided, would have improved considerably the situation of the recipients of the lowest pensions and in the highest age brackets, but the ONP did nothing about it, in spite of its significant social impact.

The present situation in the labour market evidently conspires against any improvement in the social security systems – above all, against their extension of life and risks cover especially in the field of pensions, despite the fact that demands tend to increase very noticeably with the 'ageing' of the population. In truth, the Third Age will grow significantly while the mass contributions will shrink, creating another new area of social concern.

The field with the most urgent problems in social policy is, without doubt, that of health. In this area there have been some advances with regard to cover, both through the social security system, whose capacity to meet the growing demand needs a technical evaluation and in the public health system. However, given the enormous backlog, it is evident that there is a long way to go.

In a wider view, there should be a review of the whole body of social policy, both in clearly-defined sectors, such as education, justice, the decentralization of public expenditure, and from an integral viewpoint. At present, basic social policies are based on broad assistance programmes, or on the provision of small infrastructure projects, not of a long-lasting nature. In future, it should be rooted in stable economic policies designed to widen the market economy while securing that social responsibilities are assumed by enterprises and by State, mainly by expanding social security and by significantly improving policies related to public expenditure.

It should be abundantly clear that, in the present national situation and despite the difficulties, a satisfactory social protection programme – not centralized, State-run or assistance-oriented, but based on the innate economic dynamism and in the joint acceptance of a share-social responsibility, is a prime necessity for re-establishing an adequate system of labour relations. Both interact and cross-feed, but the important thing is that, in the future, they should do so on the basis of modernization and a new approach.

The main objective, rooted in international experience and in our present situation, is to resolve the basic, structural problem of our economy, while improving levels of employment.

VII. A NEW LABOUR MARKET AND THE CHALLENGES OF COMPETITIVENESS

There are no magic wands for solving the serious problems of our labour situation. But, contrary to the general opinion we have formed, in this field there does exist a promising body of opinion concerning the most elementary needs and priorities in order to achieve progress, as we shall now see.

The principal guiding objective, in the light of international experience and our own situation, is to resolve the basic structural problem of our economy, while improving levels of employment. In other words, we must define a development model which makes us more exporters than importers, while improving employment levels and incomes in the poorest segments of the population. Neither protectionism, nor exporting raw materials, nor an indiscriminate 'open door' policy have achieved this higher aim. We must therefore build our own exporting model, with a well-administered dose of defense for the internal market, increase of national value-added and, above all, a very aggressive concertation of national effort in order to win foreign markets.

Peru has already detected abundant opportunities for exploiting resources in nearly all sectors of the economy, apart from its manifest condition of mineral exporter. Peru has nearly all the energy resources, but a noticeable decline in oil production, especially of high density crude, has made the country a net oil importer. At the same time Peru has a natural gas deposit at Camisea, whose reserves are equivalent to 20 times the present availability of energy in the country, besides new important gas deposits which could be but in production if a stable energy policy were defined which is one of the major demands of Peru's entrepreneurs. The mining and fisheries sectors also have substantial potential: in both these sectors Peru's resources are recognized worldwide.

In both cases there is an insistent demand for increased value-added – both in mineral refining and in fish-processing (which accounts for 90 per cent of total fish production) – this will help towards satisfying the need for employment, especially in the negotiation of concessions and of exploitation contracts.

The export solution to the agrarian problem will also be a fundamental past of the solution of unemployment and poverty in Peru: it would tend to de-centralize production, modernize agriculture and bring income to the poorest areas, which in turn, through migration, cause and aggravate urban overpopulation.

Undoubtedly the sector that attracts most attention is agriculture, and rightly so. First, because it will help resolve the adverse trade balance. On one hand, it would reduce imports since at least half our food is imported, despite the fact that 85% of our agricultural production goes into the home market. In the second place, because the number and sources of products which are opening up promising markets or which are potentially exportable, are multiplying daily.

To name a few products with proven possibilities: quality timber in Piura, asparagus in the coast, limes, mangos, flowers and medicinal plants from Selva and Sierra, as well as the recovery of our former production of sugar and cotton, which at present are imported. In the South, white onions, asparagus, spices, fruits (chirimoya, avocado, lucuma, grapes and their products), cereals, roots, pulses (especially the Andean species which are rich in proteins), quinua tarwi (lupinus sp.), maca and Urubamba maize. In the Selva, beside logging for lumber, there is increasing exploitation of palmito, Brazil nut, medical essences, tropical fruits and exotic flowers, as well as managed plant and animal species. The central Sierra, a traditionally poor area, has entered export markets with cochinilla, spices and flowers, andean cereals, artichokes, from the Mantaro Valley, Andean potato of very high quality (black and yellow).

Agricultural exports can also be a fundamental part of the solution to the employment problem and of poverty in Peru: it will have a de-centralizing effect on production, modernizing the countryside and bringing income to the poorest areas, which, for their part, are source areas for the migration which causes urban overcrowding. With the interior of the country immersed in the process of exporting we should have a cure for many ills, especially if this is joined to a policy expressly aimed at generating value-added in agro-industries and related sectors such as agriculture and the production of non-traditional meats, such as those of the Andean camelids, and the most recent addition, the ostrich. Still, surrounded by so many rich opportunities Peru still does not export. Just as in any branch of production, the central problem is not producing, which depends on our own efforts and is centered on cost reduction without loss of quality, but in being able to *sell*. Exporting needs a complex of port and transport infrastructure, phytosanitary services, market information, packaging, the development of which in Peru is slower than in competitor countries, including those in the Andean region, coverting Peru into a net importer. If there are no explicit, short-term policies in these areas, we shall miss our chance. Worse still, we shall be marching, almost certainly, to our own national debacle, once the balance of payments can no longer be set right by privatizations and speculative investments, while we maintain the depressive trend in our terms of trade in international trade.

These are not the only opportunities and employment potential which it is customary to quote. In the internal market, sectors like construction, or the modernization of commercial, social and entrepreneurial services, should be sources of renovation of employment. Tourism, an activity with a sustained upsurge in the world with the concentration of capital in the industrialized countries, has demand potential at present bigger than our capacity to cater for it – even if no great effort were made to attract visitors. Finally, even industry, especially for internal consumption, still has possibilities for expansion within the framework of suitable policies.

Behind the great objective of export-oriented, employment-generating development, there should be aligned the macroeconomic policy, and internal policy in general. This is the area in which generally there are the most serious confrontations, because there the interests of the different segments of production come to light. Changes in tariffs, exchange or interest rates, wages or public charges, signify costs for some and gains for others, at least in the short terms, before the external dynamics have been stabilized and before a growth structure has been established which does not de-finance the country. This policy level is undoubtedly where there will be the greatest need of national agreement, and the definition of programme for administering these reforms in order that they should not imply additional costs due to the suddenness of the changes, and the technical skill for defining targets and procedures. At the most immediate level, there is a mass of administrative measures related to employment, which a good administration of labour should be able to resolve.

Public employment programmes of an emergency nature through the medium of infrastructure, programmes directed to specific groups, development of labour education and training, temporary fiscal incentive policies in cases which merit them, credit policies and policies of credit and support for micro enterprises should be part of routine and should sustain a programme of active policies in the labour market.

VIII. SOCIAL DIALOGUE, DEMOCRACY AND A NEW LABOUR MODEL

We have seen from the foregoing that it is possible to achieve development with special emphasis on the problems of employment and wages. On the other hand, it is clear that the main condition for the viability of such a development model is the possibility of a permanent environment of national unity, broad dialogue and integration of interests between the social actors.

Likewise, it will have been noted from the ideas put forward that the re-formulation of the pattern of labour relations in Peru cannot be achieved without an understanding of its structural weakness; at present, the most important enterprises in Peru are islands almost totally cut off from the surrounding sea which is the subsistence economy. Without economic policies favourable to the population and without explicit proposals for social protection and redistribution, there is not much sense in discussing *in vacuo* modern labour relations pattern in the enterprises. In today's conditions fraught with difficulties for democratic development and with weakened institutions, this is a challenge which poses great difficulties and great responsibilities. This is specially true when one remembers that Peru's history is one of confrontation, destructuring, clashes between group interests, instability, demagogy and little opening for dialogue. At this juncture, we are at the difficult confluence of positive aims clearly visible, thanks to the availability of more information and the examples of international experience but, at the same time, in spite of the manifest possibilities, prevented from achieving these objectives by a deadlock of conflicting interest. This stranglehold on development is found, not only in the field of political differences between government and opposition and within them, but that they form an integral part of Peru's social fabric.

This is what underlines the need for a profound labour reform, as the spearhead of the effort to put in operation a new awareness of national unity and consensus. Such a project will be unfeasible if not based upon a new relationship among the social actors at enterprise level in the social 'production cells' which also are those that bear the heaviest economic burden in the nation.

As will have been seen, it is not only a matter of making new labour laws seeking an equilibrium of forces, the transparency and modernization of processes and democratic practices with suitable systems of prevision and control. The essence of any new model of labour relations lies in the alteration of the production and management structures within the enterprise. Pioneer actions in regard to social responsibility, quality culture, creation of a company-culture, production commitments and job stability, are as yet insufficient indices of this possibility, but not for that reason insignificant. It is on this basis that new patterns of labour legislation of an autonomous nature can operate, which become indispensable, but which cannot function without changes in the scenario and in the actors. Trade democracy, autonomy of parties in collective bargaining and institutional dialogue, job mobility with social protection, integration of interests and worker participation are dead letters if not accompanied by a change in organization and conduct within the enterprise. Our lagging, but hard-working modern production sector bears on its forehead the passport to new highways in our history, even in these difficult times. In these present political juncture, the challenge is greater for the lack of decisive state leadership. The initiatives will have to come from employers and employees. Despite the scarcity – one might say, the absence – of prior actions in this direction, never has the need for such action been so urgent.

There is, indeed little to find out concerning the road to be followed. What matters now is a united, dedicated effort to go forward along the road already mapped out.

13. The Labour Relations System of the United States

Efrén Córdova*

The labour relations system of the United States was born in the late 1930s when the country was still undergoing the effects of the great economic crisis, which had begun in 1929. Its appearance changed the nation's social panorama and contributed to its recovery by strengthening the income of the working population. It also signaled the recognition of the unions as full actors of the industrial relations system.

This system was the work of the Democratic Party with the great Roosveltian trilogy of the Wagner Act (National Labour Relations Act), the Fair Labour Standards Act and the Social Security Act. Its initial aim was to break the existing legislative inertia and hostility toward trade union organizations. In the course of 3 years (1935–1938) this legislation met with considerable success – by regulating various aspects – of labour relations and working conditions and setting the foundation of a social security system that now grants compensation to 45 million people. Other measures on employment creation, professional training, non-discrimination and the important law on Occupational Safety and Health (OSHA) were later promulgated. However, the legislative framework was never completed which is the reason why I have maintained on other occasions, that the system was born flexible and with big gaps that are still noticeable in its legislation.

Viewed in its historical context and despite its deficiencies, labour legislation signified a big step forward from the attitude of underestimation of trade unions, characteristic of the early stages of labour relations. Large-scale industry had already been born and the first trade unions had made their appearance in the nineteenth century when courts of justice after the *Philadelphia Cordwainers'* case (1806) declared that those organizations were criminal conspiracies whose aim was to unlawfully alter the price of products. Although that doctrine was rejected in the *Commonwealth* v. *Hunt* case in 1842, the courts soon found other means to restrict union action. One of them consisted in applying the Sherman Anti Trust Act to trade unions despite the fact that this law had clearly been conceived for corporations. Another was the wide latitude given to employers to use injunctions against strikes and related means of industrial action. The performance of US judges regarding labor matters can only be considered deplorable.

---

*   Professor at the International La Florida University, USA, Former ILO Officer.

R. Blanpain (ed.),
Labour Relations in the Asia-Pacific Countries, 147–152.
© 2004 *Kluwer Law International. Printed in Great Britain.*

Faced with the opposition of the employers and the antagonism of judges, many workers resorted to direct action. The second half of the nineteenth century is marked by violent incidents that reached their peak with the Molly Maguires' and the bloody confrontations of the Homestead and Pullman strikes. On the occasion of the sadly-famous Hay Market episode, that gave rise to the First of May celebration, eight workers, mostly German anarchists, were unjustly condemned to death for killing seven policemen (four of them were executed, one committed suicide and three were pardoned by the Governor of Illinois).

It was really surprising that in the midst of so many upheavals, Samuel Gompers opted for business unionism and founded the American Federation of Labour (AFL) in 1886 the new organization accomplished the feat of promoting collective bargaining and advancing a new type of pragmatic unionism. When summoned by Congress to explain the philosophy of his movement, Gompers explained it in one word: 'More'. During the 1930s the organization showing the greatest militancy was the Congress of Industrial Organizations (CIO) which favoured unionism at enterprise or industry level rather than by trades as in the AFL. In 1955, the two organizations merged.

Judges' partiality in favour of businessmen had its last manifestation in the annulment of the National Industrial Recovery Act and doubts on the validity of the Wagner Act. It was only due to Roosevelt's pressure that the Supreme Court ruled that the Wagner Act did not contravene the Constitution since it was covered by the Congress' power to rule interstate trade. This acceptance of federal labour legislation does not, however, alter the fact that it still lacks a constitutional basis. Unlike Canada state labour legislation is of relatively minor significance in the United States.

I. THE ROLE OF COLLECTIVE BARGAINING

The regulations in the Wagner Act guaranteed workers the three basic rights of collective labour relations: the rights to establish or join a trade union of collective bargaining and of concerted action including the right to strike, the use of pickets and certain kinds of boycotts. The system was structured on the basis of a few novel notions: exclusive workers representation by the majority union, the appropriate unit for collective bargaining, the duty to bargain in good faith, a system of unfaith labour practices and grievance arbitration. Unfair labour practices were applicable at first only against employers and later extended to unions under the Taft–Hartley Act (1946).

Encouraged by the benefits of the new climate of labour relations, there was a vertiginous growth of unionism and a significant expansion of collective bargaining. With the exception of some strongholds of paternalism or of obstinate anti-unionism, nearly all the large enterprises now accept involvement in the process of discussing collective agreements and these became increasingly voluminous and rich in benefits.

New rights for workers (such as those derived from seniority) and for unions (such as the check off of union dues) were adopted. New types of leaves appeared, payments provided by law were increased and some big gaps in the legislation were filled such as the right to paid holidays, maternity leave, family and sick leave (recently established by law, but without pay) and above all, protection against unfair, arbitrary dismissal.

The principle of 'termination at will' still holds in the United States, allowing the employers to terminate the labour relation at his discretion unless there is a collective agreement in force restricting this right. If there is no such agreement, the only cases in which the law protects the workers are those related to anti-union practices or cases of discrimination. After the latter were forbidden by the Civil Rights Act in 1964 and were later covered by other laws, the anti-discriminatory policy has meant a great protection for racial minorities, women, the disabled and the elderly (up to 70 years).

The impact of collective bargaining is felt in almost all aspects of labour relations. For example, in regard to working hours, while the law stipulates a 40 h working week and 25 per cent overtime for extra hours, in practice the weekly working hour average is 39.2 h and overtime payments are no less than 50 per cent. In many cases it reaches 100 per cent or more.

Regarding remuneration, while the minimum wage is now $ 5.15 an hour, a number of states and counties have passed living wage laws that raise minimum pay for many. The average wage per working hour in the year 2002 was:

Metal Industry	$ 18.23
Manufacturing	$ 15.35
Construction	$ 17.23
Coal Industry	$ 19.51
Health Services	$ 14.20
Land Transport (teamster)	$ 22.60

It should be noted, however, that one of the most serious potential problems in the American labour scene is the enormous and worrying gap existing between the very high salaries and benefits received by top executives in big companies and the average earnings of employees. It is the most striking difference in the world: averaging around 350–351.

Collective bargaining should also be credited with the generalization of grievances committees made up, in equal number of management and union representatives and in charge of settling labour disputes in the company. Claims are settled rapidly and free of charge, and in case of disagreement, private arbitration is accepted by the parties. Conflicts usually solved in this way are generally related to the interpretation or application of legal provisions or clauses of agreements and in that sense the committees replace labour tribunals in the United States.

Responsibility for attempting to settle interest disputes pertains to the Federal Conciliation and Arbitration Service and grievances over unfair practices are handled by the National Labour Relations Board. The efficacy of these organizations is in part responsible, for the decline in the frequency and incidence of strikes in the last few years. The main reason, however, is the non-ideological nature of the labour movement as well as the growth of an economy that has raised large sectors of the proletariat to a middle class status. Unlike Spain, France or Italy, there is not at present a strike culture in the United States. Labour agreements and the process of collective bargaining are the real axis of American labour relations. They represent a kind of workplace law that make up for legislative deficiencies and also provide means for the peaceful settlement of disputes.

The problem, however is the limited coverage offered to the working class. In order to have an agreement there must be a union, and it is clear that this situation does not exist in all work places. Only 13.5 per cent of the work force is at present affiliated to unions and although agreements cover all personnel in enterprises (unionized or not), with the only conditions that said organization be the most representative, it is probable that the universe protected by collective agreements does not exceed 20–22 per cent of the working population.

Another collective bargaining problem is its effect on the social dialogue especially because it generally takes place at the enterprise level. Such fragmented contacts among social actors along with the adhesion to the principle of free competition hamper the vision of the great macro-economic problems and even discourage interest in tackling them. Social dialogue at national level takes place only occasionally and imperfectly. Fortunately neither unemployment nor inflation have reached critical dimensions over the last two decades.

II. CAUSES FOR THE DECLINE OF TRADE UNIONISM

What is the reason for the decline of labour unions that 50 years ago affiliated more than 30 per cent of the working force and today hardly reach 14 per cent? There is no doubt it is largely due to the change that has taken place in the composition of the labour force.

The number of workers in industry has decreased. Factories where previously unionism found its natural habitat have disappeared or are sprinkled with a parallel increase in the number of workers in the service sector (less favourable to the development of solidarity ties, which are the essence of unionism). The decline has not been due to union leaders' negligence but to diminished receptivity on the part of members. Four years ago, when John Sweeny won the AFL-CIO elections, he did so supported by great activists' campaign that promised sustained increases in membership.

Efforts were made and some increase in the services areas was accomplished as well as among immigrants, but great number of workers remained indifferent and did not join unions. The United States is now living in a post-industrial society where the trade union message does not have the same appeal as before. In a globalized economy competition also tends to erode large segments of industry such as auto manufacturing and the steel industry. Is it not significant that Detroit, which 40 years ago had 2 million inhabitants, now has fewer than one million?

Paradoxically, and looking to the future, it is in the public service where the best opportunity for consolidation and expansion of unionism are found.

Public servants who before were placed outside the area of labour relations and unionism are now those who with more enthusiasm nurture its ranks. Both the Postal Reorganization Act (1970) and the Civil Service Reform Act (1978) include chapters on the right to bargain collectively. Neither postal workers nor federal employees are permitted to strike but government employees in some states are allowed to go on strike. At the federal level strikes are still regarded as a crime and are grounds for immediate dismissal. This fact was put to the test during the Reagan administration when thousands of air traffic controllers on strike were dismissed.

III. DIVERSIFICATION OF EMPLOYMENT MODES

Another factor that contributes to explain the decline of unionism and which is typical of the present labour scene is the diversification of employment modalities. There never existed in the United States the legal presumption that regular labour contracts had to be, for an indefinite period. This fact facilitated flexibility in the hiring of workers. Added to the complex requirements of the economy, this trend encouraged the proliferation of atypical employment modes.

Three of these new modes of employment have become especially important: part time, temporary and homework employment. One out of five workers is now engaged in part time employment due to his personal preferences, familiar convenience, or because it was the only available offer. In such situation it was difficult to tighten ties of solidarity and even to identify with a particular group when working less than 20 h a week and combining in some cases two part time jobs. The 'Temps' sent to work for a few months in a company and then to a totally different one, feel the same disaffection, and their numbers are rapidly growing. It was also inevitable, that advances in data processing and the popularization of computers opened new horizons for homework and made possible service away from head offices.

On the other hand, two new situations coexist in the United States, alongside the traditional classification of workers as 'blue collar' and 'white collar' workers. At the top of the executive hierarchy are privileged exponents of high technology for whom a union's message has little meaning. In the lower social strata and particularly among immigrants, an informal sector is emerging in which workers are abandoned to their own devices as in other parts of the world.

IV. THE PRESENT ECONOMIC PICTURE

During almost all the period 1990–2000, the country enjoyed a cycle of prosperity in which the unemployment rate was almost near full employment (4 per cent or less). Towards the middle of 2001 the first signs of recession began to be felt, aggravated by the events of September 11th. In the first quarter of 2002, unemployment rose to 5.8 per cent. The United States government extended the term of the right to draw unemployment compensation and took several fiscal measures intended to vigorize the economy. To some extent the incentives achieved the desired effect but in the third quarter of 2002, the economy had not yet fully recovered. As a result concessionary bargaining (wage and beneficients) is now making a comeback.

The unemployment problem is linked to the large number of illegal immigrants (between 7 and 8 millions) living in the United States. In 1986 it became illegal to employ these persons, but the employers were reluctant to assume the responsibility for refusing to hire 'undocumented' immigrants. Undocumented workers contribute to social security but do not enjoy its benefits, for the law requires 10 years' contribution and citizenship or legal residence. In the agricultural sector, there is an abundance of migrant workers from Mexico and the Caribbean. The economic slow-down brought a sharp increase in the number of insolvencies, while the pressures of globalization made for more mergers. Both these phenomena have produced disproportionately large number of dismissals. The tendency of American capitalists to order massive stand-off as soon as their balances go into the red can be correlated with their other obsession – for making short-term profits.

The working class has suffered the effects of the tendency. One would be tempted to think that Marx was right when he referred to the inexorable law of capital concentration and its catastrophic consequences. What the fathers of Communism could not foresee was the market system's capacity of economic regeneration. The big enterprises generate complementary enterprises and their accidental bankruptcy or disappearance for other motives is made up for by the proliferation of middle-sized and small enterprises. What the United State labour system needs is for this economic vigor to be accompanied by greater social progress. There is a need to bring coherence to labour law, of which the first and most promising instrument, the Wagner Act was later impaired in its application by the Taft–Hartley and Landrum Griffin acts. Since it is unlikely that American Labour Law will be codified or will acquire constitutional rank, efforts should be made to fill the major gaps in the legislation which affect the employees' rights. Meanwhile it is only thanks to sophisticated labour administration that workplace relations and conditions are kept within acceptable levels that characterize the United States economy.

14. Industrial Relations in ASEAN
A Comparative Analysis*

Balakrishnan Parasuraman†

I. INTRODUCTION

National industrial relations system is the product of interaction between actors and environments. There are three main actors in industrial relations: labour, management and government (Balakrishnan, 1998, 2001). These actors are influenced by four major environmental sub-systems (economic, legal, political and socio-cultural) (Sharma, 1996). All four environments contribute to the shaping of the emerging patterns of industrial relations system, but the economic environment plays a predominant role.

The trust of these countries at different stages of structural transformation generates different requirements for capital accumulations. Policies on capital accumulation affects patterns of labour orientation and evolving strategies of industrial relations, employing the stage structural transformation and the capital accumulating requirement as distinguishing criteria. Three separate patterns of labour orientation and industrial relations strategies have been identified. These three patterns are known as political-paternalistic, repressive-confrontative and accommodative-co-operative, in least-semi and newly industrialized countries.

Therefore, this chapter will discuss the comparative analysis of industrial relations in the member's countries of the association of the Southeast Asian Nation (ASEAN). This comparative analysis will provide similarities, differences and patterns on ASEAN industrial relations. The focus of study concentrates only on Malaysia, Thailand, Philippines, Indonesia and Singapore.

II. SIMILARITIES

Among three major institutional forces of workers, employers and government, the third force plays a central role in ASEAN industrial relations systems. It is

---

*   Indonesia, Malaysia, Philippines, Singapore and Thailand.
†   Program of Industrial Relations, Social Science School (UNB), Kota Kinabalu, Sabah East, Malaysia.

R. Blanpain (ed.),
Labour Relations in the Asia-Pacific Countries, 153–159.
© 2004 *Kluwer Law International. Printed in Great Britain.*

because the so-called Asian model of industrialization is based on the interaction between government guidance and market competition where companies compete vigorously to meet the goal set by government (Fallow, 1995, p. 445). Extending this argument to industrial relations, one could state that both unions and employers are required to conduct their relations in line with industrialization strategies of the government.

The dominant approach to industrial relations in ASEAN is collective bargaining complemented by compulsory arbitration. However, collective bargaining cannot be effectively participated in the absence of a comprehensive legal framework.

Now the main concern of the ASEAN government has been to maintain stable and harmonious industrial relations system. At the heart of this remains the search for a viable mechanism, which is capable of promptly resolving and settling labour disputes. To achieve this goal the government has passed labour legislation creating mechanism for dispute settlement, of which compulsory arbitration is the dominant mode.

The ASEAN region belongs to the 'last frontier of fast growth'. Catching up with the industrialized world is a major national economic policy; thus boosting labour productivity has high priority with the ASEAN governments. In practice to achieve this goal includes encouraging worker participation, for example, the workers committees at the enterprise level in Singapore and the Labour–Management Co-operation Committees in Philippines. It is notable in this regard that ASEAN has been attempting to emulate the Japanese experience by adopting measures such as joint labour–management consultation and quality circles (Balakrishnan, 2000).

In summary, there are significant areas of industrial relations where close similarities exist. The question that arises is whether there will be eventual convergence of the various industrial relations systems in the ASEAN region? It is so necessary first to consider the major differences between them.

III. DIFFERENCES

Although government is at the centre of industrial relations in ASEAN, variations in its ability to direct and control labour organization exist. Indicative of this is the pattern of the relationship between the government and labour movement in each country. In Indonesia, labour and government collaborate in that the Serikat Pekerja Seleruh Indonesia (SPSI) functions almost as an organ of the government. The government has become more repressive whenever threats to its ability to control appeared. The case of Marsinah and the role of local police in 1993 are one of many examples pointing out this development. In Thailand, while there is close contact between the Free Labour Congress and the Internal Security Operations Command (ISOC), other prominent labour unions have maintained some distance from the government. This pattern is intensified in the case of the Philippines.

Although the Philippines Trade Union Congress (PTUC) is often called the official trade union congress, other trade union strongly oppose the government such as the Kilusang Mayu Uno. In Malaysia, the relationship between the Malaysian Trade Union Congress (MTUC) and the government are clearly conflictual, illustrated by the cold war, which took place between them in the course of amending the Industrial Relations Act in the 1980s. With the coming of the Malaysian Labour Organization (MLO), this tension has been further exacerbated. The government saw it fit to promote in-house unionism in the private sector to promote Japanese-style labour–management relations. In fact, the number of in-house unions in the private sector in 1984 was only 43. This increased to 85 by 1988, accounting for 38.2 per cent of the total in-house union in Malaysia (Arudosthy and Littler, 1993; Kuruvilla, 1995). The government has also made it sure that trade unions do not penetrate the electronics industry, the flagship sector for export-oriented industrialization in Malaysia. As Kuruvilla and Arudhsothy (1995) indicated, the government of Malaysia has been pursuing a repressive industrial relations policy. A heavy dependence on foreign direct investment and an ambitious State-led Plan to make Malaysia graduate to become a developed country by the year 2020 have become the underlying forces behind such a policy. In Singapore, there is full co-operation between the labour movement and the government, evidenced by the fact that a number of leaders of the National Trade Union Congress (NTUC) have become Members of Parliament, ministers and even the President of the country.

With respect to the structure of trade unions movements, some are highly fragmented, such as those in Thailand and the Philippines, while other are more unified. In Malaysia, the movement was fragmented due to the conflict between the MTUC and earlier CUEPACS, recently the MLO. However, the disbanding of the MLO has been indicated a prospect for unified labour movement in Malaysia. Indonesia enjoyed a unified labour movement in the aftermath of the promulgation of the pancasila labour philosophy, but the labour movement is becoming more fragmented in recent years. Still, its pattern of trade unionism is political as the SPSI retains a strong link with the present government.

The ASEAN members also have differences with respect to the degree of legitimization of industrial action on the part of industrial works. In Indonesia, strikes are legal, but not tolerated. They were banned in Thailand between October 1976 until January 1981 and in the Philippines after the promulgation of martial law until January 1981. Malaysia allows strikes, but those motivated by sympathy or inspired by political agitation are illegal. In Singapore, strikes are legal but the referral of an industrial dispute to the Arbitration Court can always bring about their early demise.

Employers and their associations play an important role in industrial relations systems and their strength will determinate to a considerable extent the effect they may have on broader issues. Employers associations and federations in Malaysia and Singapore are resourceful and strong, compared to those in other ASEAN countries. The primary organizations, their major functions and the extent of resourcefulness are summarized in Table 1.

Table 1: Confederations of employers associations in ASEAN

Country	Primary organisation	Major function
Indonesia	Indonesian Employers Association	Represent employers on tripartite bodies; promote industrial peace; review labour law and regulation.
Malaysia	Malaysian Employers Federation	Represents employers on tripartite bodies; provides assistance to members regarding collective bargaining.
Philippines	Employers Confederation of the Philippines	Represents employers in tripartite bodies; provides assistance on matters related to industrial relations
Singapore	Singapore National Employers Federation	Represents employers in tripartite bodies; provided assistance on mattersrelated to industrial relations.
Thailand	Employers Confederation of Thailand	Represents employ in tripartite bodies; provides assistance in collective bargaining.

Source: Sharma (1996) Industrial Relations in ASEAN: A comparative study, p. 101.

Table 2: Variations in aspects of industrial relations in ASEAN

	Indonesia	Thailand	Philippines	Malaysia	Singapore
Pattern of labour–government	Political–conflictual	Conflictual	Conflictual	Conflictual	Accommodative
Nature of the government	Fragmented	Fragmented	Fragmented	Fragmented of unified	Unified
Federation of employers association	Very weak	Very weak	Weak	Strong	Strong
Power of trade union registrar	Little	Little	Little	Considerable	Considerable
Statutory limits on bargaining issues and procedures	Procedural	Procedural	Procedural	Substantive	Substantive
Strikes	Allowed and tolerated in the private sector, but not in state enterprises	Allowed and tolerated	Allowed and tolerated	Allowed and tolerated	Allowed and tolerated

Source: Sharma (1996) Industrial Relations in ASEAN: A comparative study, p. 101.

Nonetheless, employer's strategies have also been changing. In response to pressures of global competitiveness and eroding cost advantages due to low wages, employers have demanded more flexibility in terms of production process as well as employment relations.

Significant variations, based on the discussion presented in the preceding chapter are also found in other characteristics, such as the degree of unionization, the power of the registrar of trade unions, the statutory limits on bargainable issues and so on. Table 2 summarizes a number of these issues.

IV. OVERALL OBSERVED PATTERN

An examination of the variations in aspect of ASEAN industrial relations system indicated that Indonesia and the Philippines stand at one extreme, Singapore at the other, with Malaysia and Thailand somewhere in-between. At the risk of over simplification, the Indonesia and Philippines pattern in-between as conflictual. How can this variation be explained?

One explanation for the observed variations in ASEAN patterns of industrial relations may be found in the degree of the need for capital accumulation. Some indication of such a need is reflected in the enactment of various investment incentives Act. In addition, it was argued that governments would enact legislation in order to effect labour relations consistent with the dictates of industrialization.

In fact, there is a close correspondence between the timing of legislative enactment concerning investment incentives and labour relations. For example, the Indonesian government enacted Foreign Capital Investment Law in 1967; the Manpower Act was passed the same year. The Malaysian government passed the Industrial Relations Act in 1967; this was followed by the investment Incentives in 1968. In Philippines, the General Order No. 5 of 1972 and labour code followed the Investment Incentives Act of 1967 and the Export Incentives Act of 1970 in 1974. The Singapore government passed the Industrial Relations Act in 1968; this was followed by the Investment Incentives in 1970. The Thai government enacted the Alien Business Law in 1972; this was followed by the Labour Protection Ordinance of 1972. There have been subsequent amendments to this legislation over the years. However, the correspondence between investment incentive acts and industrial relations acts has remained very close. It is also important to note that these legislation and policies enshrined in them are guided by stage-specific industrialization policies pursued by government (import-substitution vs. export-oriented; labour intensive vs. capital incentive/skill incentive and capital accumulation requirements therewith.

What is clear is that social, political and economic factors affect the institutional framework for industrial relations. Conversely industrial relations phenomena affect the socio-political and economic structure.

V. CONCLUSION

Although there are many similarities among ASEAN's industrial relations systems. The variations in some important aspects appear to be striking and are likely responsible for generating the different patterns noted earlier. If all ASEAN members shared on single pattern, then the scope for co-operation and the prospect for convergence would be much greater. However, the scope for co-operation in the field of labour and industrial relations within the regional framework of ASEAN appears to be rather limited. Moreover, since each pattern is dynamic, countries having a particular pattern at one point in time may move to another at a later date. The determining factor of which is often tied to the will of the government in power. In other words, the limited scope for co-operation at present may change if more positive conditions for convergence though economic dynamics emerge in the future.

REFERENCES

Ahmad A. Talib (1983), 'Mahathir advises unions against imitating west' *Union Herald* Vol. 63, No. 299, pp. 25–29.

ALEC Staff (1946), 'Emergence and development of labour unions in the Philippines', *Labour Review* Vol. 1, No. 1.

Allen, J. (1967), *The Malayan Union*. New Heaven, Yale University Press.

Aminuddin, M. (1999), *The Malaysian Industrial Relations and Employment Law*, 3rd Edition, McGraw Hill, Singapore.

Arudsothy, P. (1990), 'The state and industrial relations in developing countries: The Malaysian situation', *Asian Economic Bulletin* Vol. 6, No. 3, pp. 307–329.

Arudsothy, P. and Littler, C. (1993), 'State regulation and union fragmenation in Malaysia', in Frenkel, S. (ed.), *Organised Labour in the Asia-Pacific Region: A Comparative Study of Trade unions in Nine Countries*. ILR Press, Ithaca.

Balakrishnan Parasuraman (1998), 'Industrial relations in Asia Pacific: A comparative perspective', *Philippines Journal of Labour and Industrial Relations* Vol. XVIII, Nos. 1 & 2, pp. 78–91

Balakrishnan Parasuraman (1999), 'The effects of economic development on industrial relations: The Malaysian experience' in *Proceedings II Congreso Regional de Las Americas: Las Relaciones de Trabajo en el Siglo XXI*, Lima, Perú, 13–17 September 1999.

Balakrishnan Parasuraman (2000), Industrial relations in East Asia: A review, *Journal of Kinabalu* No. 4, pp. 23–26.

Balakrishnan Parasuraman (2001), 'The effects of the economic development on industrial relations: The case of Malaysia', *Asian Profile* Vol. 29, No. 1, pp. 17–30.

Bernhard, B. (1983), *Wage Policy and European Integration*. Gower Publishing Company Limited, Aldershot.

Dekker, L.C.G. (1989), 'The concept of corporate from and industrial relations perspective', in Barbash, J. and Barbash, K. (eds.), *Theories and Concepts in Comparative Industrial Relations*. South Carolina Press, Columbia. pp. 42–58.

Dunkley, G. (1982), 'Industrial relations and labour in Malaysia', *Journal of Industrial Relations* Vol. 24, No. 3, pp. 424–442.

Fallow, J. (1995), *Looking at the Sun: The Rise of The New East Asian Economic and Political System*. Vintage Book, New York.

Islam Iyanatul (1989), 'Management and Industrial Relations in ASEAN', *Labour and Industry* Vol. 2, No. 2.

John, W. (1982), *ASEAN Economies in Perspective: A Comparative Study of Indonesia, Malaysia, the Philippines, Singapore and Thailand*. Macmillan, London.

Jones, G.W. (1981), 'Labour force and development since 1961', in Booth, A. and Mccauley, P. (eds.), *Indonesian Economy during the Soeharto Era*. Oxford University Press, Oxford, pp. 218–261

Kuruvilla, S. (1995), 'Economic development strategies, industrial relations policies and workplace industrial relations/HR practices South East Asia', in Wever, K.S. and Turner, L. (eds.), *The Comparative Political Economy of Industrial Relations*, Industrial Relations Research Association Series, Madison, pp. 115–150.

Kuruvilla, S. and Arudsothy, P. (1995), 'Economic development strategy, government, labour policy and firm-level industrial relations practices in Malaysia', in Verma, A *et al.* (ed.), *Employment Relations in the growing Asian Economies*. Routledge, London.

Sharma (1996), *Industrial Relations in ASEAN: A Comparative Study*. International Law Book Services, KL.

Venkatraman, A. (1990), *Singapore Industrial Relations*. McGraw Hill, Singapore.

Verma, A. Kochan, T. and Russell, D. (1995), *Employment Relations in the Growing Asian Economies*. Routledge, London.